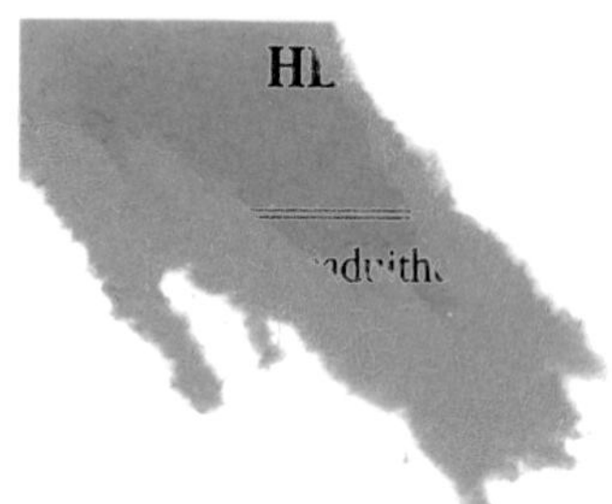

Instant Sound Forge®

Jeffrey P. Fisher

San Francisco, CA

Published by CMP Books
an imprint of CMP Media LLC
600 Harrison Street, 6th Floor, San Francisco, CA 94107 USA
Tel: 415-947-6615; Fax: 415-947-6015
www.cmpbooks.com
email: books@cmp.com

Distributed in the U.S. by:
Publishers Group West
1700 Fourth Street
Berkeley, CA 94710
1-800-788-3123

Distributed in Canada by:
Jaguar Book Group
100 Armstrong Avenue
Georgetown, Ontario M6K 3E7 Canada
905-877-4483

For individual orders and for information on special discounts for quantity orders, please contact:

CMP Books Distribution Center, 6600 Silacci Way, Gilroy, CA 95020

email: cmp@rushorder.com; Web: www.cmpbooks.com

ISBN: 1-57820-244-2

This book is for all the instructors, lab aids, and students, past and present, who make teaching at College of DuPage Multimedia Arts such a wonderfully enriching experience for me.

Contents

Tech Editor's Notes

Welcome to the VASST Series from CMP Books and VASST. VASST is an acronym for Video, Audio, Surround, Streaming, Training. VASST is the only training company in the world that provides one on one training, live roadshow training, DVD-based training, and of course, printed training such as what you are holding in your hand.

Jeffrey P. Fisher's instructional style and years of experience using Sound Forge caught our attention a few years back, when we invited him to present at Seybold in San Francisco. Impressed by his talent and easy manner, we then invited him to do a book and DVD on Sound Forge, and here is the result of that invitation.

This book is for anyone who has even just a passing interest in editing audio for any purpose. It is also directed at professionals who might not be aware of faster, more efficient and effective workflows, and we assure you, those faster and more efficient workflows are found in these pages.

In addition, this book is for the video editor wishing to create high quality audio for their video productions, prepping audio for DVD or broadcast, general noise cleanup, or specific, sample-accurate repair of damaged audio. All of these workflows, techniques, and tips are found here.
Of course, musicians will find this writing a true gem in the pile of information found in the audio world today. Specific tasks related to music production are covered in topical selections, allowing readers to quickly find the solution to any specific problem they might be facing.

As a technical professionals, we found that we were learning new methods of workflow as we worked through Jeffrey's writings, and we've been using Sound Forge since the time the creators of Sound Forge were selling this product out of their basement on floppy discs! There is always more to learn, and we were delighted that Jeffrey shared not only the obvious aspects of Sound Forge in this book, but he also uncovers some of the lesser known functions and possibilities of the application. It is not only an honor, but a delight to be able to be part of Jeffrey's project.

VASST is dedicated to providing techniques, tips, and solutions to all your multimedia needs in a concise and methodical manner, so that you are able to quickly get up to speed in the multimedia application of your choice. Jeffrey's book is a continuation of that dedication to excellence in teaching.

Learn it FASST with VASST.

Douglas Spotted Eagle
Managing Producer
Technical Editor

Mannie Frances
Managing Director

Updates

Want to receive e-mail news updates for Instant Sound Forge? Send a blank e-mail to instantsoundforge@news.cmpbooks.com. We will do our best to keep you informed of software updates and enhancements, new tips, and other Sound Forge resources.

Chapter 1

Introduction

Sound Forge® is a powerful mono and stereo digital audio recorder and editor. The software includes several tools and effects for fixing and sweetening audio files. Beginners and professionals use the program for a variety of audio production duties to develop content for personal use, radio, TV, film, video, animation, music, multimedia, and the Web.

Sound Forge is a highly graphical program that can be used on many levels. A beginner can use its basic recording and editing functions to realize great results fast. As skills grow or tasks become more sophisticated, you can employ additional tools. These advanced features, coupled to Sound Forge's shortcuts and streamlined workflow, also appeal to professionals who crave creative tools and speed.

Instant Sound Forge is a graphical "cookbook" of specific techniques for using the program including ways to both fix and sweeten audio. Fixing involves using the tools to hide mistakes, repair errors, and such. Sweetening implies using the tools to make your recordings better.

Since the software is so visual, it makes sense to have a visual guide to using it instead of large blocks of type and esoteric detail. If you want to know how to accomplish specific tasks -- get rid of background noise, break bigger files into smaller chunks, mix music and voice together, and so forth -- this resource presents the step-by-step solutions in a highly visual manner.

Ye Olde Days

It was all analog recording when I began my career a few decades ago. Sure, digital was there, but out of my price range at the time. Although arguments continue today over the merits of analog, these diatribes rarely applied to my world. For me, in the land of 1/4" and cassette multitrack, analog was an inferior format. Distortion, tape hiss, loss of quality and fidelity through successive generations all added up to disappointment. I'd slave over recording guitars, drums, and vocals only to hear them degenerate into mush. It was GIGO of a different sort: good in, garbage out.

I also cut my teeth editing magnetic tape. Actually, I cut my fingers as the tool of choice was a plain razor blade. There was no visual guide to the audio you'd recorded. Instead, you rocked the tape back and forth across a tape machine's playback head and mark edit points with a grease pencil. Then, you'd place the tape into a splicing block, grab a trusty blade, and slice the tape (and occasionally your finger). Next, using a piece of adhesive tape, you'd edit the pieces together. If this sounds like a lot of work, you're right. And though you can become rather efficient in this arcane world of magnetic tape editing, you'd never approach the power and speed of digital tool such as Sound Forge.

And then digital become affordable, first as the musical instrument digital interface (MIDI), next in stereo form as digital audio tape (DAT), then modular digital multitrack (MDM), and finally, computer software. At first, it was rough going as the computer hardware could barely keep pace with the bandwidth demands of audio. As computer power increased with faster processors, cheaper and better RAM, and larger hard drives, digital audio became a mainstay on computers. And although Apple led the way for several years, programs such as Sound Forge helped the PC emerge as a viable professional choice for audio (and video) work.

I began using MIDI in the middle 80's, DAT in the 90's, and then skipped over MDMs to PC work by 1994. Other than a few client demands, I've never returned to the analog world. Slowly, I've eliminated most of the hardware in my project studio (it was once packed with gear of every sort) and now comfortably use computers for my music, audio, video, writing, consulting, training, and media production services. Sony products—Acid®, Sound Forge®, and Vegas®—have been at the epicenter of my production work from the start. I began with Forge at version 4.5 and both Acid and Vegas at version 1. And as of this writing Sound Forge is at version 7 with Acid at 4 and Vegas at 5.

How far we've come. I can't wait to see what the future brings.

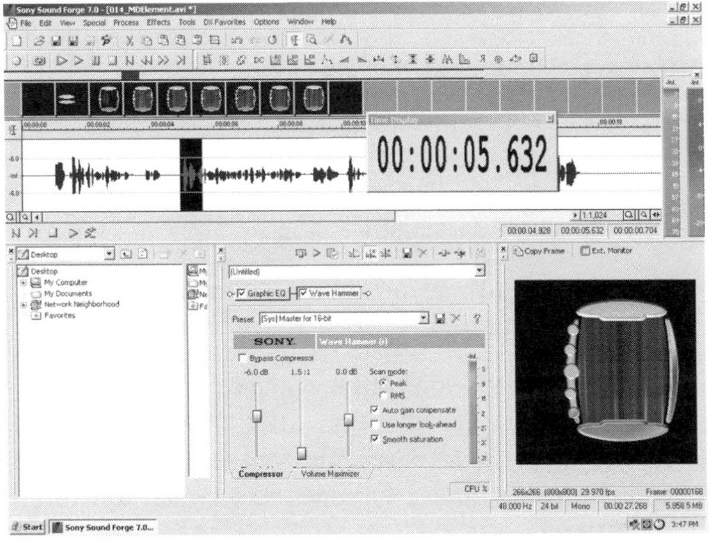

How to use Sound Forge

Today the latest version of the software brings unparalleled audio power to your PC. Along with a basic complement of tools and functionality, there are features that make Sound Forge the best choice today for recording, editing, fixing, sweetening, mastering, and delivering audio in different formats. You can use Sound Forge to:

- Record high-quality digital audio (music, voice, and sound effects) into a desktop or laptop PC
- Make unattended, timed recording of material
- Edit digital audio on a sample-by-sample basis
- Fix mistakes, reduce or eliminate noise, and overcome other audio problems
- Restore old recordings from analog tape, vinyl, and other formats
- Archive audio material
- Rip audio from CDs, such as sound effects, and quickly edit and tweak them

- Manipulate audio in new and unique ways for musical or sound design projects
- Create, edit, and save Acid loops
- Audition effects and other processes non-destructively
- Master audio for CD and finalize audio for video projects
- Convert to the popular Web formats (MP3, Windows Media, etc.)
- And accomplish so many more audio tasks

The latest Sound Forge version 7 adds these new features:

- Automatic file mixing and conversion
- Automated time-based recording
- Clipped peak detection and marking
- DirectX® effects plug-in automation
- Drag-and-drop CD extraction
- Enhanced Spectrum Analysis tools
- Media Explorer with file previewing
- New fade curves
- Project files
- Threshold recording
- Undo past save
- Vinyl Restoration plug-in
- Volume and pan envelopes
- VU/PPM meters
- White, pink, and brown noise generators
- Windows Media® 9 Series import and export
- QuickTime® 6 import and export, RealMedia® 9 export

For many, Sound Forge is their preferred application for recording and editing when multitrack isn't needed. For my audio classes, we use the software for every project. Even when students learn the Vegas multitrack, Sound Forge is still a significant part of their productions. In fact, Sound Forge and Vegas work together quite well giving you even more power on your desktop. I'm forever going back and forth between the programs with my work, and I couldn't accomplish so much without either of them.

What about the box?

Sound Forge's minimum system requirements are modest. As is true of most software, exceeding these minimums usually makes for a better working experience.

- Microsoft® Windows® 2000, or XP
- 400 MHz processor

- 60 MB hard-disk space for program installation
- 64 MB RAM (128 MB recommended)
- 24-bit color display recommended
- Windows-compatible sound card
- CD-ROM drive (for installation from a CD only)
- Supported CD-Recordable drive (for CD burning only)
- Microsoft DirectX® 8 or later
- Internet Explorer 5.0 or later

To this list, I would add a separate hard drive as an absolute necessity. You don't want your programs and operating system on the same drive as your work. Working with audio (and video for that matter) is faster and less problematic with a second drive onboard. Don't be fooled by a "virtual" second drive as some computer manufacturers partition a single drive to look like multiple drives; it's not the same thing and performance is often worse.

For this additional drive, choose a 7200 RPM drive with enough space to hold your work. Audio consumes about 10 Mb per minute for stereo CD quality sound (44.1kHz / 16 bits). A 60-80 GB drive is sufficient for most audio applications. If you work with video, your space needs will be greater.

Also, if you plan on doing any serious recording, such as voice-overs, music, or restoration, you'll want to avoid the cheap soundcard that came with your computer. If you're working on a laptop, you'll definitely want a better sound. Invest in a high-quality computer audio interface device. Choices range from PCI and Cardbus interfaces to Firewire- and USB-based designs. Many have on-board preamps for microphone recording and line-level inputs for connecting other sources. What's most important is these devices offer far better analog to digital conversion that is quieter and more pristine than typical cheap soundcards. Some let you work at higher sample

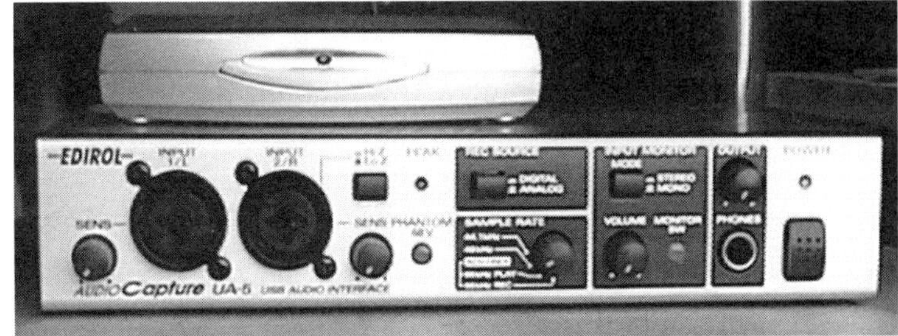

rates (48 kHz up to 96 kHz) and bit depths (24 bits) which Sound Forge can handle with ease.

In some cases, you may require a dedicated analog-to-digital converter to assure you make only the most pristine recordings. Apogee products are well-respected in this arena.

Other tools

Monitors. Accurately hearing what you are doing is critical to working with sound. While some computer speakers are adequate for recording, editing, and finishing a basic recording, those built-in to laptops are useless. Therefore, invest in some decent powered speakers and use them to monitor your work. Choose speakers designed for critical music monitoring such as those made by Event, JBL, M-Audio, and Tannoy. The self-powered versions (often called active monitors) are more convenient than the traditional passive speakers with separate amplifier combination. Position your monitors so they form two points of an equilateral triangle (with your head as the third point). Keep the tweeters at ear level, too.

Headphones. Pick up a pair of closed-ear headphones. There are many brands available and an even wider range of prices. I don't feel you have to use the top-of-the-line components here because you should never make critical sound decision based on a headphone mix. Speakers rule, and therefore you should rely on them for accuracy. Headphones are useful when recording with mics (to avoid feedback), when working in noisy environments (airplanes, for example), or for keeping your work from disturbing others. Other than that, use speakers!

Microphone. To get acoustic sound into Sound Forge, you need a microphone. Don't use the crummy little one that came with your computer. High-quality, inexpensive mics abound and sound far better than that trash. For basic voice work, I'd suggest either the Shure SM57 or SM58. These are rugged, good-sounding dynamic

M-Audio LX-4 stereo monitors with subwoofer (www.m-audio.com)

microphones. The '58 is especially suited for female voice as it reduces sibilance (excessive esses) somewhat. Males can choose either. Both mics are available from music or audio equipment suppliers for under $100.

Moving up to a large diaphragm condenser mic can result in better fidelity and reproduction. There are many solid choices available from Audio-Technica, AKG, Marshall, Rode, and Shure. Condenser microphones need power to function so make sure your mixer, preamp, or computer interface can supply the 48v phantom power. Also, get a proper mic cable and a stand to hold the mic. Adding a boom to the stand gives you placement flexibility.

Microphone preamp. Microphones put out such a low amount of electricity that their signal needs to be boosted. The soundcard's mic input includes the necessary preamplifier. Unfortunately, much like the cheapo mic that shipped with your box, most sound card mic preamps are too noisy for serious work. In a pinch you could use it, but at least, use it with a better mic.

When you're ready to jump to the professional world, get a better preamp. Choose either a small mixer to work with your mic or a dedicated device. Mixers essentially let you connect several microphones and other devices (such as a turntable) to one place and adjust their volumes independently. Mixers from Behringer, Mackie, and others are popular choices. Alternately, you could choose a stand-alone preamp such as those made by DBX, ART, and others. Remember that some Firewire- and USB-based external soundcard options include preamps.

Obviously, the more you invest in higher quality mics, preamps, and a dedicated computer audio interface, the better your resulting recordings could be.

Quiet recording space. If you need to record voice or other acoustic sounds, you need keep noise out of the finished recordings. It costs a lot of money to soundproof and treat a recording environment. You can buy acoustic supplies from several manufacturers to both reduce room noise and make the room sound better. Also, there are solutions available for small, portable vocal booths. These issues are far beyond the scope of this book, but that doesn't reduce their significance. Acoustic suppliers, such as Auralex (www.auralex.com), have information on their Web sites that can provide the primer you need to make your recording and monitoring rooms sound accurate and good.

Contour Design ShuttlePro V2. This handy device includes 15 fully-programmable buttons and a jog/shutle wheel that work flawlessly with Sound Forge. The ShuttlePro V2 plugs in via USB and programming the buttons (if you don't like the default assignments) takes seconds. You can greatly speed up tasks by using keyboard shortcuts, and accessing many of these shortcuts with the ShuttlePro V2 is even easier. Plus, if you mouse as much as I do, it's good to give your other hand something to do for a change.

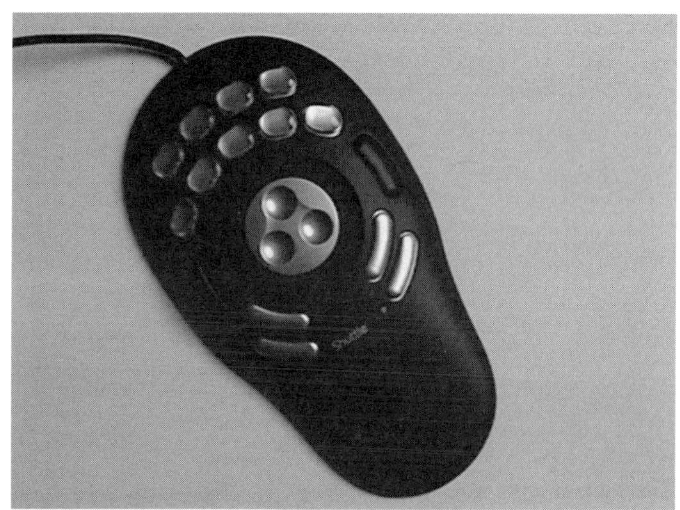

DirectX® plug-ins. Though Sound Forge comes with a versatile complement of effects, you can also purchase third-party plug-ins to work with the program. From reverbs to equalizers and everything in-between, you can find plug-ins to help you realize your sonic dreams. Tools are available from many sources, many as shareware and freeware. For an up-to-date listing, and links to download demos and trials, visit www.directxfiles.com. Here are two I highly recommend:

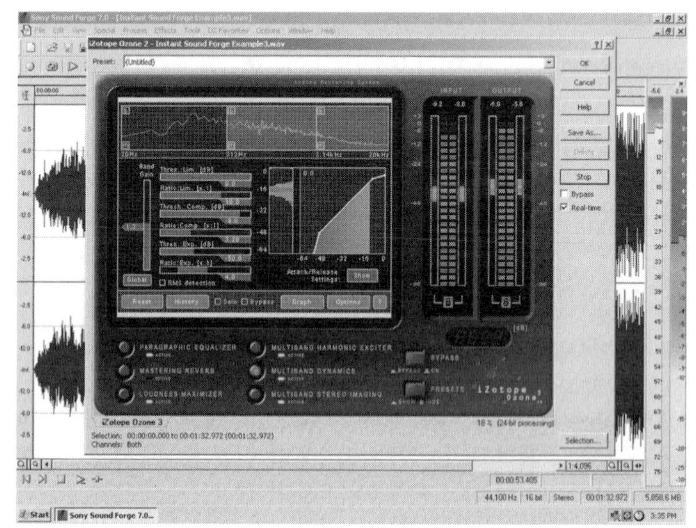

- Izotope Ozone 3 is a multi-effects processor ideal for mastering music and audio for video (www.izotope.com).
- Sony Noise Reduction 2. If you will use Sound Forge to fix audio problems, and since noise is a number

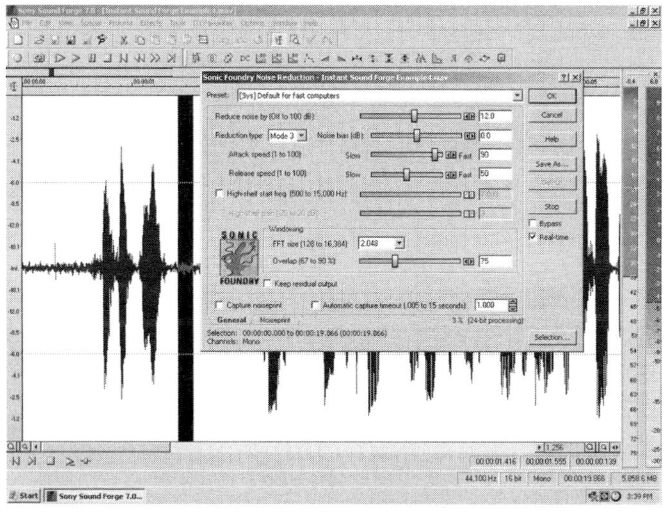

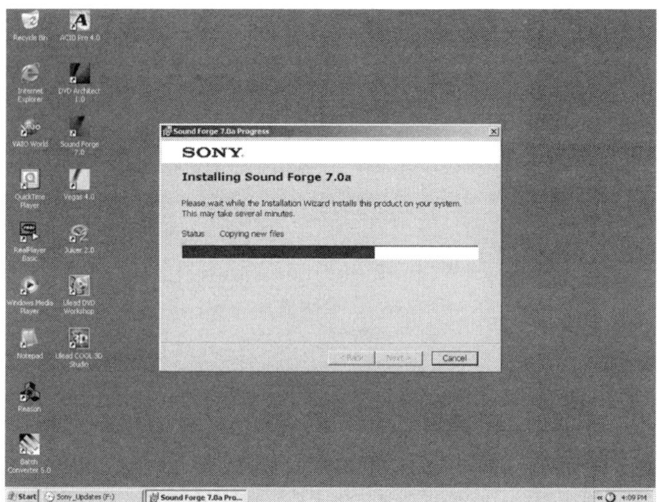

one problem, you should seriously consider the Sony Noise Reduction plug-in. This tool is an amazing workhorse that actually does what it purports to do—and does it very well.

Installing Sound Forge

To start working with Sound Forge, drop the CD in your drive or double-click the executable you downloaded from Sony and follow the onscreen prompts. You'll be asked to register the product which you can do either via the Internet or by phone. Once you've completed these steps, you are ready to begin.

Let's go ...

Sound, analog, and digital

Before using Sound Forge, it's important to know a little about how sound works in the world and the difference between analog and digital recording. Here's a basic primer.

Sound is vibration. Stretch a rubber band tightly and pluck it to see how the bands vibrate back and forth until they run out of energy. Sound travels through air, water, and other solid surfaces moving at approximately 1.1 feet per millisecond (1/1000th of a second) in air.

Sound moves out in all direction from the source that created it. The most common analogy is to drop a pebble in a pool of water to see the waves move out from the center. Like the water wave, sound has crests and troughs, called compression and rarefaction respectively. The wave metaphor extends over to the two-dimensional "waves" you see on your monitor when using Sound Forge and .wav is even the primary audio file format used on PCs.

The primary components of sound are pitch and loudness.

From at rest to maximum compression through at rest again to maximum rarefaction and back to at rest is called one cycle of the wave. The more cycles a wave has, the higher its pitch; less cycles, lower pitch. The frequency of a sound is its number of cycles per second, called Hertz (Hz). Normal human hearing range is from 20Hz to 20,000Hz (20kHz).

The power of the wave, how high its crest and low its trough is the sound's amplitude which we perceive as loudness expressed as decibels (dB). The decibel scale starts at the threshold of human hearing and continues up through the threshold of pain where a sound is so loud it hurts. A typical level in a house is between 40-50dB; a rock concert over 100dB. The decibel is logarithmic meaning that a 6dB increase is a doubling of the energy. Perceptually, people need a 9-10dB change before they respond to a sound being "twice as loud".

Analog

When we think about sound only three sources typically come to mind: voice, music, and noise. We often use analogy when describing sounds, such as a cat that sounds like a baby crying. In the root of analogy is the word analog. Understanding this key concept, and the analog signal flow, is important before moving on to grasping digital audio.

How does the ear work? The outside of the ear, called the pinna, serves to collect sound and funnel it into the ear canal. At the end of the ear canal is a piece of tightly stretched skin called the ear drum. As sound strikes the ear drum, it vibrates in an analogous way to the sound energy. Three bones, the hammer, anvil, and stirrup (called ossicles) transfer the vibration from the ear drum to the inner ear or cochlea. The bones work much like a piston. The cochlea is filled with fluid and thousands of tiny hairs. The sound energy from the ossicles creates a wave pattern in the fluid that, in turn, moves the hairs. This movement creates an electrochemical response that travels to the brain which interprets it as sound.

Quite simply, the ear converts the energy moving in the air to mechanical energy and then converts that mechanical energy into electricity. A microphone works the same way. Sound strikes a tightly stretched diaphragm that vibrates in turn. The diaphragm's energy gets converted to electricity that can then be amplified and sent to an analog tape recorder. At the recorder, the electricity moves magnets that arrange tiny particles of metal on the tape into a pattern that matches the original sound.

Of course, there can be distortion at any and all of these stages with distortion defined as any time the output wave is different from the original sound source.

Digital

Computers know only two numbers, 0 and 1. By stringing together these zeroes and ones, more complex computations are possible. If we substitute a digital recorder for the analog tape recorder from above, we need a process to convert the electricity into numbers.

The analog to digital conversion analyzes the electrical waveform by taking digital snapshots or samples over time. For CD-quality sound, the computer takes 44,100 samples each second. To prevent a form of distortion called aliasing, the sample rate must be twice the highest frequency sampled. With human hearing ranging from 20 to 20kHz, a filter blocks any frequencies above 20kHz from the computer. However, since a brickwall filter is impractical, the anti-aliasing circuit employs a gentler filter that limits the frequency response to 22.5kHz, and therefore the sample rate is 44.1kHz.

The computer then assigns a value to each sample to represent the waveform's amplitude. CD-quality uses a bit depth of 16 for 65,536 possible amplitude steps (2^{16}). Distortion can result because the computer must round or quantize to the nearest value (called quantization error). This process of converting analog to digital creates a stair-step pattern in the resulting digital file. To overcome this, an analog filter (used when playing back a digital file) helps smooth the stair-step digital pattern back into the original wave shape.

What should be obvious is using higher sample rates and greater bit depths results in a more faithfully reproduced sound with greater fidelity.

A single minute of stereo digital audio consumes about 10 megabytes of space; a monaural file about half that. Several audio compression schemes, such as MP3, use psychoacoustic masking to reduce the file size while maintaining acceptable fidelity. The encoding process scans a file and throws out information the ear doesn't hear. For example, a cymbal crash covers up or masks other sounds in a song for a brief moment. By encoding the frequencies of the cymbal, and ignoring everything else, the file's size can be reduced. Apply this process dynamically over time, and significant reductions in file size are realized.

Chapter 2

The Grand Tour

For the beginner, Sound Forge® is a straightforward program. Recording is as simple as pressing a button or two. Editing is akin to word processing with sound. And the program makes extensive use of the Windows GUI meaning many operations are drag and drop affairs and common keyboard shortcuts are those you may already use daily in other programs. Of course, the program is highly visual so you can see and hear what you are doing at every step of the way.

Learning the basics of this program takes minimal effort. Once you record a few things and edit a couple of projects, you'll have the basic functions down. Then, you can explore the other options available to both make your work better and improve your efficiency.

For professionals moving from other software, Sound Forge will quickly become a comfortable friend. Although the tools may be in a different place, the concepts and workflow are what you've been used to. For pros entering the computer editing environment for the first time, Sound Forge offers software equivalents for many of the hardware tools of which you may already be familiar. Most of you will find the visual paradigm a refreshing way to work (once you get away from scrubbing, grease pencils, and blades).

'Round here

When you first launch Sound Forge, its main screen looks something like Figure 2.1.

Across the top are the typical Windows menus: File, Edit, View, Special, Process, Effects, Tools, DV Favorites, Options, Window, and Help.

Many of the basic functions are duplicated with the icons on the main toolbar. The transport controls dock below with the level meters along the far side. The large, empty space is the work-space. Navigational elements (zoom, amplitude zoom, scroll bars, etc.) are along the bottom, but only display when you load a file.

Destructive vs. non-destructive editing

It's important to recognize that Sound Forge is part destructive and non-destructive in the way it handles files. As you work on a file, changes are non-destructive. That means the original file is unaffected by what you do. This way you can try out ideas without affecting or ruining your original file. You have complete undo and redo history, too.

However, once you save the file, and overwrite the original, you make your changes destructive and permanent. You can't Undo operations after a save. That said, version 7 lets you work non-destructively and recapture your undo history even after a save. See Sound Forge Project File below for how to use these functions.

Another work around is to always work on a copy of your original file. That way you can always return to the original should you make a mistake.

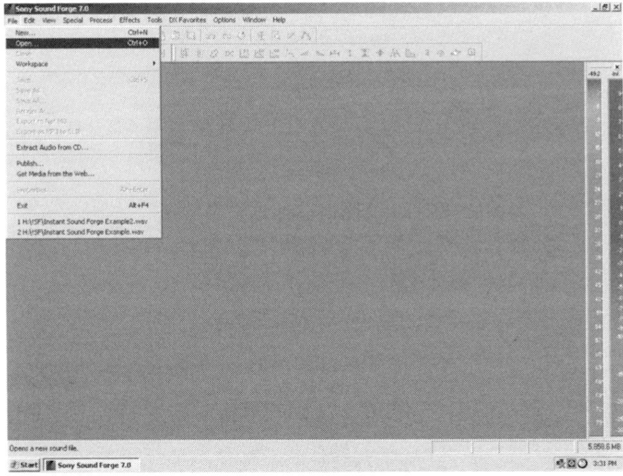

Open the original file by choosing File > Open.

Navigate and select the file.

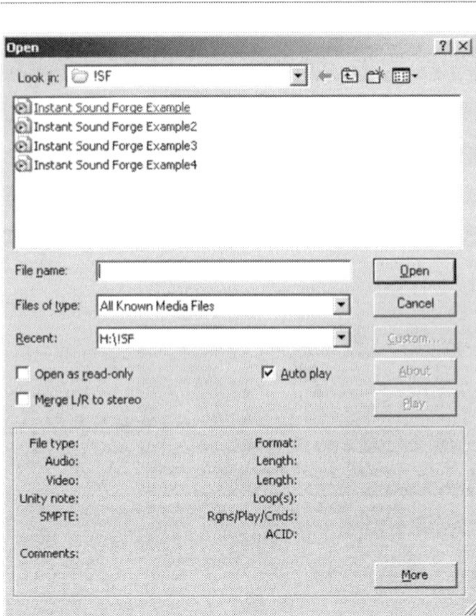

It will open in the Sound Forge workspace.

Choose File > Save as.

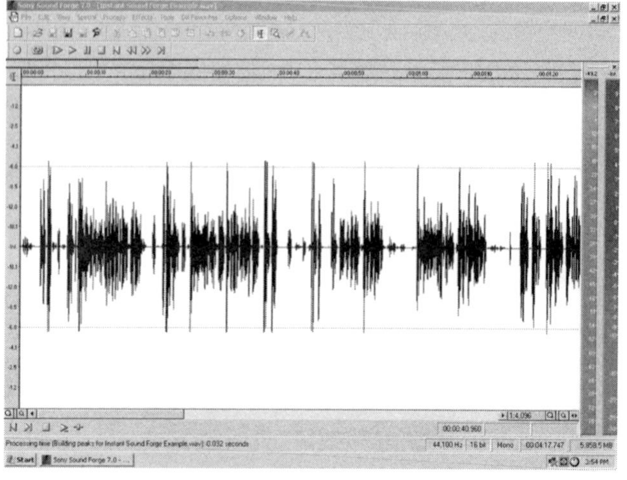

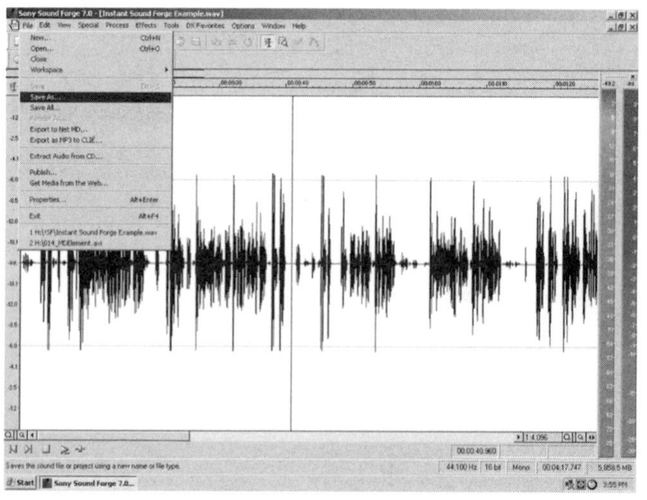

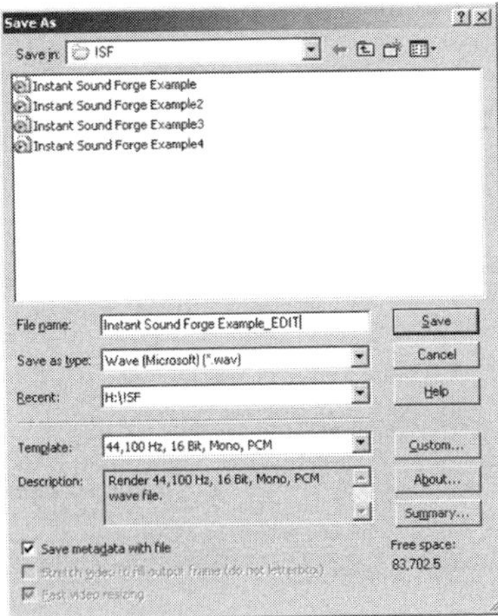

Give the file a different name, such as filename_edit, and click OK.

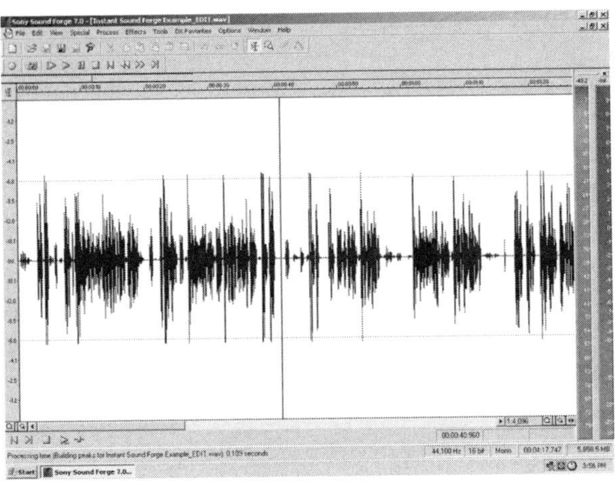

Continue to work on the copy. To save subsequent changes, click File > Save or use the CTRL+S keyboard shortcut.

You may even want to save different versions as your work progresses (use File > Save as). These subsequent saves serve as back-ups should something unfortunate happen in the future (such as a file corruption). When teaching, I caution repeatedly on the need for backing up work. Still, nearly every quarter a student loses some (or all) of his or her work due to a lack of back-ups. Which would you rather do? Go back to the beginning? Or perhaps just your last save a few minutes ago?

Get in the habit of covering your own backside though diligent back-ups. When something happens to you, and inevitably it will, you'll be glad you took the time. Also, make sure these back-ups are someplace other than your main working hard drive. Keep backups on another drive (such as an external Firewire/USB drive) and/or burn them to CD regularly. If you lose the primary drive, you're covered.

Sound Forge in a Nutshell

Sound Forge offers a complete suite of functions for recording, editing, processing, and encoding your audio along with CD burning and video functionality. Here's the lowdown:

Recording

- Record anything that makes a sound—musical instruments, voice, CDs, and more. All you need is a soundcard and, optionally a microphone.
- Make up to 24-bit recordings (depending on soundcard capabilities).
- Program Sound Forge to record automatically or when sounds exceed a certain level threshold.
- Prerecord buffering means you'll never miss the start of a take again.
- New VU meters make checking average levels easier.

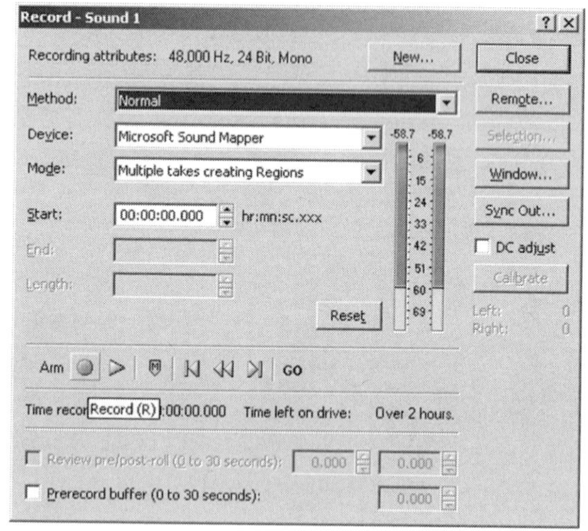

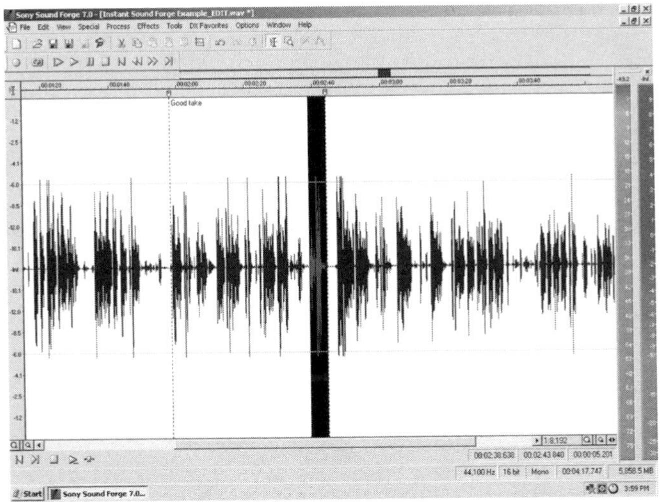

Editing

- Slice, dice, and chop audio fast all the way down to the sample level with dozens of processing tools.
- Edit nondestructively without losing your valuable originals.
- Media Explorer makes finding and working with files faster and easier.
- Import and process high-quality sounds and/or compressed formats. Work with video, too.
- New Sound Forge project file format retains your edit history with unlimited undos and redos.
- Use markers and regions to organize your work.
- Spectrum Analysis tools reveal details about your audio.
- Find clipped audio automatically.
- Use the Vinyl Restoration™ plug-in to reduce noise from records.
- Change Volume and Pan over time using envelopes.
- Customize Sound Forge toolbars and other settings, float or dock windows, and save and recall the workspace as needed.

- Background processing helps speed your workflow.
- Preset Manager organizes your processing settings and lets you share them with other users.
- Record, edit, and save ACID®-ized loops.

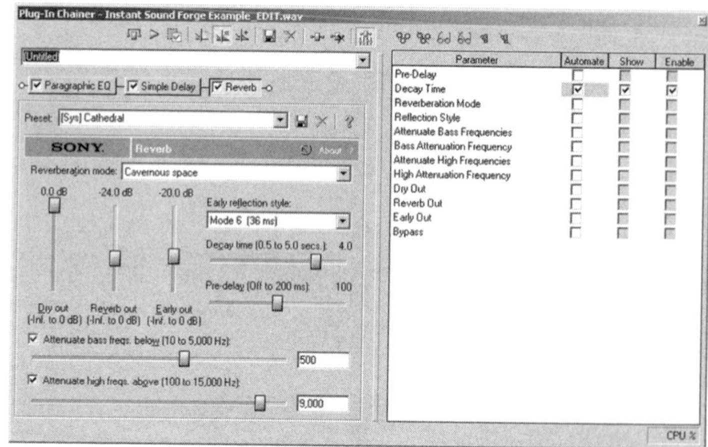

Effects and Processing

- Access over 40 built-in audio effects and processes. Support for third-party DirectX® Plug-Ins, too.
- New automated effects give you even greater control over your audio.
- Chain multiple effects and preview the results in real-time
- Time compress or expand audio while preserving pitch.
- Create audio test tones and/or use the built-in synthesizers for sound design
- Master your recordings with the Wave Hammer®

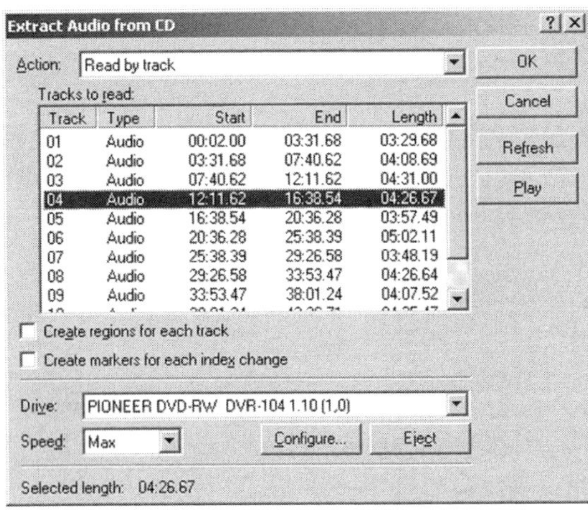

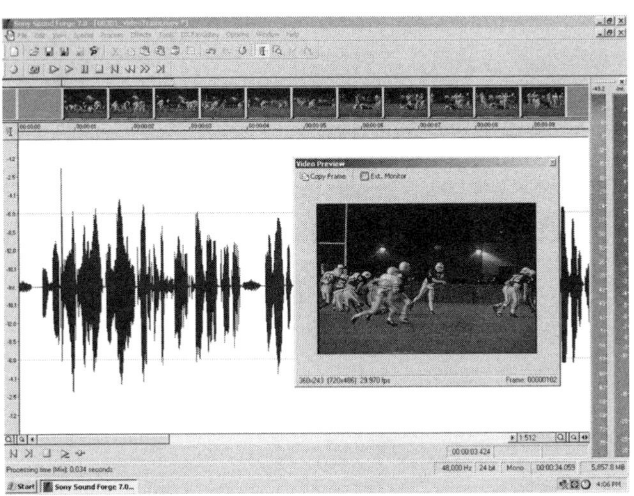

CD

- Easily extract audio from CDs and save to a variety of audio formats including MP3.
- Burn track-at-once CDs directly from Sound Forge

Video

- Import AVI, MOV, WMA, and MPEG-1 and MPEG-2 video, including 24p footage.
- Save and render the video to a variety of formats.
- Preview video in real-time and frame-by-frame on the computer or on an external monitor (via an IEEE 1394 device). Audio and video stay in sync with sub-frame accuracy.

Encoding

- Render and encode your audio to many formats including WAV, MP3, Windows Media® 9, RealMedia® 9, and QuickTime® 6 formats.

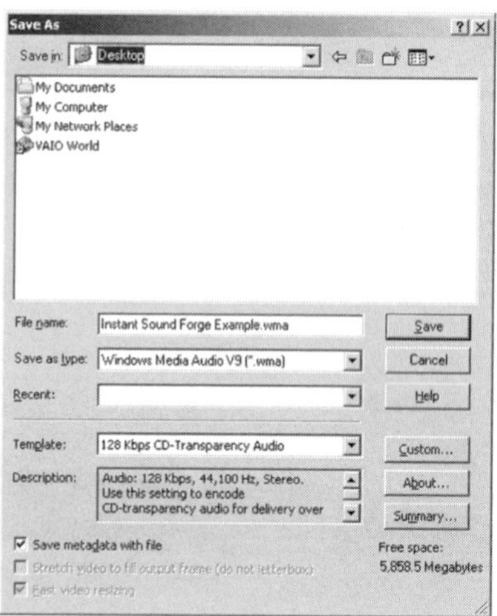

File formats

Sound Forge supports these file formats:

- AIF/SND Macintosh® AIFF
- AU/SND NeXT/Sun (Java) (PCM, µ-Law)
- AVI Microsoft® Video for Windows® (including 24fps DV video files)
- DIG/SD Sound Designer 1
- IVC Intervoice (ADPCM, µ-Law, A-Law)
- MOV Apple® QuickTime® Movie
- MP3 MPEG-1 Layer 3 (Audio)
- MPG MPEG-1 or MPEG-2 Video
- OGG Ogg Vorbis
- PCA Perfect Clarity Audio™
- .QT Apple QuickTime 6
- RAW Raw Files (8- and 16-bit data: signed, unsigned, and Motorola and Intel byte ordering)
- RM RealNetworks® RealAudio® 9

- RM RealNetworks RealVideo® 9
- VOX Dialogic VOX (ADPCM)
- W64 Sony Pictures Digital Wave 64™
- WAV Microsoft Wave®
- WMA Microsoft Windows Media® 9 (Audio)
- WMV Microsoft Windows Media 9 (Video)

Sound Forge Project File

New to version 7 is FRG the Sound Forge Project File. This is not a stand-alone multimedia format. Much like project files in other Sony applications, such as Acid® and Vegas®, the Sound Forge Project File lets you work non-destructively on your audio without affecting the original media.

Use File > Save as and choose Sound Forge Project File (*.frg) from the Save as type list. The program creates a subfolder with everything needed to continue working on your session. Best of all, the file's Undo history remains intact, even after a subsequent save.

Since the Sound Forge Project File is not a multimedia format, to finish up the work, render the project into a supported file format. Click File > Render As and select the format. The program converts the project to your chosen file format.

Keyboard shortcuts

Sound Forge supports dozens of keyboard shortcuts to speed up your work and reduce mousing. Many should be familiar to seasoned Windows users such as open (CTRL+O), save (CTRL+S), cut (CTRL+X), copy (CTRL+C), paste (CTRL+V), and undo (CTRL+Z). The Spacebar toggles start/stop which returns the cursor to the start point. If you want to pause, press Enter while the file plays.

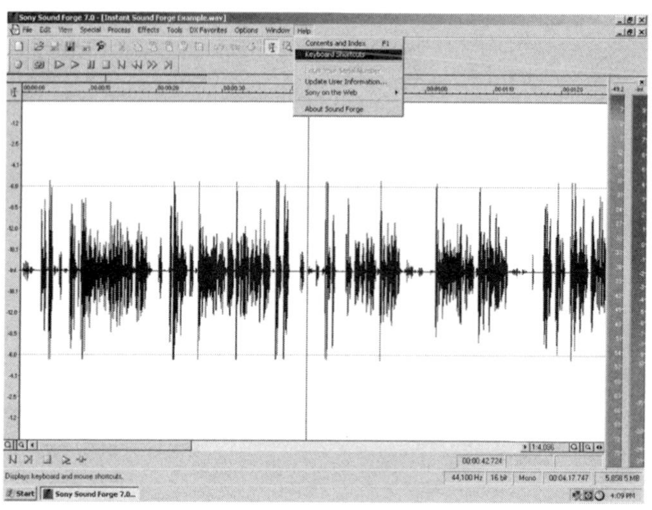

There are many others, and you should try to learn them. Click Help > Keyboard shortcuts.

To see the handy dandy list.

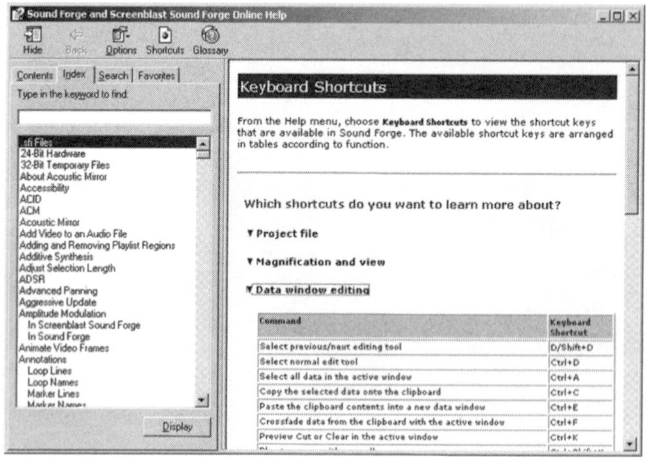

To adjust the sliders in various dialog boxes, click with your left mouse button and drag it. This can be a rather coarse adjustment. For finer control over the settings, click both the left and right mouse buttons and drag the slider at the same time.

If you use a Contour Design ShuttlePro V2, assign your most used shortcuts to its programmable buttons to greatly speed up your workflow.

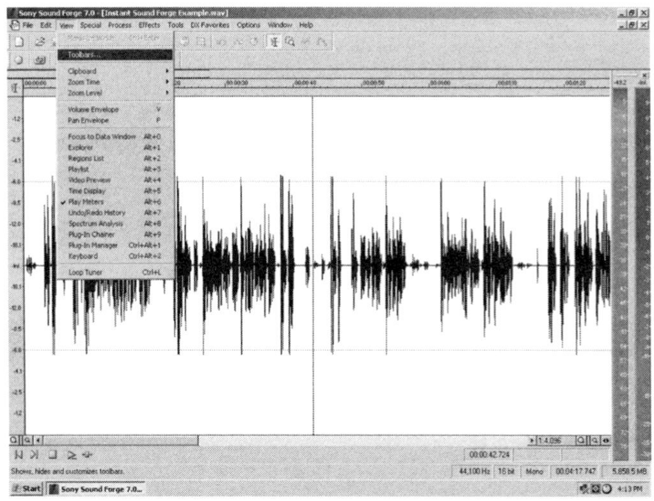

Custom Workspace

Sound Forge gives you the ultimate flexibility for customizing your workspace. You can choose the toolbars you want to see. Choose View > Toolbars.

Place a check in the box for the specific toolbars you wish to use.

Preferences

General | Display | Editing | File | MIDI/Sync | Perform
Playlist | Previews | Status | Toolbars | Wave | Video | Other

Toolbars:

- [x] Standard
- [x] Transport
- [ ] Navigation
- [ ] Views
- [ ] Status/Selection
- [ ] Regions/Playlist
- [x] Process
- [ ] Effects
- [ ] Tools
- [ ] Levels
- [ ] ACID Loop Creation Tools
- [ ] Play Device

Customize...

- [x] Show Tool Tips

OK Cancel Apply

They can dock or float.

For a list of other elements you can view, depending on your personal choice and project needs, go to the View menu.

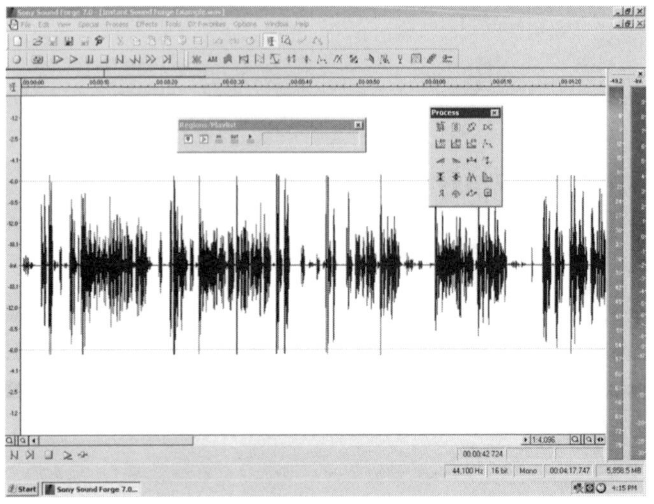

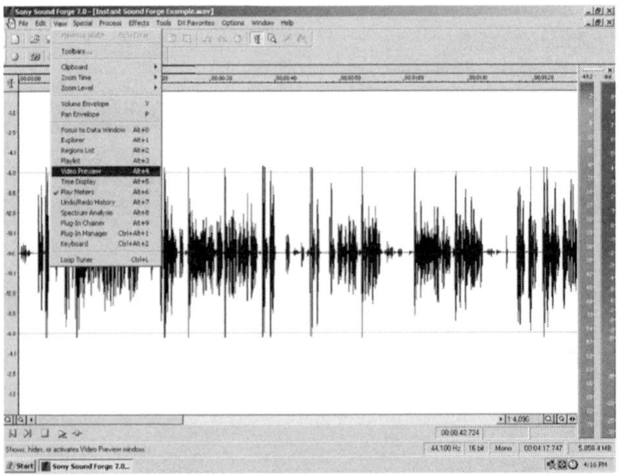

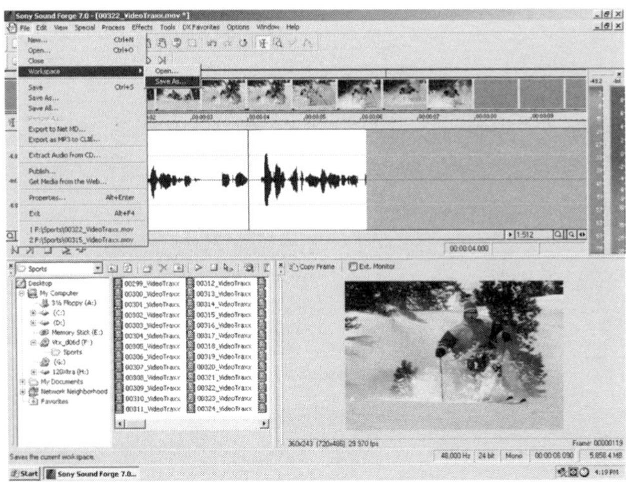

Also, you can save your workspace and recall it at any time.

Click File > Workspace > Save as to save your workspace and File > Workspace >Open to recall it.

Name the file and click OK.

Chapter 3

Basic Procedures

To Open an existing file, click File > Open (or CTRL+O). You can also click the File folder icon in the main toolbar.

The open dialog box displays. Navigate to find the file, select it, then click OK. Note that when you select

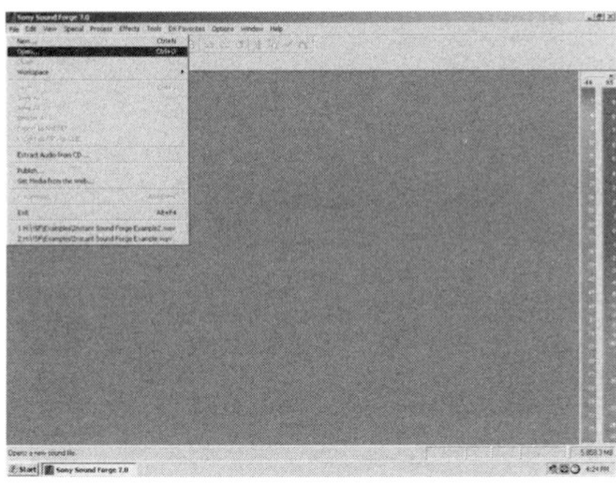

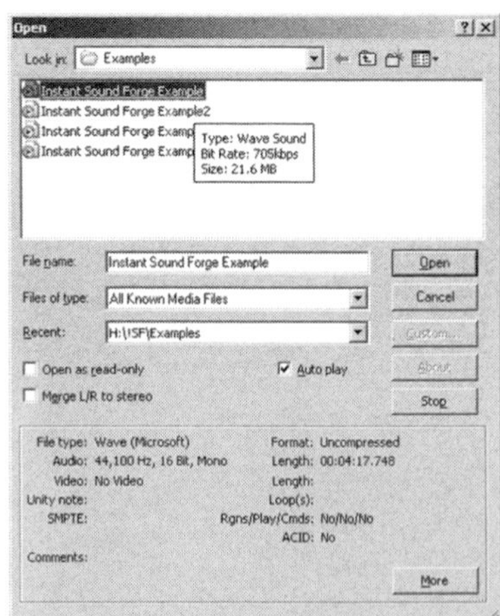

the file, its attributes display. You can Shift+click to select a range of files or CTRL+click to select multiple files to open.

You can choose to search by a specific file type by selecting from the Files of Type list first.

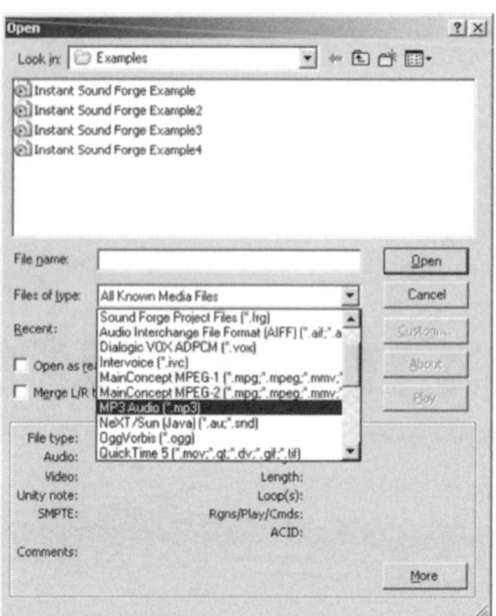

Once you've selected the file, it displays in the workspace. Now you can work on it as needed. To save your work, click File > Save or use the shortcut CTRL+S.

Get into the habit of saving and backing up your work regularly. However, if for some reason you experience a crash, such as a unexpected power loss, Sound Forge® includes a handy crash recovery feature. When you relaunch the program after the crash, Sound Forge will tell you that your last session did not end properly and ask if you want to recover the file. Answer yes and immediately do a File > Save as to recover the temporary file and give it a permanent name.

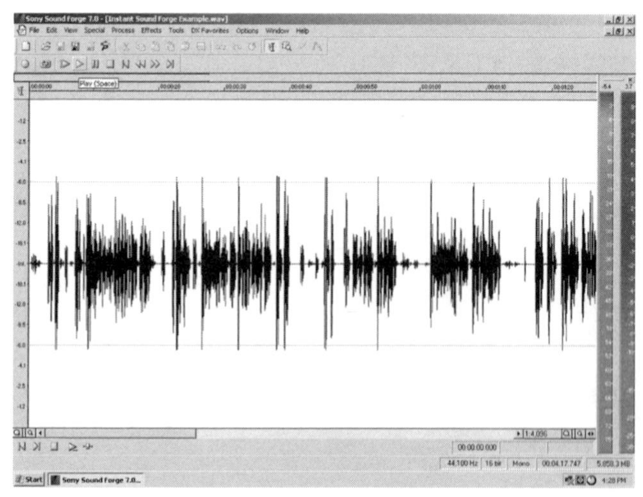

Navigation

The transport toolbar gives you tape machine-type controls over file playback.

From left to right are:

- Record. CTRL+R launches the record dialog box
- Loop. Plays the file continuously. The Q key also toggles this feature on and off
- Play All
- Play (from cursor position). The spacebar duplicates this function
- Pause. The Enter key duplicates this function.
- Stop (and return to the cursor start position). Press the spacebar again or hit ESC.
- Go to the start of the file. W is the keyboard shortcut
- Rewind (in small amounts)
- Fast Forward (in small amounts)
- Go to the end of the file. E is the keyboard shortcut

Use the Magnify tool to zoom in. First, select the tool.

Next, drag the tool over the area you wish to zoom while holding down the left mouse button.

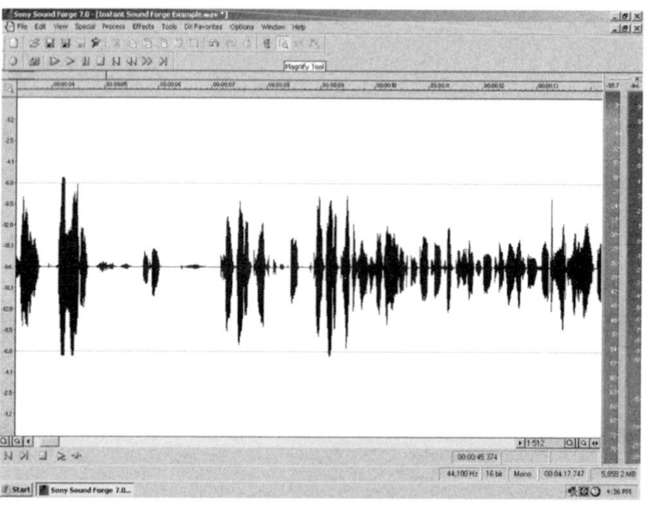

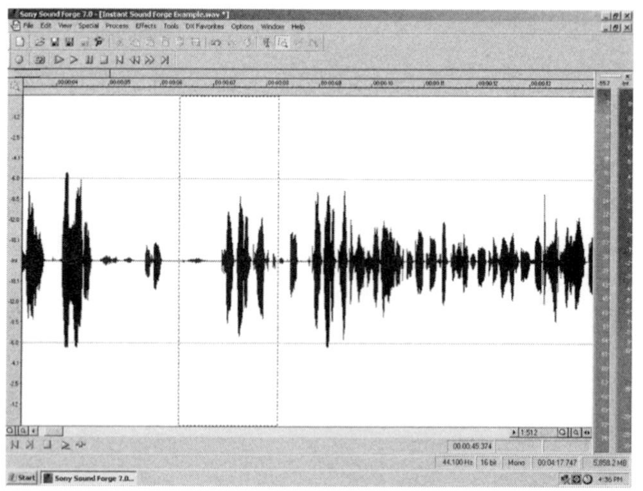

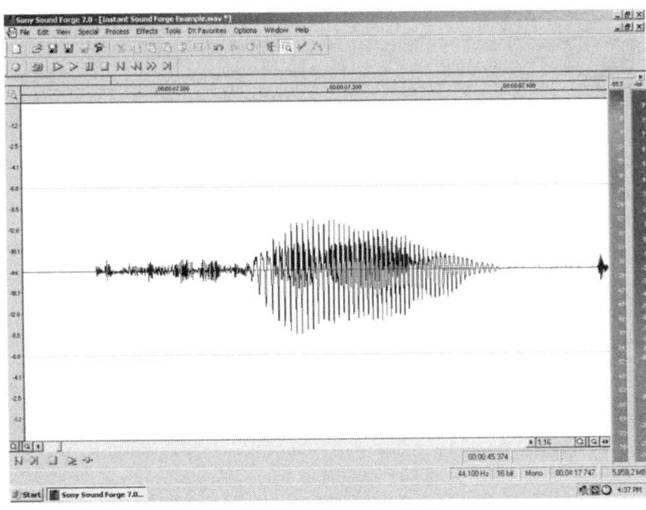

Release the mouse button and Sound Forge magnifies the part of the file you selected.

If you have a scroll wheel mouse, rotating the wheel allows you to zoom in and out of your file. Alternately, click the right mouse button for additional zoom options.

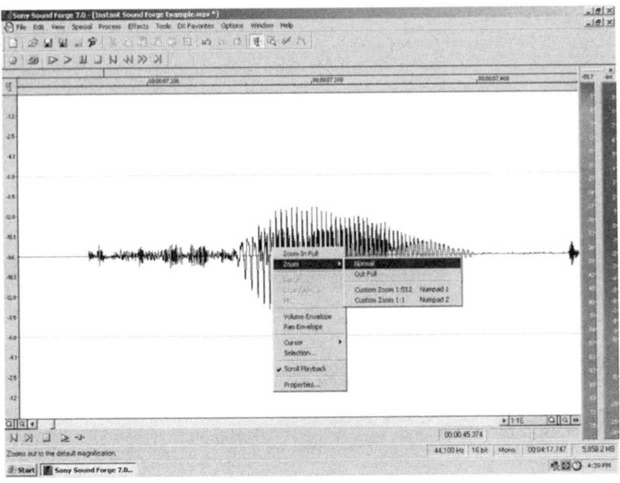

In the lower right corner of your workspace, there are zoom in and out tools as well. Click them as needed. Also, if you click and drag the small bar between the two magnifying glasses you can further control your zoom. The zoom ratio displays to the left of these zoom tools.

In the lower left corner are two additional zoom tools. However, instead of magnifying time, these magnify level or amplitude. They essentially change the scale of the Sound Forge workspace. To use this tool, click the amplitude zoom buttons or click and drag the bar. Notice how the decibel scale along the far left of the screen changes.

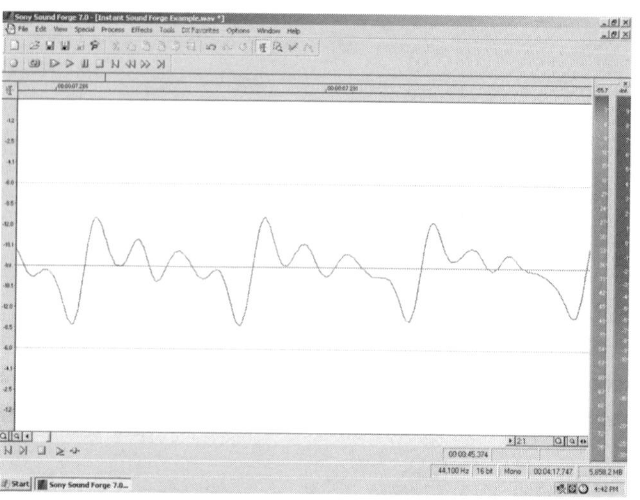

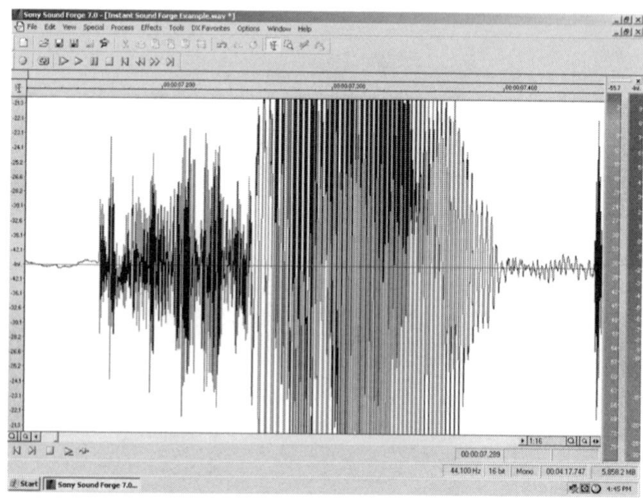

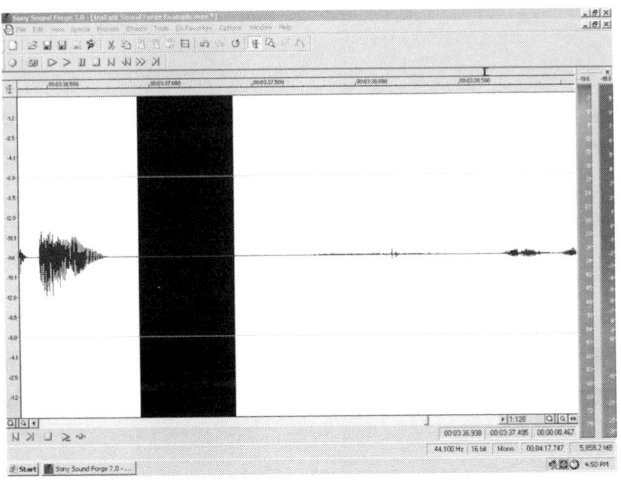

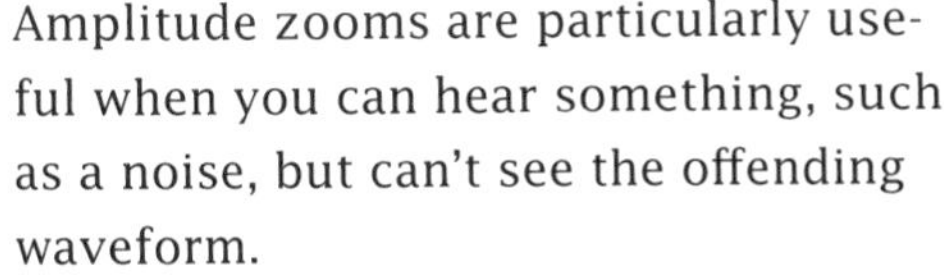

Amplitude zooms are particularly useful when you can hear something, such as a noise, but can't see the offending waveform.

Zooming the amplitude can reveal the source of the noise.

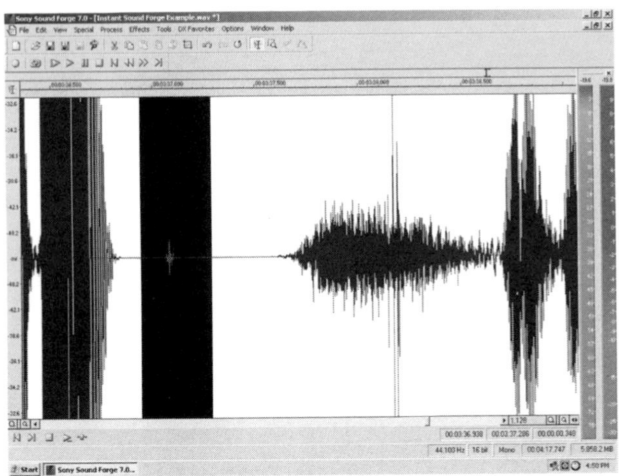

Sound Forge lets you set two custom zoom levels that you access by pressing the 1 or 2 key on your keyboard number pad. To set these custom zoom levels, go to Options > Preferences and click the Display tab.

If your file is larger than what can fit on the screen, use the standard scroll bar along the bottom to move through your file. This function is duplicated by clicking and dragging the bar directly below the time ruler.

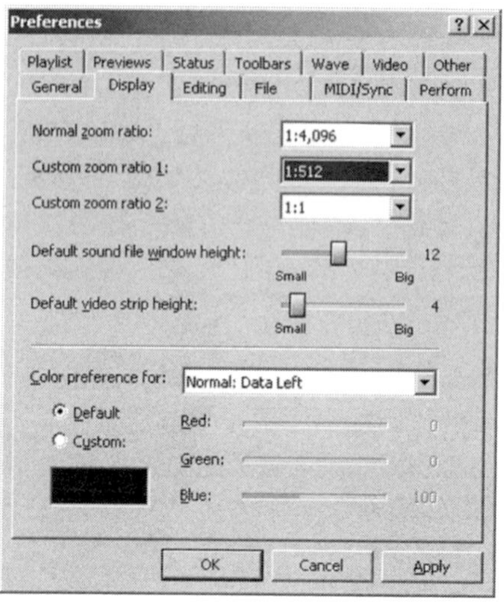

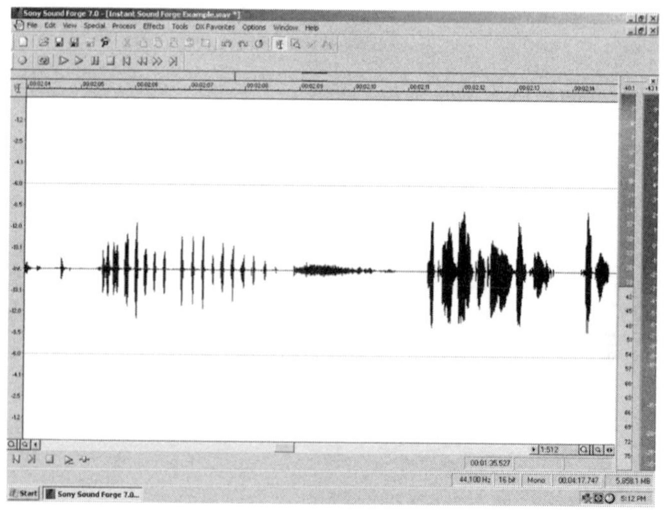

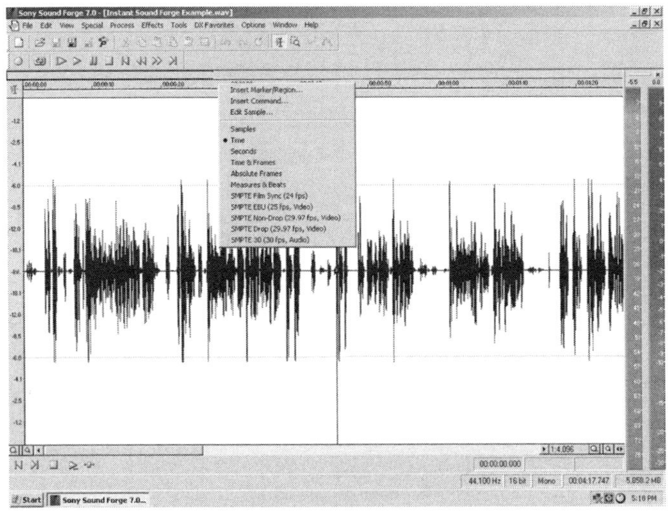

Alternately, position your mouse pointer in the small area above the time ruler and click and drag to move quickly, or scrub, back and forth through your file. You'll hear the file when you navigate this way, sped up or slowed down depending on how you click and drag.

Notice also how the scrub bar indicates the part of your file displayed in the workspace and also shows your current cursor position.

Right click the time ruler to adjust its display options. You can choose:

- Samples
- Time
- Seconds
- Time and frames
- Absolute frames
- Measures and Beats
- And a variety of SMPTE time code formats

Right clicking the tool icon in the upper left corner of the data window gives you display options for the various navigation and informational tools available to you. Once again, Sound Forge lets you easily customize your workspace to your needs.

In the right corner are details about attributes of the file. In this example, the file was sampled at 44,100 Hz, 16 bits, is a single, monaural (mono) file, and is 1 minute and a little over 25 seconds long. The final number indicates the disc space available on the hard drive from which this file originates.

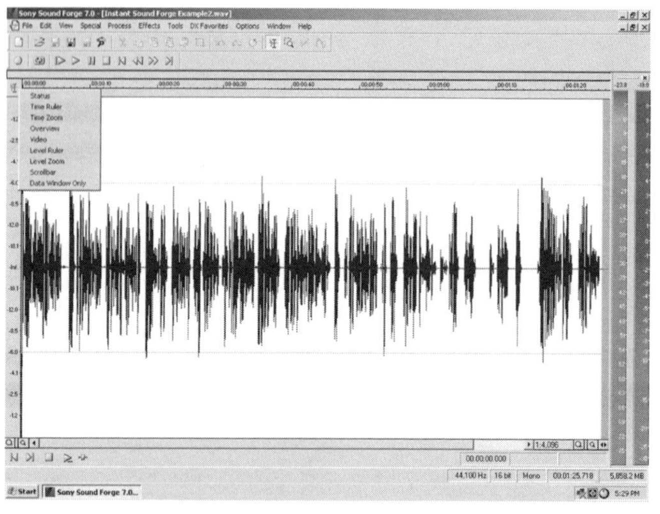

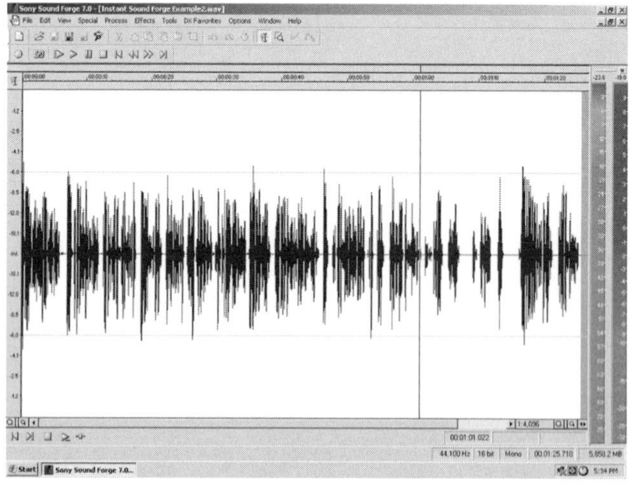

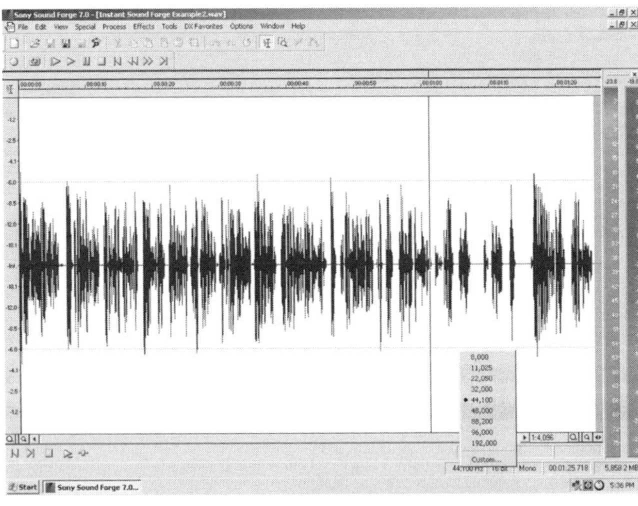

Right click any of these attributes to quickly change them.

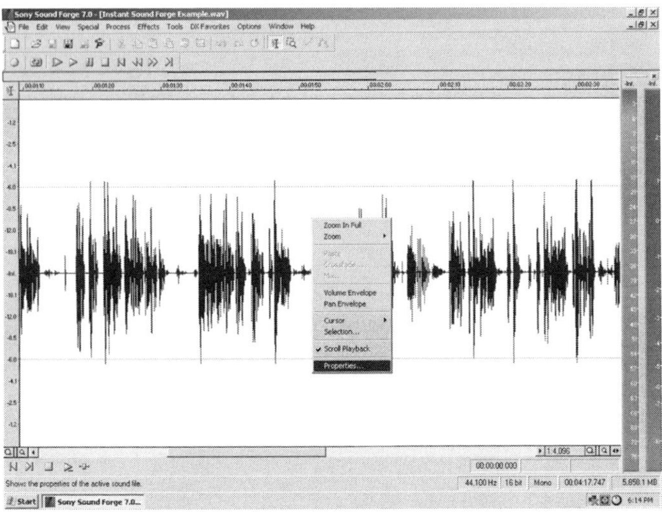

You can find additional information about a file by right clicking it and choosing Properties.

The Properties dialog details the file's General attributes and more.

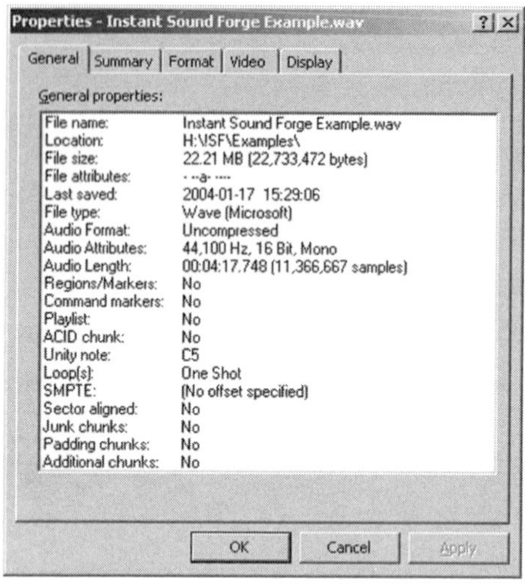

Meters

When you record and/or play back a file, Sound Forge shows the level. The meters on the far right offer two different ways to measure the loudness of your files. The left meter is a peak meter that indicates decibels full scale (dBFS). The right meter is a VU meter that indicates a more average level (called RMS).

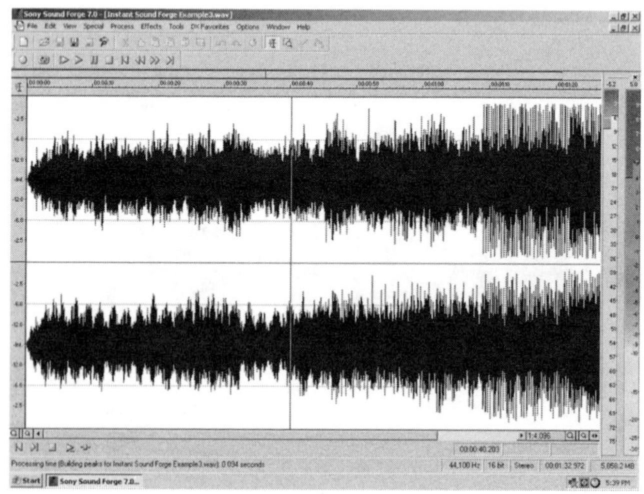

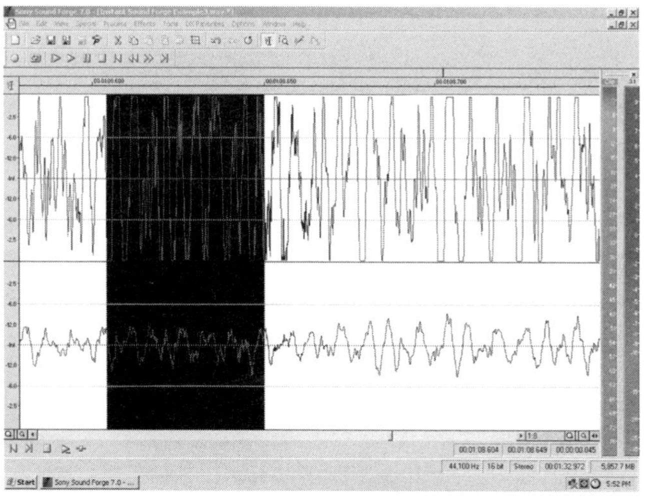

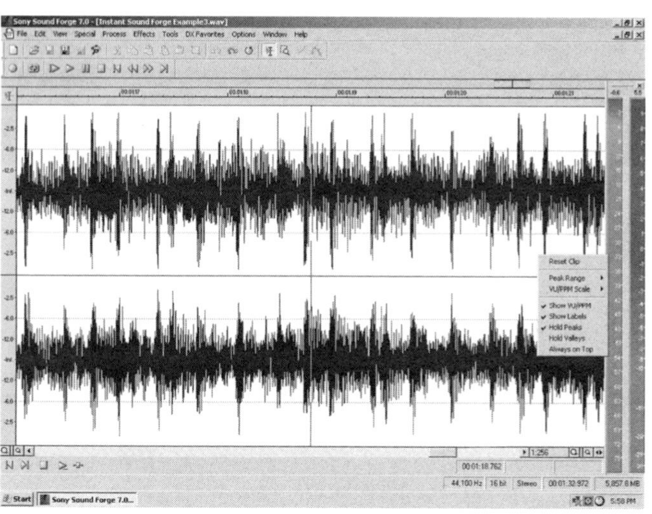

The peak meter is useful to make sure parts of your digital audio files do not exceed 0 dBFS, the absolute top of the digital scale. Any audio that exceeds digital 0 will be chopped off, or clipped, and sound gravely or distorted. As an added feature, the peak meter displays the word "clip" when your level goes above this point.

Important: Never, ever exceed 0 dBFS or your files will sound bad!

The VU meter is useful to monitor the average level of your source material. This average level is a better indicator of how loud a file really is. Sudden loud peaks do not necessarily make a file sound louder to our ears.

Right click the meters to change the options. You can change the scale and other features, such as the peak hold indicator.

Go to Options > Preferences and click the Other tab for additional VU meter setup. Here you can indicate how 0 VU relates to decibels full scale and its integration time (basically how long it takes to respond to incoming data). Typically, VU meters are slow to respond to fast transients with the result being a better idea of the average sound level.

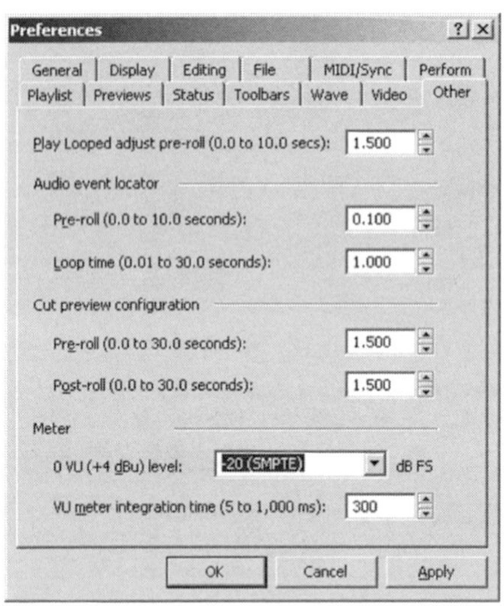

Markers and Regions

Sound Forge provides two handy ways to keep track of sections in your files. You can insert markers and/or you can designate regions in the file. Markers designate a single point in time where regions indicate a section. Use markers and regions to indicate edit points and other information you want to keep with the file—think of them as sticky notes.

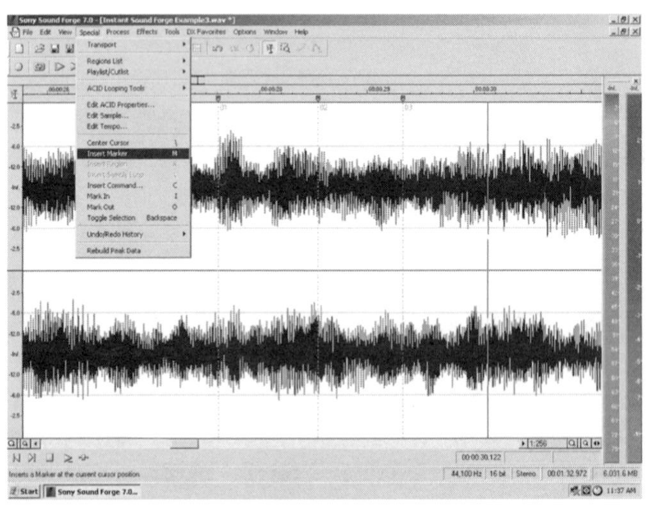

For example, when editing a voice over, you could insert markers at blown lines and wrap regions around good takes. Then, following your "notes", you could assemble a rough cut quickly. Later, you'll learn some additional uses for regions.

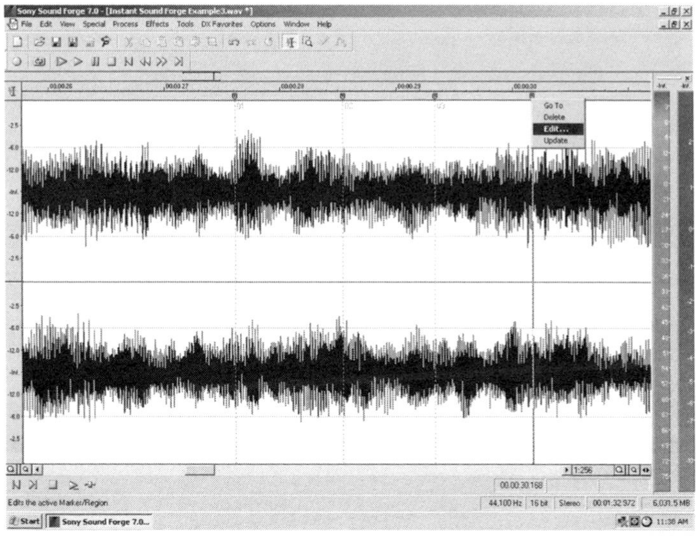

Sound Forge saves the markers and regions with the file—a very nice feature when you need to return to a session at a later time. Also, if you use Sony's Vegas, any markers and regions you insert in Sound Forge will show up in the Vegas trimmer and in events on its timeline.

To insert a marker, position the cursor and either choose Special > Insert Marker or simply hit the M key. The M key shortcut is very handy as you can insert a marker while the file plays (and even while recording).

Sound Forge assigns numbers to the markers you insert. To rename them, right click the marker and choose Edit.

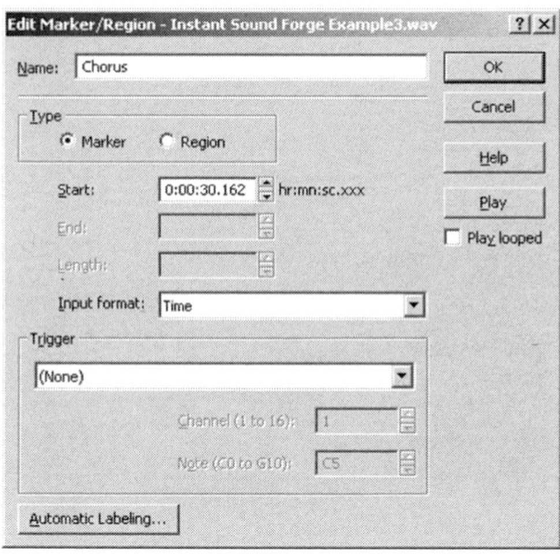

Rename the marker in the dialog box that displays.

Note the name now appears for that marker.

To insert a region, make a selection and choose Special > Insert Region or simply hit the R key.

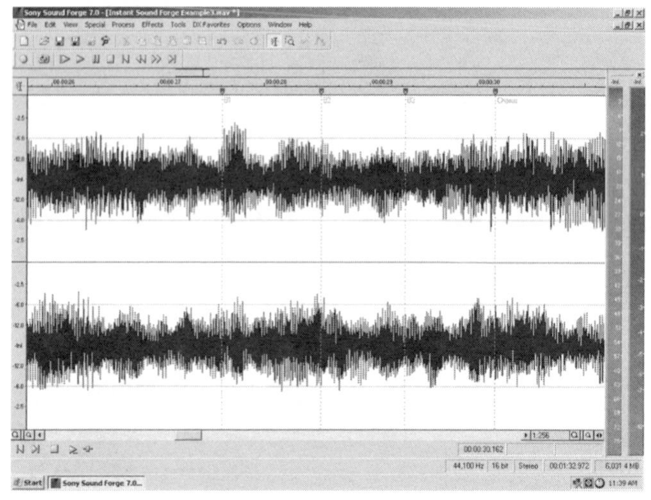

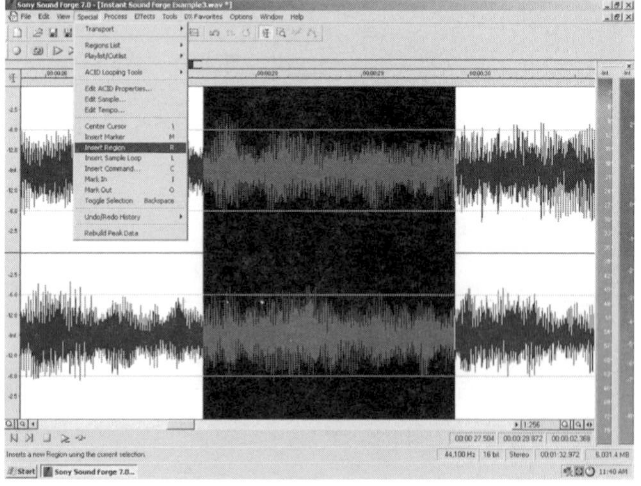

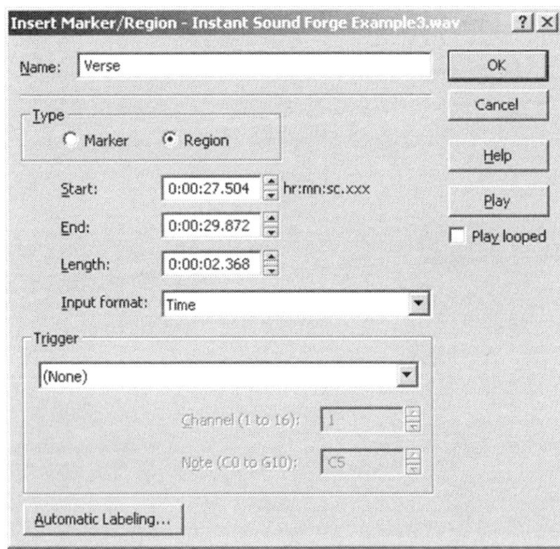

Name the region using the dialog box that displays.

Note the region name now appears for the region you selected.

To clear Markers and Regions applied to a file, click Special > Regions List > Clear.

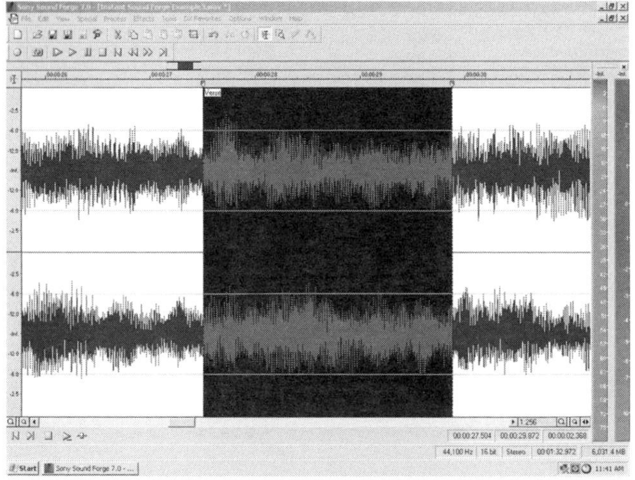

Chapter 4

Recording

Sound Forge® is a very capable monaural and stereo recorder. It is not a multitrack recorder, though. It does not have overdub capabilities (though you can "mix" audio with it). For recording voice-overs, single instruments, and general stereo and mono audio projects, for example converting music from vinyl to digital or capturing a live concert, Sound Forge has a feature-rich toolset.

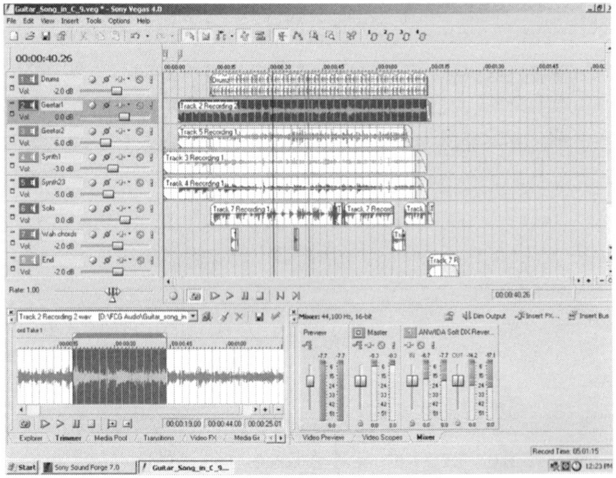

If you need traditional multitracking where you record multiple instruments, such as drums, guitars, and vocals, in sync on independent tracks, you will need to use separate multitrack audio software. Sony's Vegas is an ideal tool for this situation. As a bonus, Vegas® and Sound Forge work together as complementary tools for a variety of audio tasks.

Here's the recording workflow

- Connect an audio source to your computer
- Set the levels using the soundcard software
- Launch Sound Forge and Arm the recording
- Choose the settings you need in the record dialog box
- Begin recording
- Save the files to the high quality .wav format
- Alternately, extract audio from CDs using the built-in utility.

Setting levels

To get started recording with Sound Forge, you'll need to hook up the audio source to your computer. For example, if you are using a mic to record someone speaking, connect it to the appropriate input on your computer soundcard. You may be using a external mic preamp or a mixer, therefore connect the mic to the mixer first and the mixer to the line inputs on your soundcard. Refer to the instructions that came with your soundcard for details about hooking up audio sources.

You need to set audio levels using the software that controls your soundcard. Refer to your soundcard's instructions for specific information

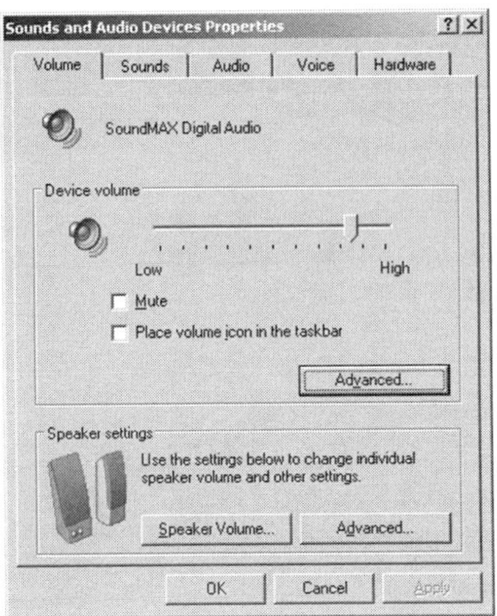

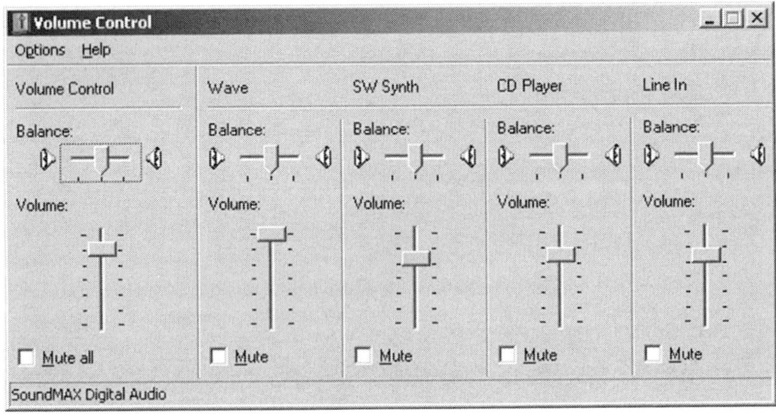

about setting levels. For example, to find the standard Windows soundcard controls, go to Start > Control Panel > Sounds and Audio Devices. If there is a speaker icon in the Taskbar, you can click that to access the same tools.

Click the advanced tab to show the Windows volume control. The default shows the playback levels of the various sound devices connected to your computer system.

Click Options > Properties to switch to the soundcard's recording settings

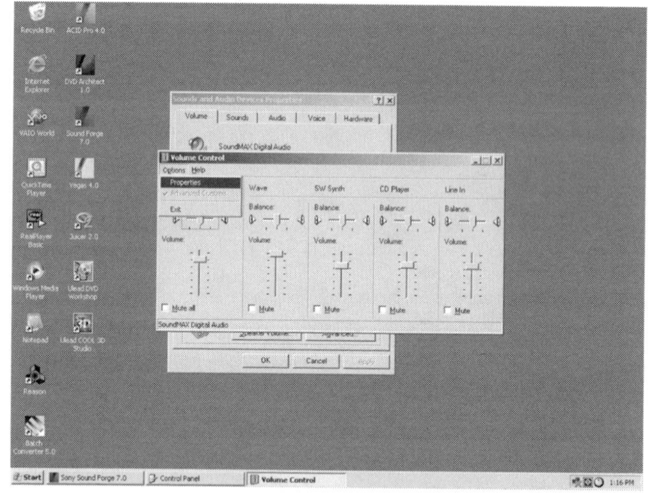

Select the Recording button and click OK.

Choose the appropriate input device. In this example, click the checkbox under Line in and use the slider to adjust the level. Alternately, select microphone and adjust the level accordingly. Under the Advanced tab are additional microphone settings.

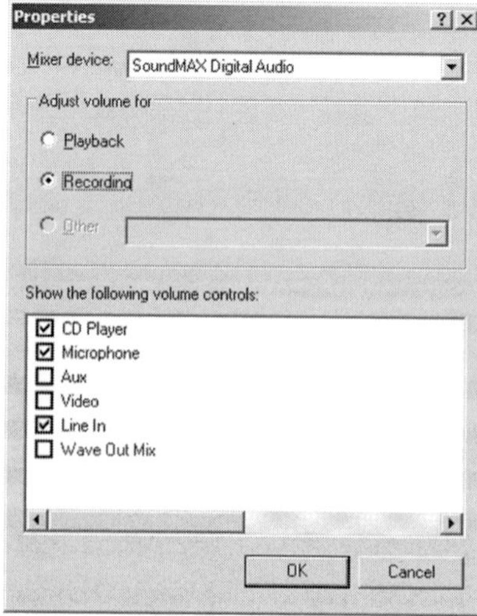

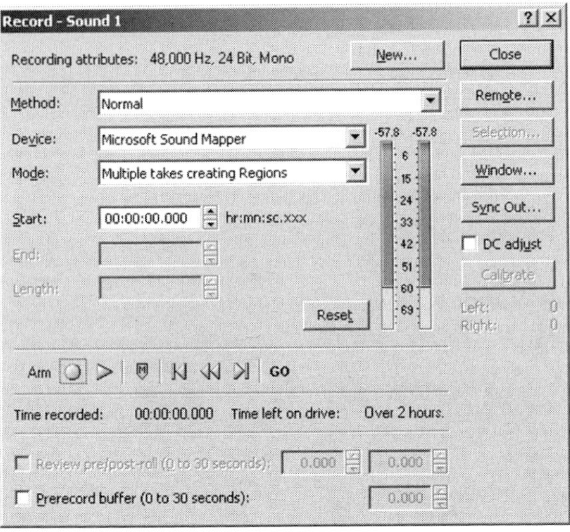

It will help to have the Sound Forge record dialog open so you can monitor levels while you make these adjustments.

Here is the software interface for controlling the M-Audio Sonica Theater USB-based surround sound audio interface. This external device can accept a stereo line level input which can be recorded by Sound Forge.

Some USB- and Firewire-based audio interfaces do not have software that controls the volume input into Sound Forge. Instead, you must set levels on the other hardware (e.g. mixer) connected to that audio interface. For example, the Edirol UA-5 has level knobs for mic and line level inputs on its external hardware interface. There is no software control for this device's levels.

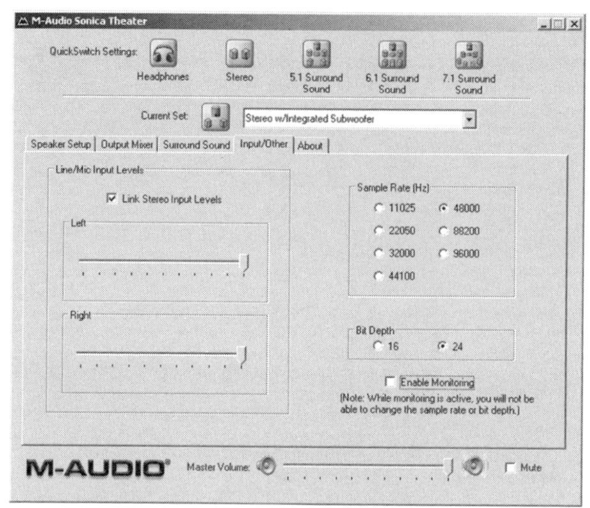

Record dialog

After making appropriate connections and setting levels, start recording with Sound Forge by clicking the red record button on the transport toolbar. The keyboard shortcut is CTRL+R .

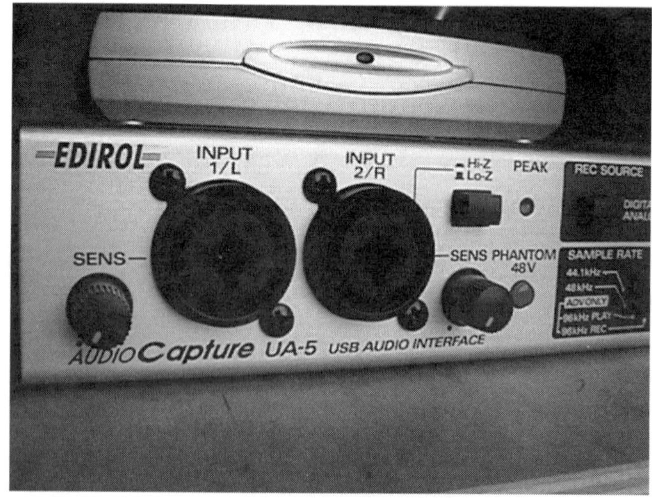

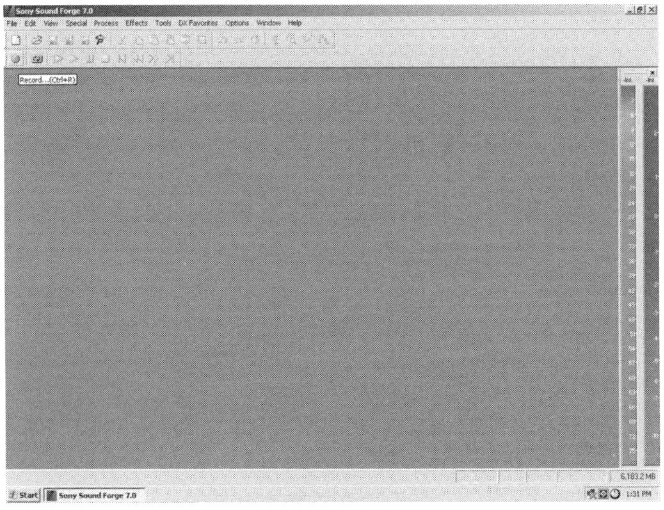

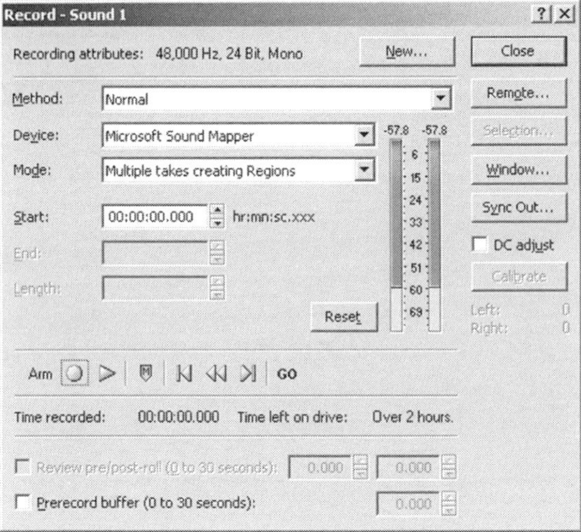

The record dialog displays. At this point, you are in record ready and not recording yet. There is a lot of information in this dialog box that affects your recordings.

First, notice the Recording attributes at the top. Here is where you set the properties for your recording. If the current settings do not match what you need, click the New button and make appropriate changes.

Alternately, before you press the Record button, go the File > New to set the attributes. A blank data window displays, and when you hit record, this file's attributes will display in the record dialog box.

Sound Forge supports bit depths of 8-bit, 16-bit, 24-bit, and 32 bit/64bit and sample rates from 2kHz to 192kHz. Note that your ability to record at higher sample rates and bit depths is wholly dependent upon the soundcard hardware that you use. Not every soundcard supports all settings. Check your documentation for details.

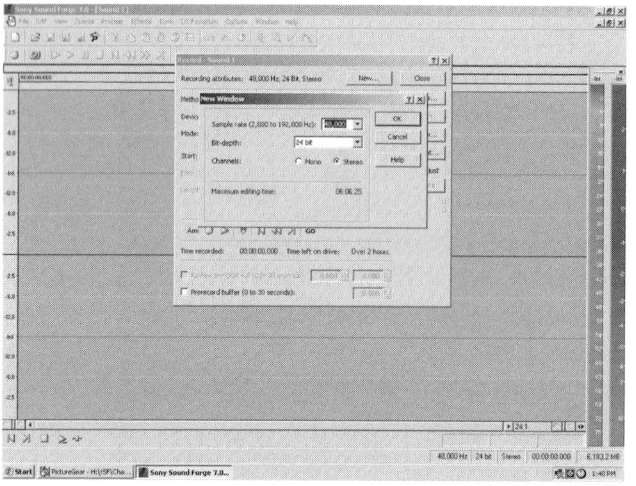

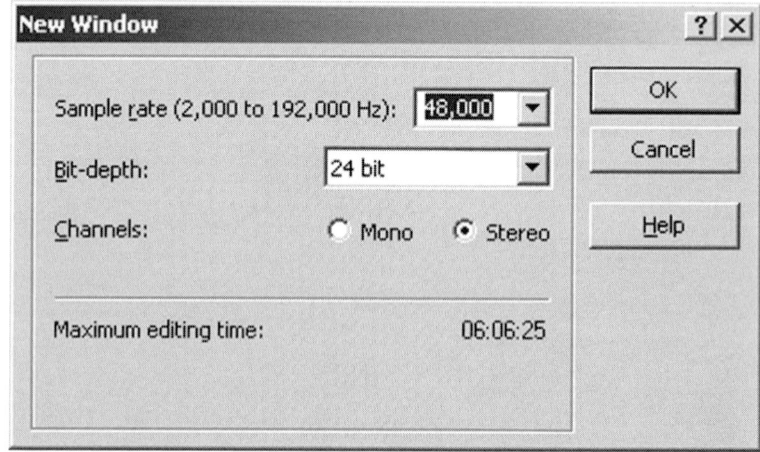

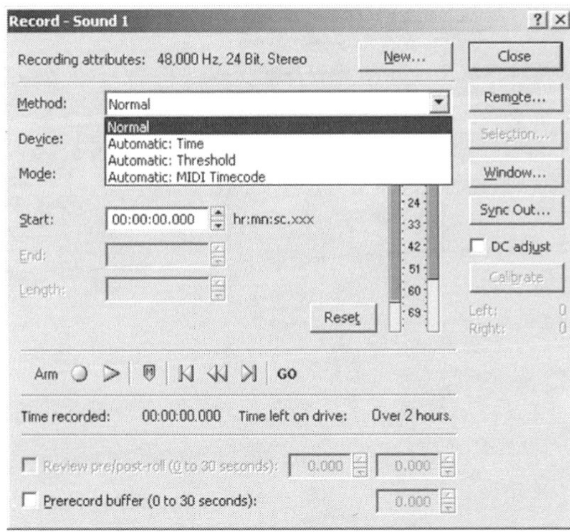

Select the Method of recording. Sound Forge provides several.

- Normal is the standard, default recording method where you start and stop the record process manually.
- Automatic: time lets you specify when a recording will start and stop. This is useful for recording events, such as a radio program, unattended.
- Automatic: threshold let's you set a specific volume level that must be exceeded to start a recording. When the level falls below this setting or threshold, the recording stops. This is useful for recording a meeting or lecture where there may be gaps when nobody speaks. This method would eliminate those gaps.
- Automatic: MIDI Timecode puts Sound Forge into record based on data received from a MIDI device connected to your computer.

I'll return to the automatic settings for additional details later.

Select normal for this example, if it's not already indicated. Use the Device drop down list to select the appropriate soundcard. In most cases, the default Microsoft Sound Mapper will route the audio from your soundcard to Sound Forge correctly. In instances where that doesn't work, or in cases where you need more specific control, select from the list.

Use the recording Mode to select the way you handle subsequent recorded takes. There are several modes from which to choose.

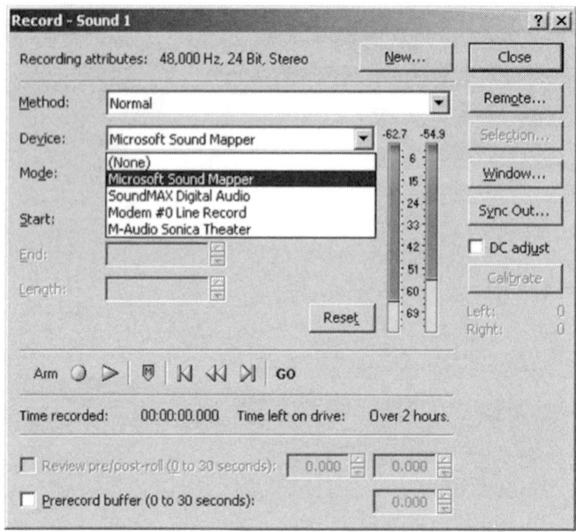

- Automatic retake (automatically rewind). Every time you hit stop when recording, and then go back into record mode, the previous take will be erased by the new one. This is a potentially dangerous recording mode as you might accidentally destroy a recording you need.
- Multiple takes creating regions. This is the default setting that places regions around each take as you go in and out of record mode. Each subsequent take is added to the end of the file. This mode is very helpful when recording multiple takes making it easier to zero in on the recording you want when editing.

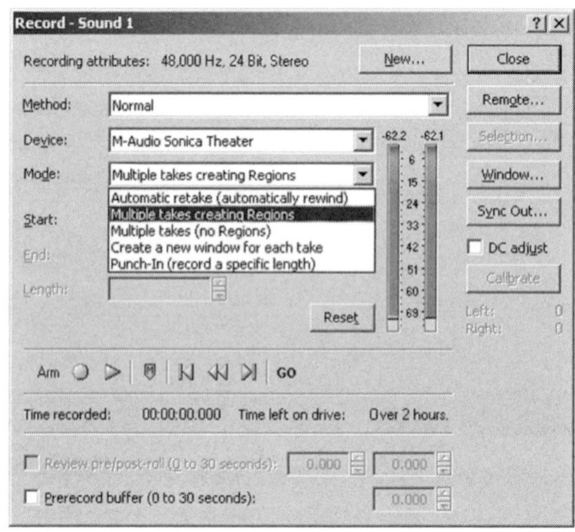

- Multiple takes (no regions). Subsequent takes are added to the end of the file, but without regions.
- Create a new window for each take. Each take gets its own data window.

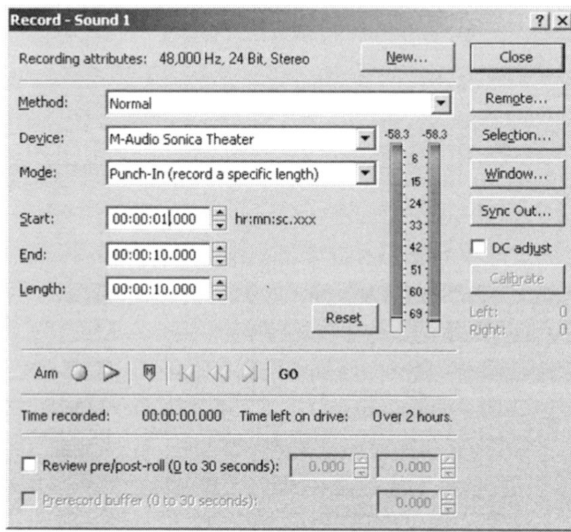

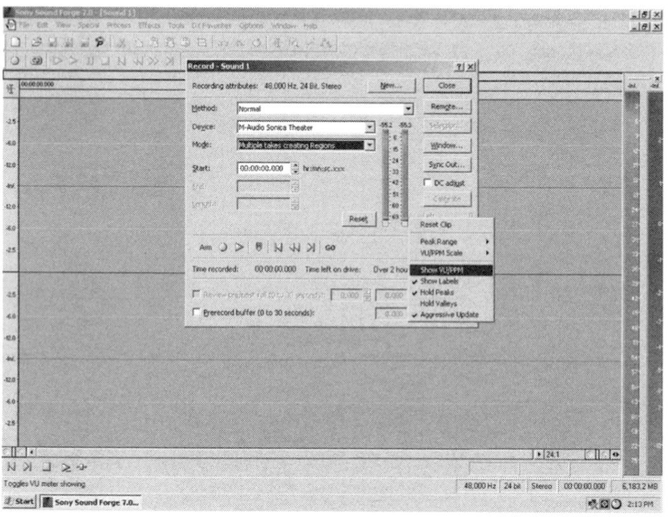

- Punch-In (record a specific length). Here you indicate a specific region to record into. This is useful when you need to replace a single problem such as a blown word or bad note.

Specify the start time for your recording, if applicable. If you choose the Punch-In mode you can also indicate the end time. The length displays automatically.

To the right of these settings are the record level meters. The default displays only the peak meters. Right click the meters to choose alternate meter views.

Monitor these meters in connection with the hardware and/or software level settings (as described above) to set and record the best level for your recordings. Generally, you want to get as close to zero on the peak meters without going over on loud sounds. For the VU meters set levels to hover around its zero point with occasional jumps above and below depending on the source you're recording.

Because of the peak hold feature, click the Reset button to clear the meters at any time.

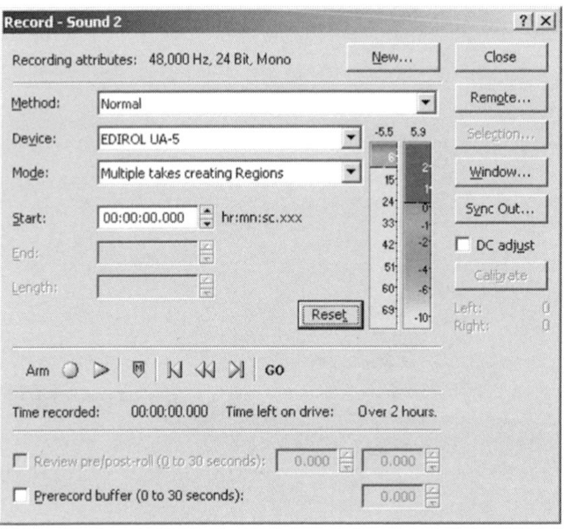

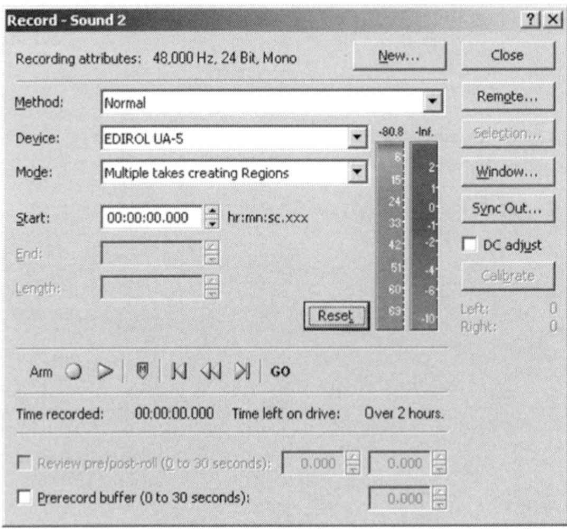

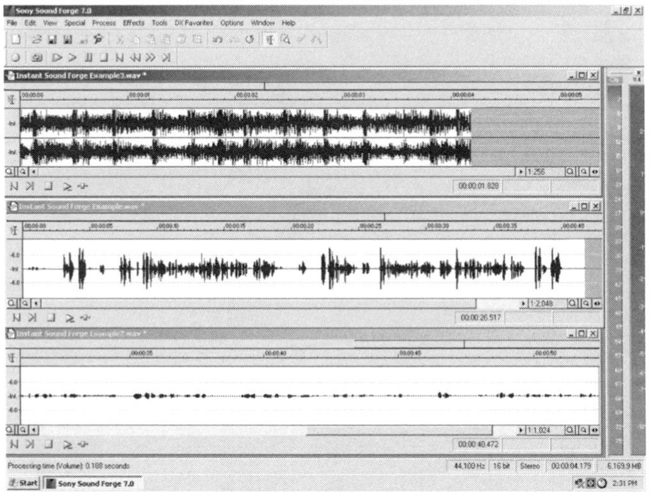

To give you an idea of proper recording levels, look at these three recordings. The top level is too high with clipping (distortion), the middle level is right for a voice recording, and the bottom level if far too low. Setting proper levels takes some practice, but you'll soon learn it.

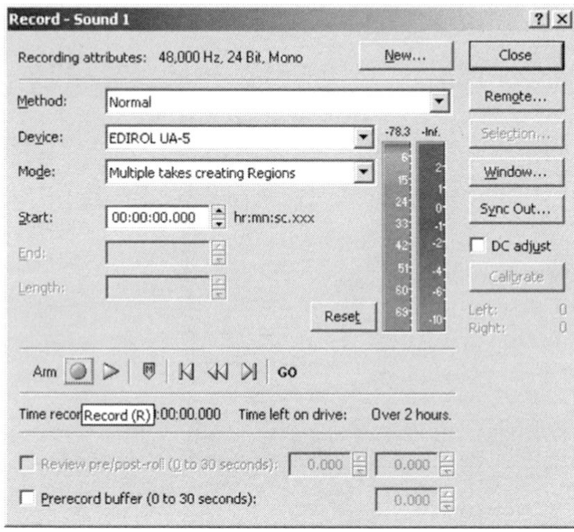

To start the recording, click the red record button (next to the word Arm) to begin recording.

The record button automatically changes to a stop button once you begin recording. Also, notice the word "recording" flashes. To stop the recording, click the stop button (or hit ESC).

Notice how the recording displays in the data window behind the record dialog.

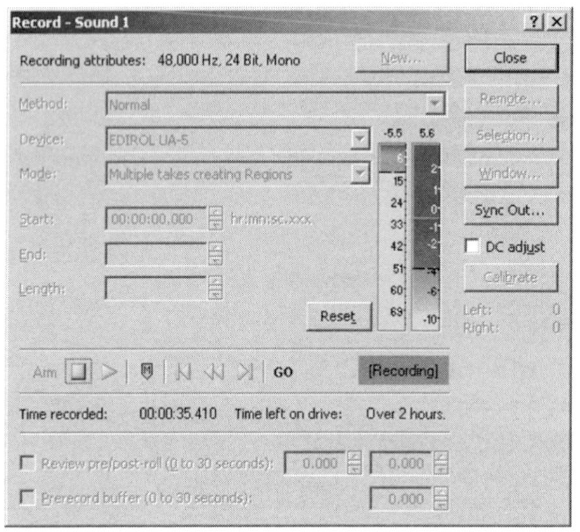

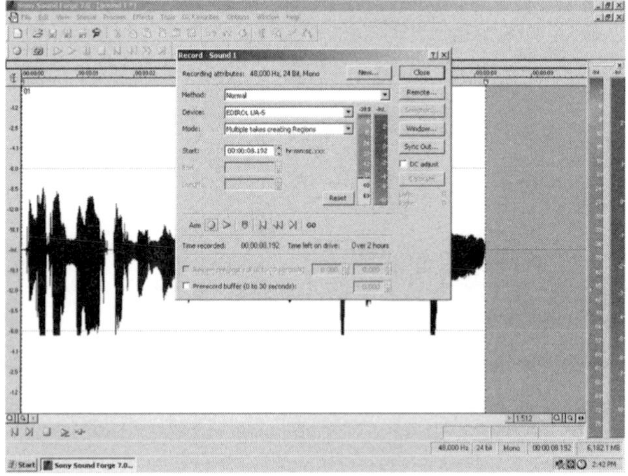

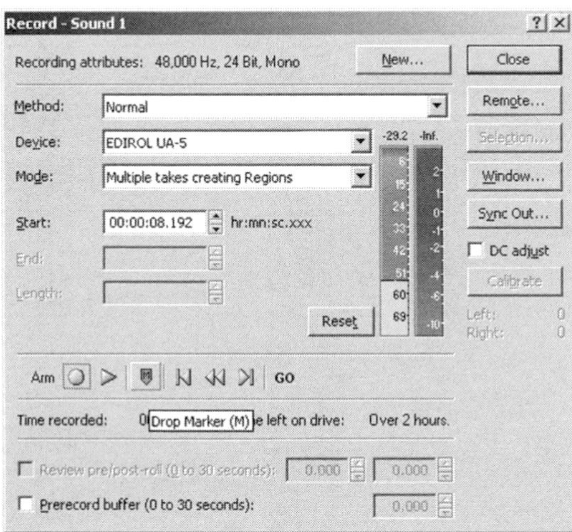

You can then use the transport controls to review what you recorded without having to close the record dialog box. This makes it easier to check your recording and return to record mode, if needed. Notice you can insert a marker while recording or while playing back the file, too.

The Time recorded shows the length of your file and the Time left indicates the drive space in recording time at the current attribute settings remaining on the drive.

If you select the Punch-In mode, you can specify the Pre/post-roll. This let's you play back a portion of the file both before and after the punch-in section.

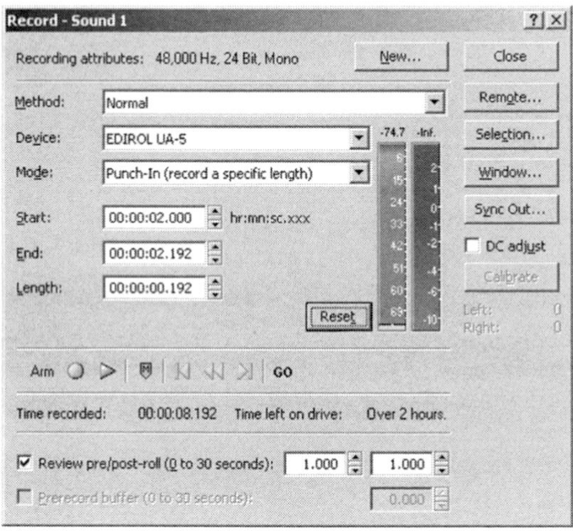

Select the Prerecord buffer checkbox and enter a value to setup this buffer. Sound Forge automatically records this amount into your file before you hit record. This feature can keep you from missing the start of a recording because you didn't click into record fast enough.

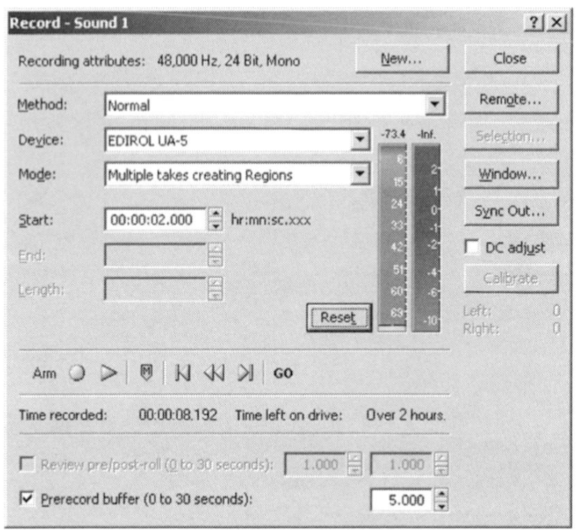

Along the right side of the record dialog are a few other buttons. Click Close to exit the record dialog.

Click Remote to minimize the Sound Forge window leaving you with a streamlined recording interface. Click back to return to the full window.

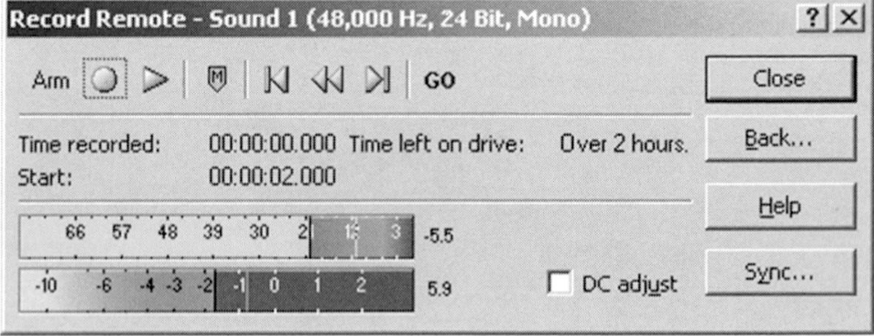

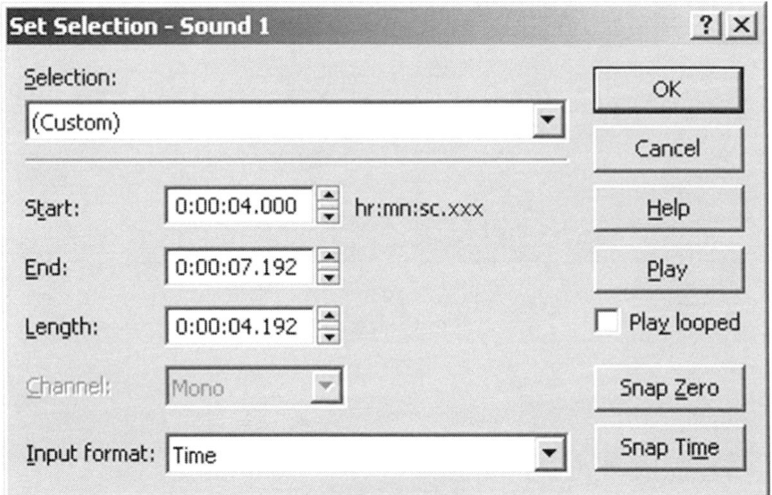

If you are using the Punch-In mode, Selection helps you set the right start and end points.

Because Sound Forge lets you have several windows open at once, click Window to choose where you want to direct the latest recording.

The Sync Out button lets you select if Sound Forge should send MTC/SMPTE timecode to an external device .

Enable the DC adjust checkbox to automatically adjust for any DC offset introduced into your recording by your hardware. Some soundcards add direct current (DC) to recordings with the effect of misaligning the zero crossing (where a sound wave crosses the center line). Sound Forge can automatically compensate for this. After checking the box, click the calibrate button and set the proper adjustment.

If you prefer, you can check and compensate for DC offset before editing your file instead of using this recording feature.

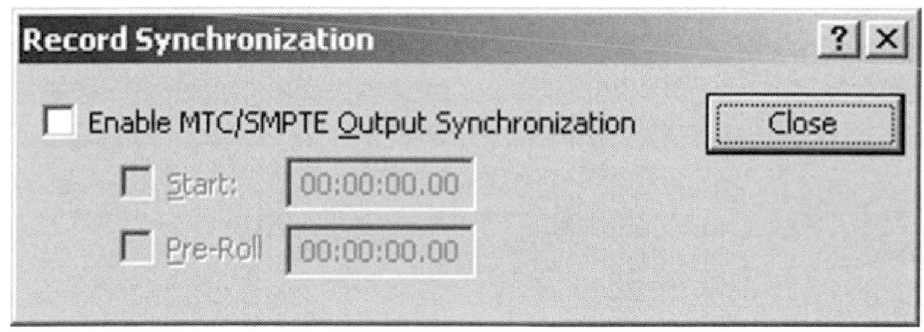

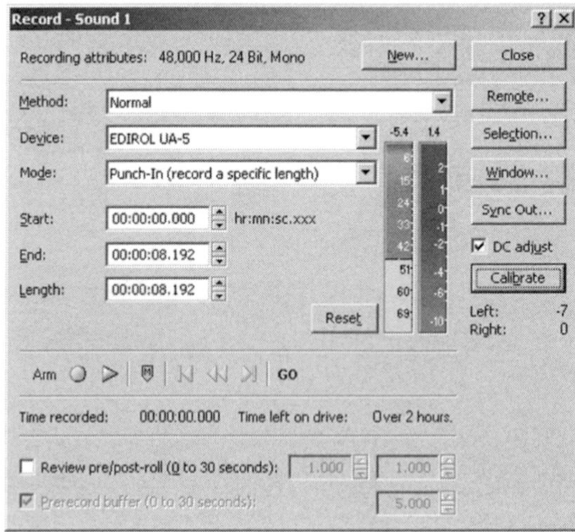

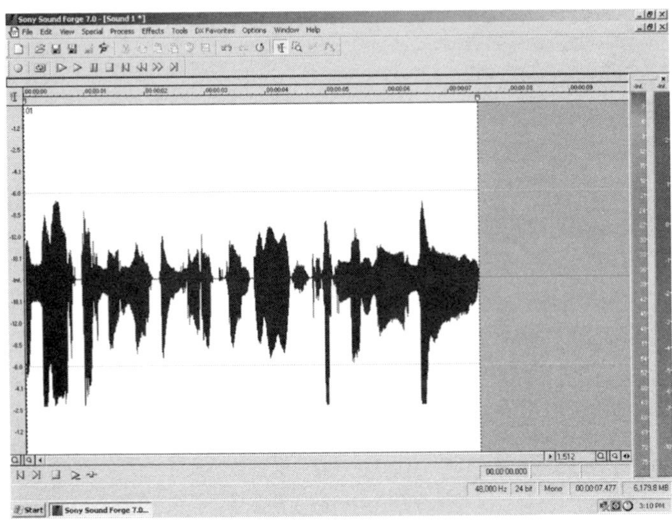

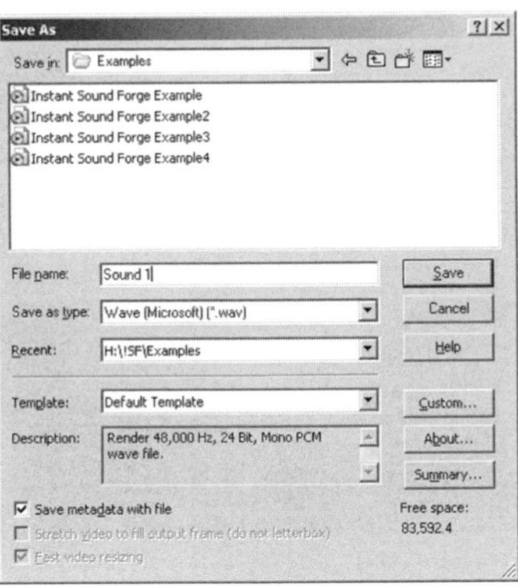

When you are satisfied with your recording(s), close the record dialog box. Notice that Sound

Forge has named your file Sound 1 (Sound 2, Sound 3, etc.).

Click File > Save as to give your file a proper name. I recommend always using Save as because you have more control over the disposition of your file. You can name it, convert to a different type, and direct where you want to store it. In the template box you can also double-check to make sure you are saving it in the format you want. With the Save metadata with file checked, markers and regions are saved along with the file. Also, if you use Acid® tools, the file (discussed later) and the information needed by Acid® get stored as metadata.

CD extraction

Another method for getting digital files into your computer is by extracting the data from an existing CD. For example, you may have purchased a sound effect or production music library that comes on audio CDs.

Click File > Extract Audio from CD to display the dialog box. Here you can extract individual tracks, a time range, or the entire CD. Use the play button for preview. You can even extract multiple tracks to one file and automatically create regions for each track and markers for each index change.

Once you've selected the track, Sound Forge automatically handles the file conversion.

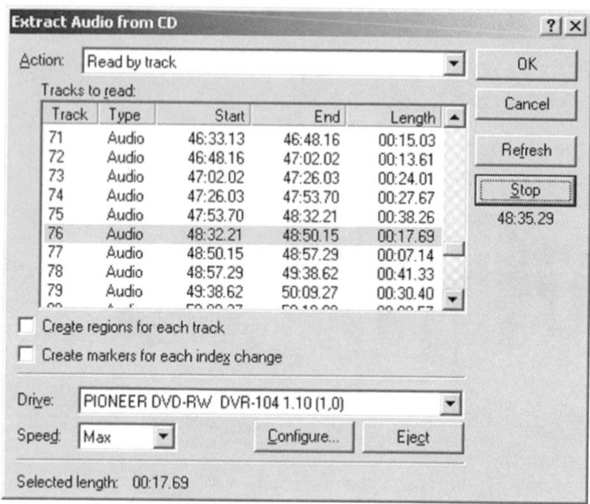

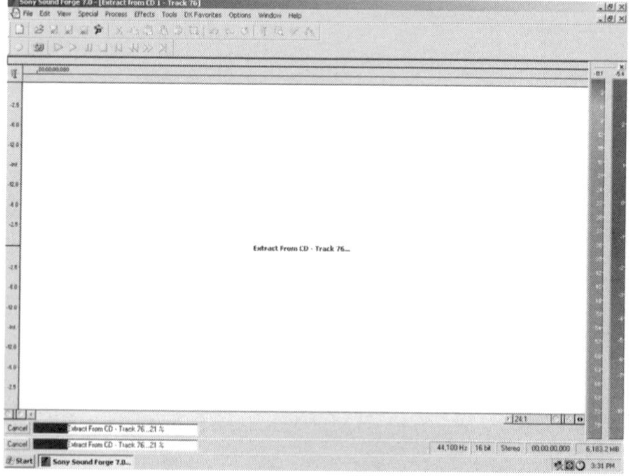

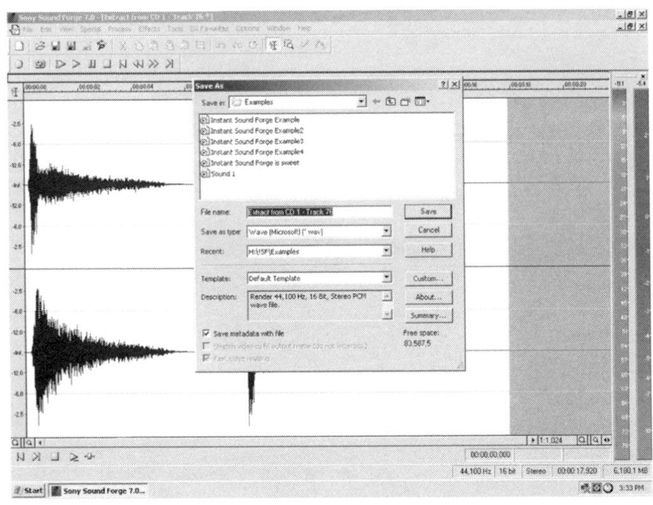

Then you can use File > Save as to name the file.

Another method for extracting from audio CDs is to use the new Explorer. Choose View > Explorer (or ALT+1). Navigate to the CD in your drive, select the track you want, and then drag and drop it on the Sound Forge workspace.

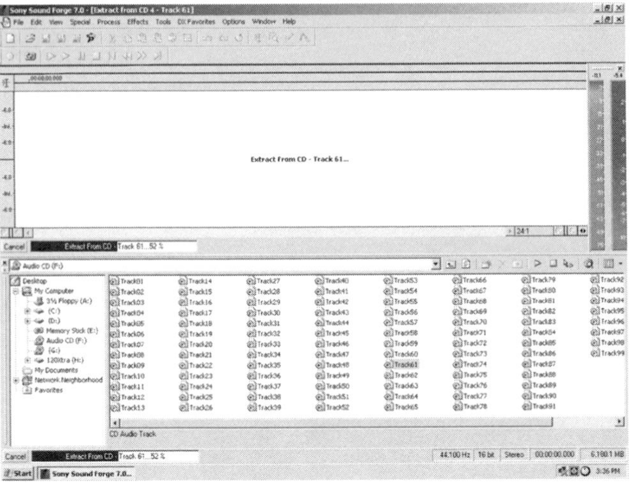

You can CTRL+Click multiple files and even preview tracks all from within the Explorer.

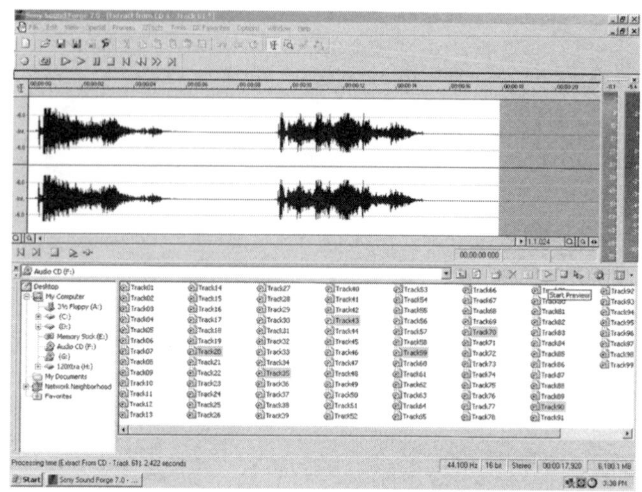

Some sound effect and production music libraries come in .wav format (a few as MP3s) on CD-ROMS. In this case, you do not need to extract the audio and can simply copy the files from the disc to the hard drive using the standard Windows Explorer / My Computer tools.

Sound Forge will open many different file formats. To convert from one format to another, open the file, click File > Save as, and choose the appropriate format from the Save as type list. Sound Forge converts the file automatically.

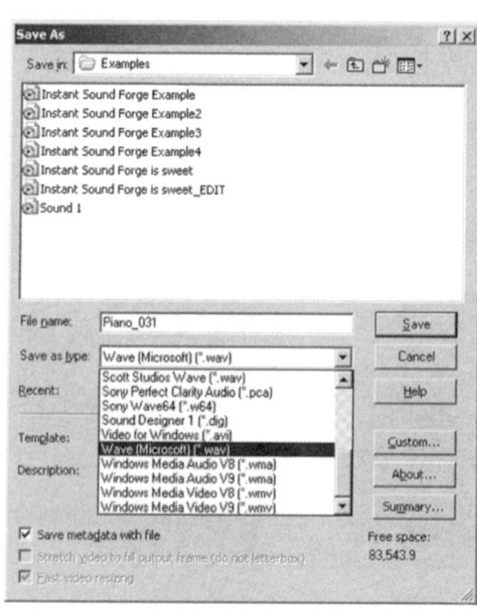

Some encode formats have options you can set. Choose from the templates for the file format and/or click the Custom button for more options.

Automatic recording modes

As mentioned earlier, Sound Forge has three automatic recording modes. These tools can make recording certain situations easier.

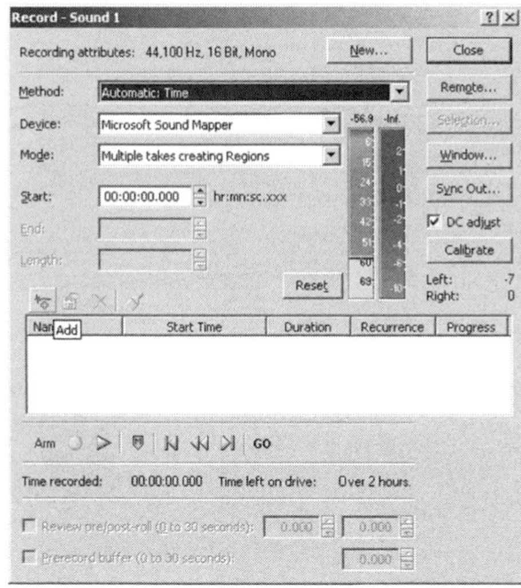

Launch the record dialog by either clicking the red record button on the transport toolbar or using the CTRL+R shortcut. Click the Method of recording. Also, click the Window button to choose the proper destination for the timed recording.

Choose Automatic: time when you want to specify unattended start and stop times for recording.

To program events, click the Add icon.

In the dialog box, name the event and choose One Time, Daily, or Weekly for the Recurrences.

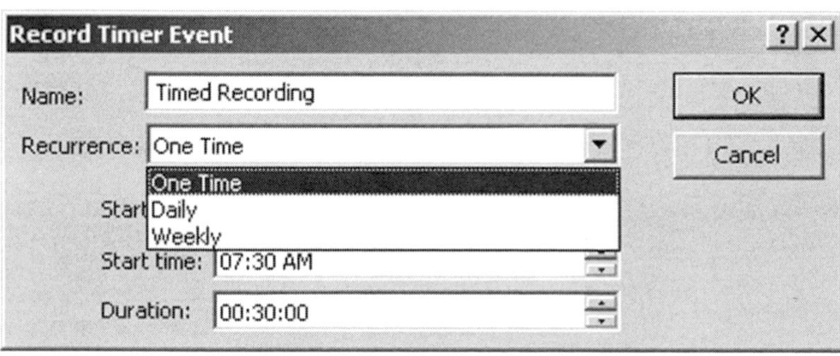

Indicate a start date. Either type the date or use the calendar.

Program the start time, duration, and then click OK. The programmed event appears in the list. Select an event to edit or delete it. Use the sweep tool to clear all events.

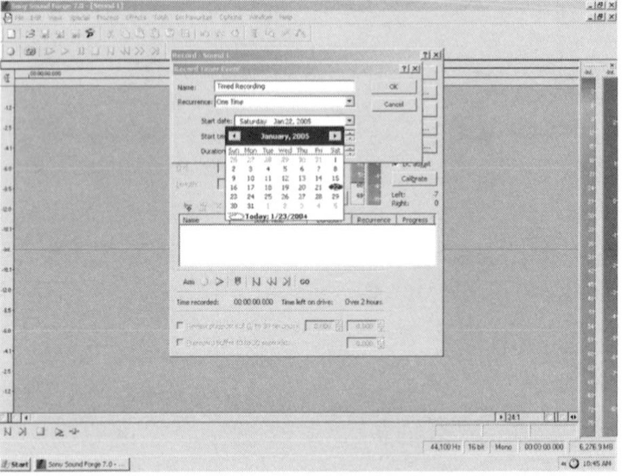

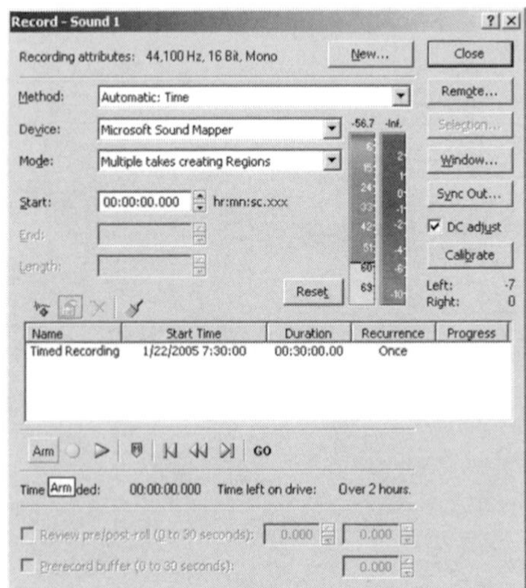

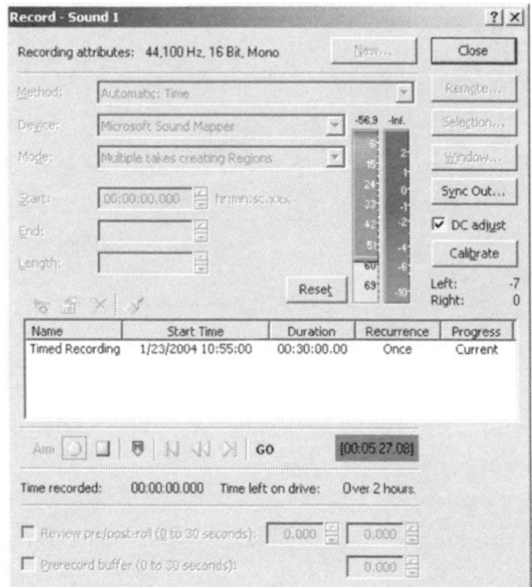

When finished programming, click Arm and Sound Forge will begin counting down to the next event. When it reaches the time, recording starts and stops automatically. You can click Stop manually if you need to interrupt a recording.

Remember to leave Sound Forge running with the Record dialog open and armed or the timed recording will not work. You can use Remote mode, but you must click that before you click Arm.

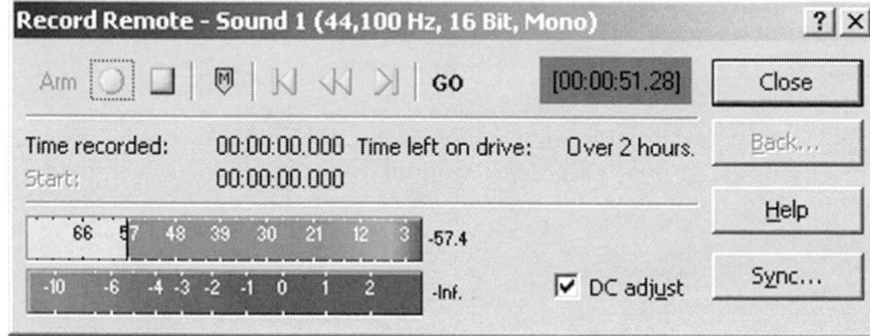

Choose Automatic: threshold to only record sound that exceeds a specific volume level. Set the Threshold using the slider. Only sounds that are louder than the setting trigger the recording. The Release controls how long after a sound drops below the threshold to stop recording. This critical setting helps prevent exiting record mode during a very brief pause or low level sound.

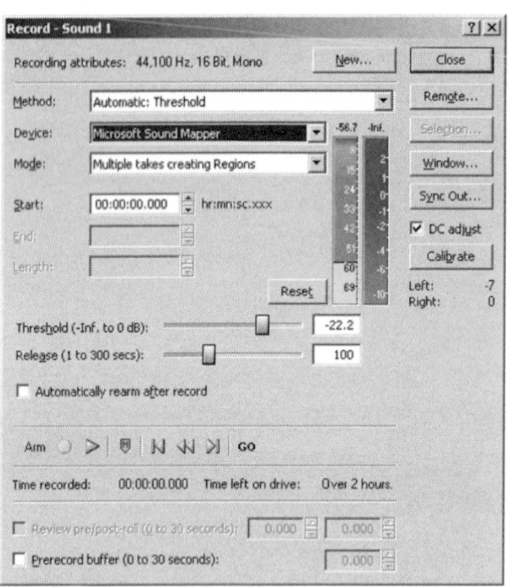

To prevent missing the start of a sound, click the Prerecord buffer and enter a value. Sound Forge will add this amount to the start of the recording once sound exceeds the threshold. Again, it's a safety feature to help prevent missing a part.

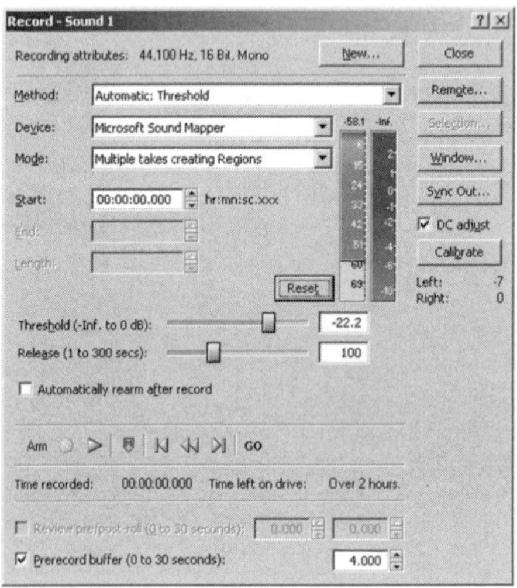

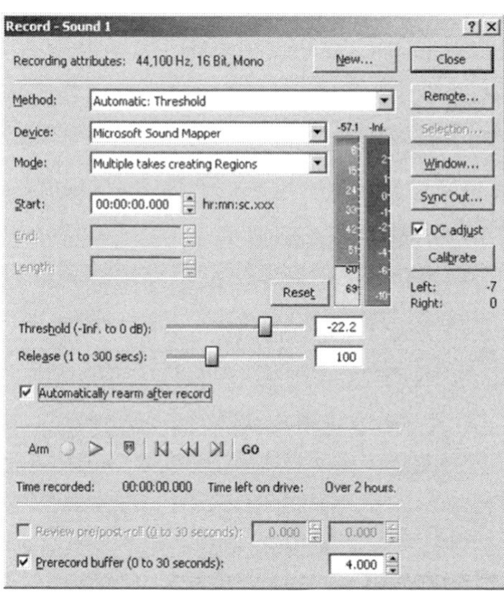

Click Automatically rearm after record if you want to keep recording new sound, such as a meeting. If this is just a one-shot recording, leave this box unchecked.

Once again, click Arm to begin the process.

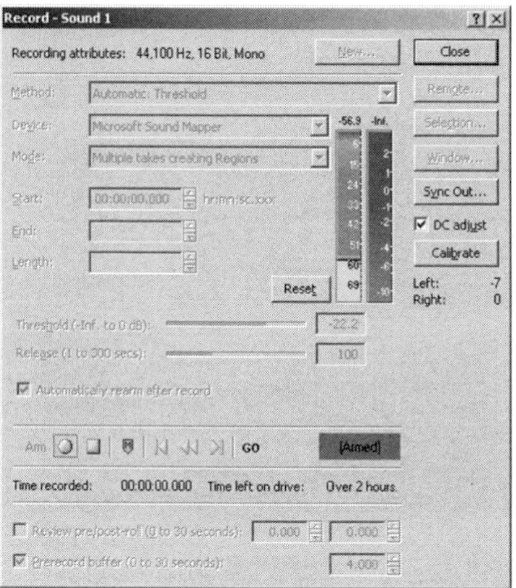

Use the Automatic: MIDI Timecode recording method to put Sound Forge into record based on data received from a MIDI device connected to your computer. Click the MIDI timecode start and/or the MIDI timecode end and type in the values. Click arm to ready the software. When the MIDI timecode is received, the recording begins and/or ends based on the settings.

Setup specific MIDI details using Options > Preferences > MIDI/Sync.

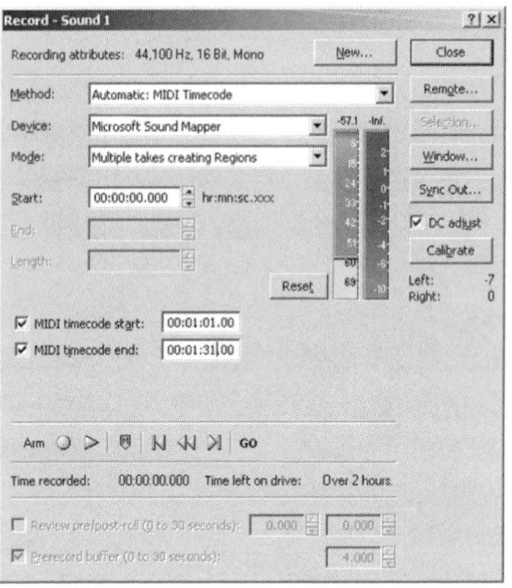

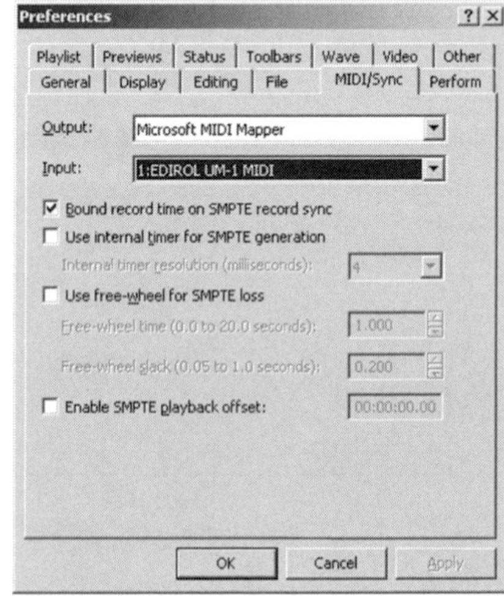

Chapter 5

Editing

The real power of Sound Forge®, and the reason so many people choose to use it, is the control you have over your files. You can literally edit down to the sample level and tweak your audio in ways limited only by your imagination. There is a full complement of tools available for both basic and critical editing that allow you to both fix problems and sweeten the final result.

As said before, audio editing is a bit like word processing with sound. You can cut, copy, paste, delete, mute, and rearrange pieces of audio into a final presentation. Here's the editing workflow:

- Listen to the recordings first. Even if you recorded the audio yourself, and especially if you received the audio from another source, take the time to go through the file and just listen. There may be mistakes or audio glitches that you didn't hear before. If you're listening for the first time, knowing what you have before you start editing is critical.
- Listen again, but this time follow along with the script. Now you can check for accuracy against the script, if that applies to the project, and note any discrepancies.
- Use File > Save as to make a copy of the audio file. This way you don't accidentally ruin your original recording and can return to it if need be.
- Run the DC Offset utility. More on this below
- Use markers and regions to make notes about the

file. You might want to indicate all the good parts and alternative good takes, making it easier to trash the junk.

- Start editing. You have the choice to edit in a single window or multiple ones. Find out which method works for you.
- Save often. If the project is particularly large or involved, I use Save as to save different versions as the work progresses, usually adding the date and time to the file name.
- Get a rough cut together. Obviously, delete the parts you don't need -- the warm-up, the mistakes, and anything else you won't use.
- Take a break to rest your ears and clear your head. (You did save your work, right?)
- Listen to the rough cut and look for ways to improve the edit.
- Clean up the edit further and begin to sweeten the audio by working with volume and other creative effects.
- Save the final file in the high quality .wav file format.
- Save the file in any other formats you need, such as encoding the file to MP3.
- Backup your work to another drive or CD/DVD (or both!).

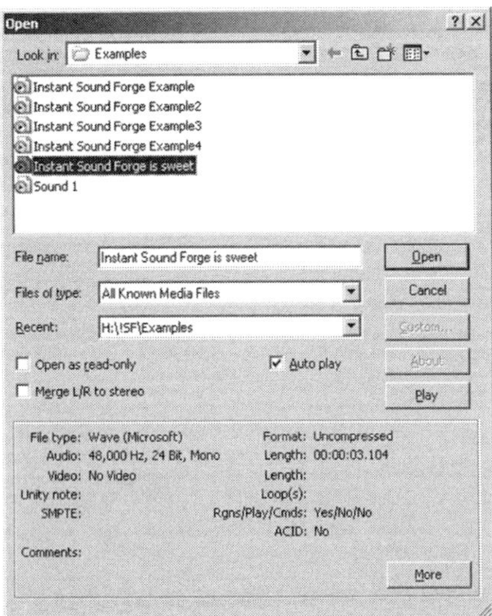

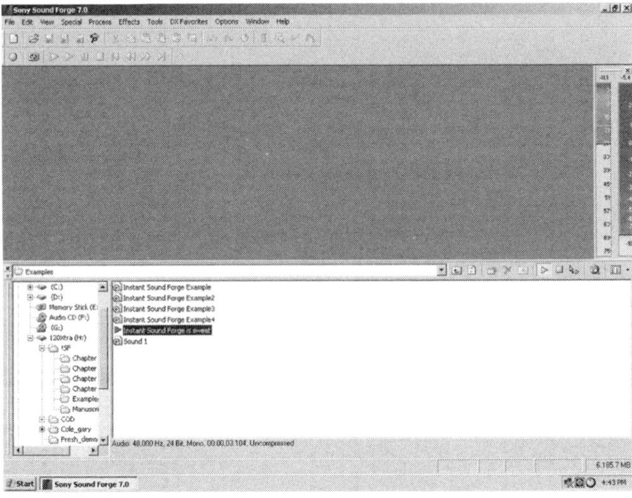

Opening files

To Open an existing file, click File > Open, CTRL + O, or click the File folder icon in the main toolbar. In the open dialog box, find the file, select it, then click OK. You can Shift+Click to select a range of files or CTRL+Click to select multiple files.

Alternately, use the Explorer. Choose View > Explorer (or ALT+1). Navigate to the file, click to select it, then drag and drop it on the Sound Forge workspace. You can CTRL+Click multiple files and even preview your file from within the Explorer

Run the DC offset utility on the file. Go to Process > DC Offset. You can change the settings in the dialog box, but Automatically detect and remove is satisfactory. Some sound cards apply DC current when recording. This anomaly can misalign the zero crossing of the waveform. You should always make your edits where the waveform crosses the center line otherwise a glitch or click may occur. But first, you need to make sure the center line is represented accurately by using this tool.

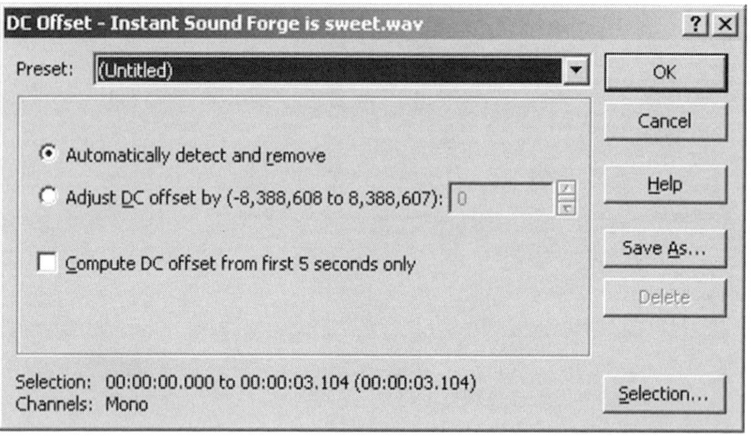

Next, use File > Save as to make a copy of your file. I usually just add EDIT to the filename. Continue to work on this copy. Save your original file as a backup.

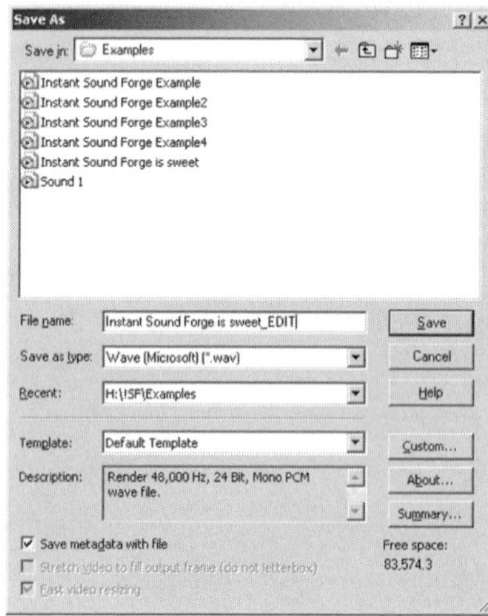

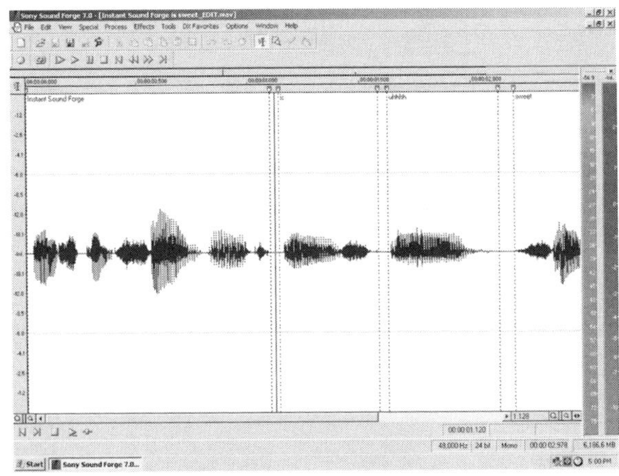

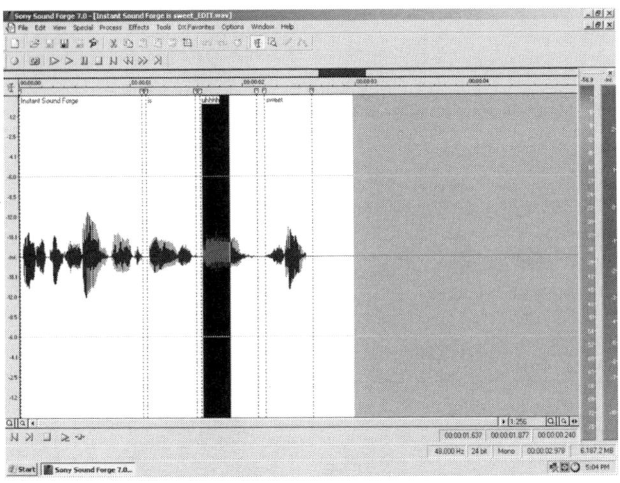

Listen to the file and add any markers or regions to the file. In this example, the regions surround the words in the phrase: Instant Sound Forge is, uhhh, sweet.

Basic edits

To delete the "uhhh", select the word by dragging the mouse over the waveform while holding down the left mouse button. You can trim the selection as needed by grabbing either end of the selection with the mouse and making the adjustment. Alternately, position the cursor, hold the SHIFT key, and use the arrow keys on your keyboard to make a selection.

With the entire word selected, click Edit > Delete or press the keyboard Delete key.

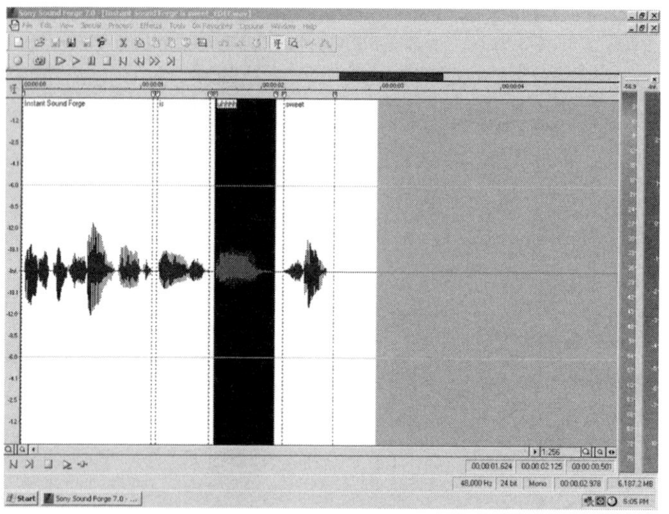

The word is gone. Note that the region referring to the word is still there. You can right click the region and delete it, too. Play the file to hear how it sounds with the mistake missing.

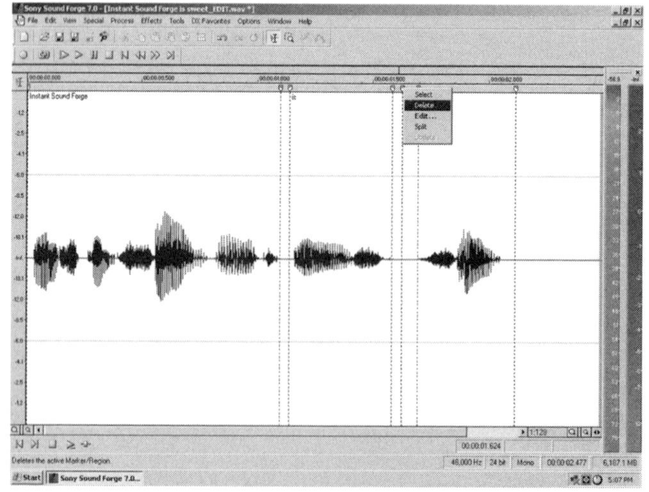

If you are not happy with the edit, you can undo it. Click Edit > Undo, the Undo tool on the main toolbar, or the shortcut CTRL+Z. Now you can make a new selection to edit.

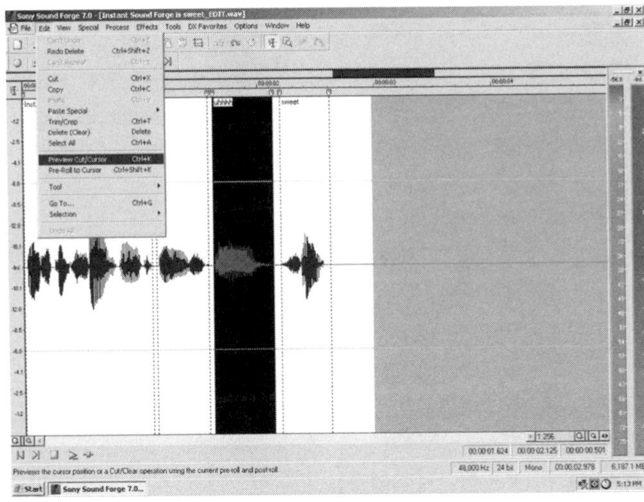

You can preview an edit, too. Select what you want to delete. Click Edit > Preview Cut/Cursor or use the shortcut CTRL+K.

Sound Forge will play the file beginning just slightly before the edit, skip the selected section, and then play a little more of the file after the edit. This way you can preview the edit, make any adjustments, and then proceed. Adjust the Cut preview pre-roll and post-roll times using Options > Preferences > Other tab.

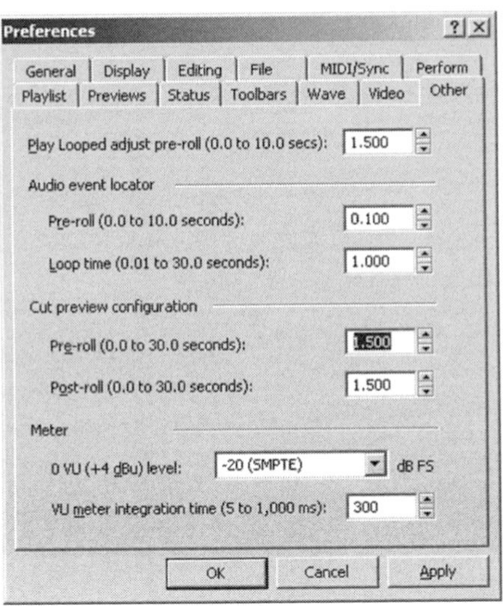

Instead of deleting a section, you can select and mute it instead. This is useful when you want to eliminate something while keeping the timing intact. Make the selection as before then click Process > Mute.

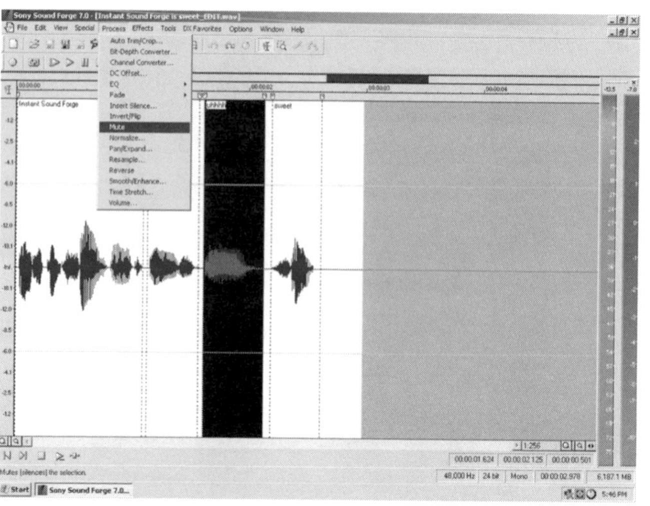

Notice how the waveform for "uhhh" is missing, but the space it occupied remains.

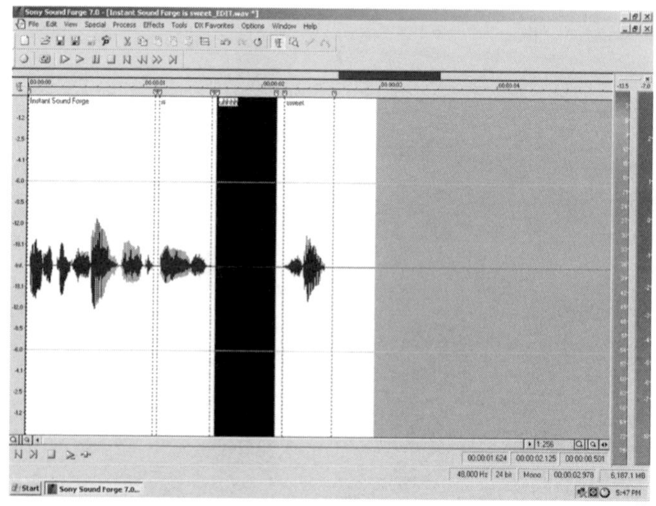

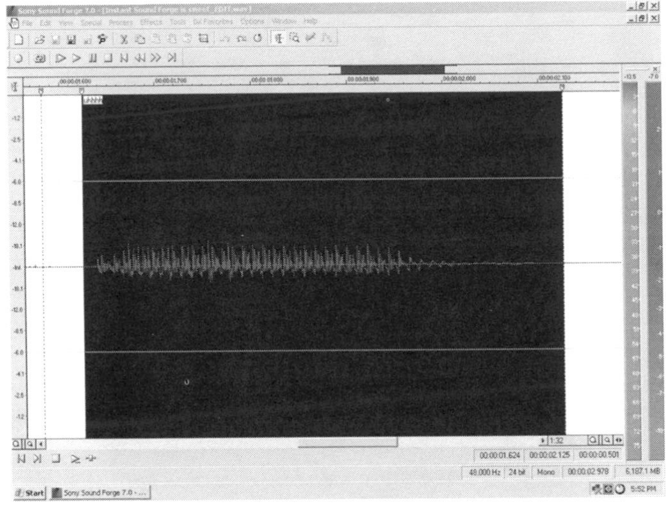

When editing, it is important to make cuts where the waveform crosses the center line and/or during silences. The only way to be sure you are cutting at the zero crossing is to zoom in when making your selection. Too many novice Sound Forge users forget they can zoom in to really focus on small parts of the waveform. If you're having trouble editing, try zooming in a little closer.

Here the cuts are not at the zero crossing.

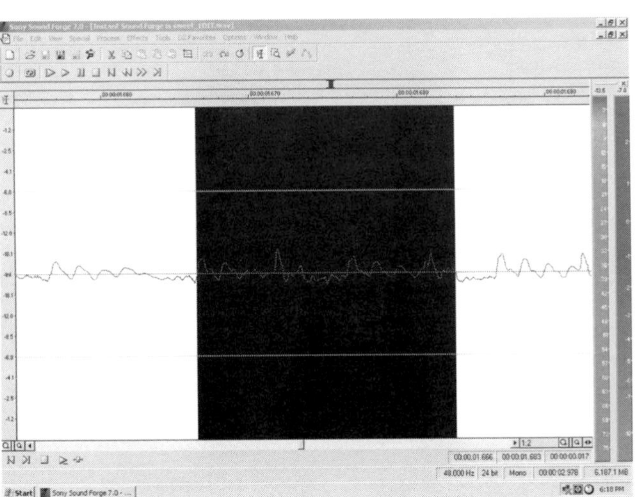

After the edit, see how the waveforms stop and start unnaturally?

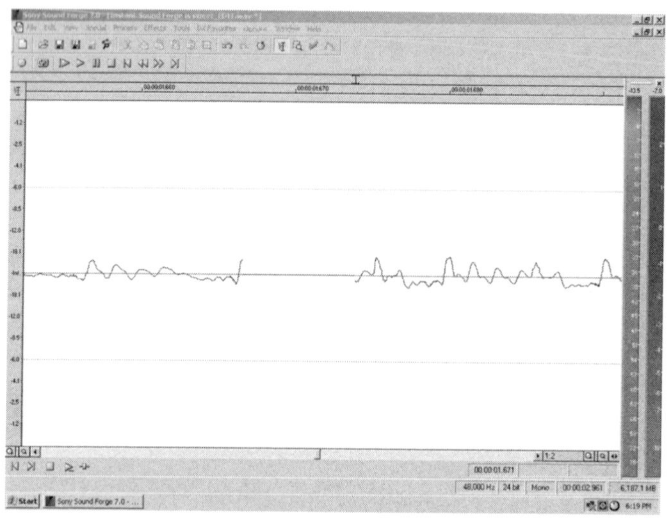

Zooming in further reveals that Sound Forge has snapped the waveform back to the center line. Look by the markers to see this. Not cutting where a waveform crosses the center line can create a tick, click, or other glitch when you play back the audio.

So, make sure you cut where your waveform crosses the center line. After making a selection, click Edit > Selection > Snap to Zero or use the keyboard and type Z. Both edges of the selection will move to the nearest zero crossing. Check to make sure this is an acceptable edit point before proceeding.

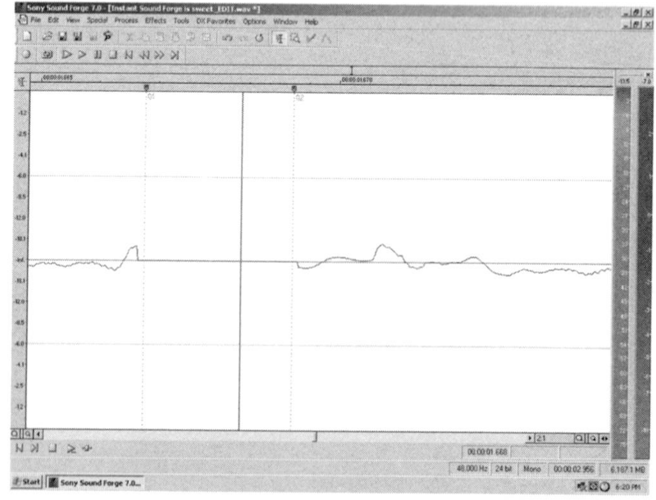

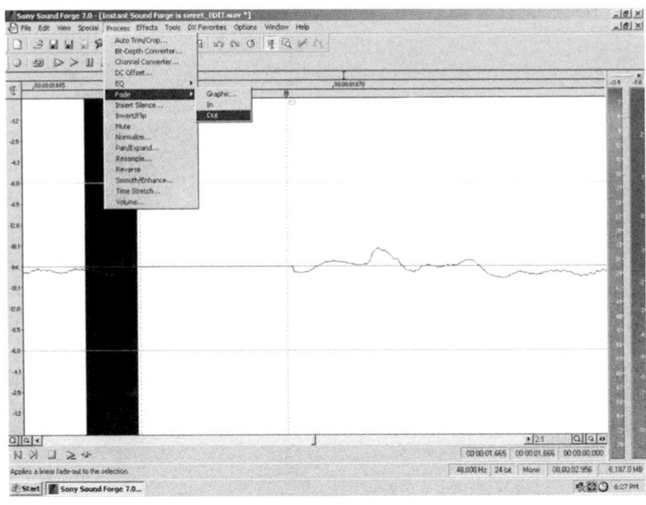

If you forget to cut at zero crossings, and later hear a tick when you play back the file, zoom in where you hear the glitch. Select a small portion of the waveform, including the tick, and choose Process > Fade > Out if it is at the end of a wave.

Select and click Process > Fade > In if the tick starts a new wave.

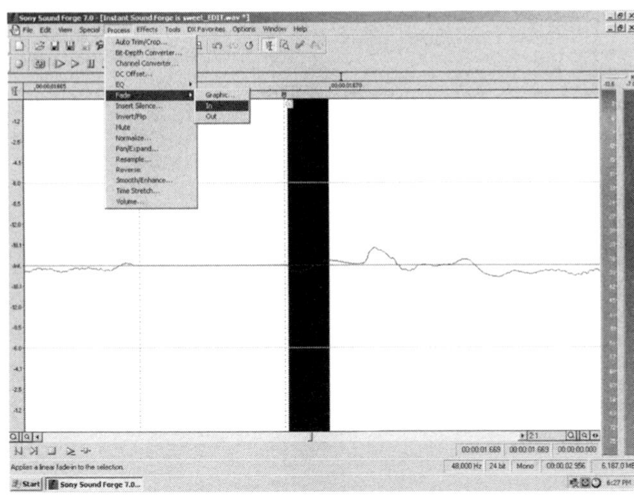

These minuscule fades, in our example less than .001 of a second, will get rid of the glitch and be so small as to be imperceptible to the ear. Tiny fades in and out can really disguise both bad and difficult edits, such as when you have to cut tightly on a word or syllable.

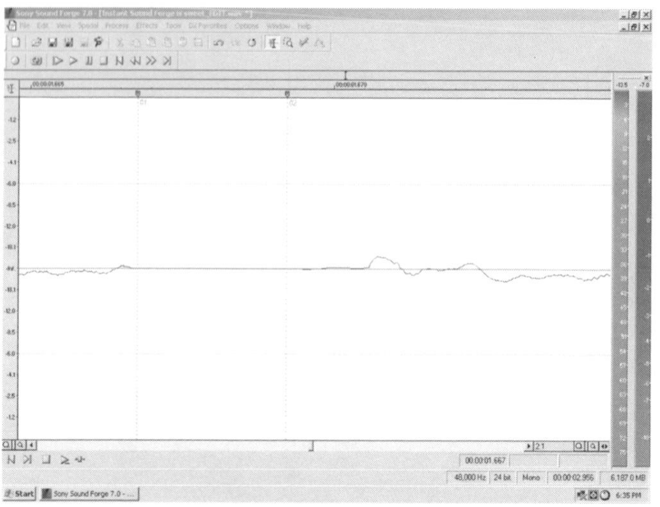

Cut, copy, paste

Just like word processing, you can also cut, copy, and paste with Sound Forge. Make a selection and choose Edit > Cut (CTRL+X) to remove what you selected from the file and place it on the Windows clipboard. The clipboard is a temporary holding place for data. But be forewarned, only one chunk of data can be on the clipboard at a time.

Alternately, make a selection and choose Edit > Copy (CTRL+C) to make a copy of what you selected and place it on the Windows clipboard. The original selection remains.

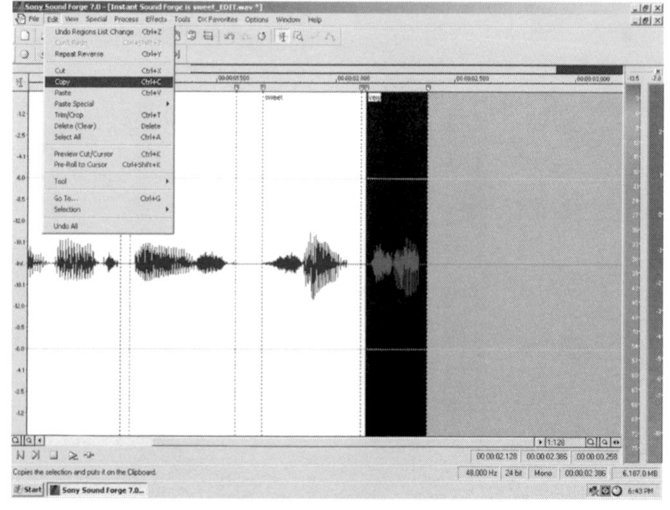

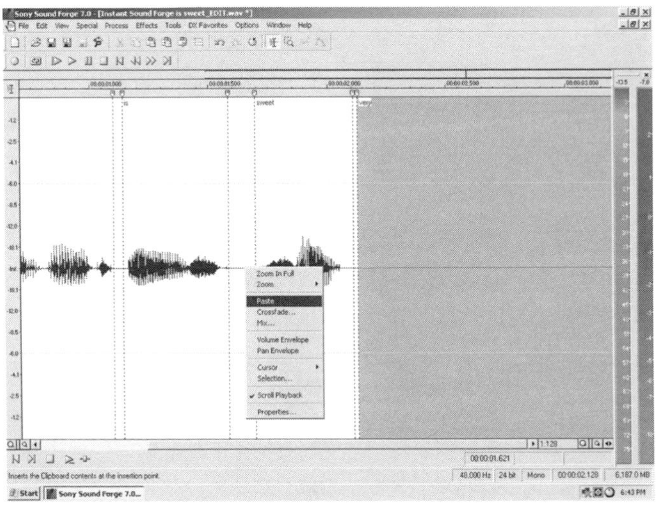

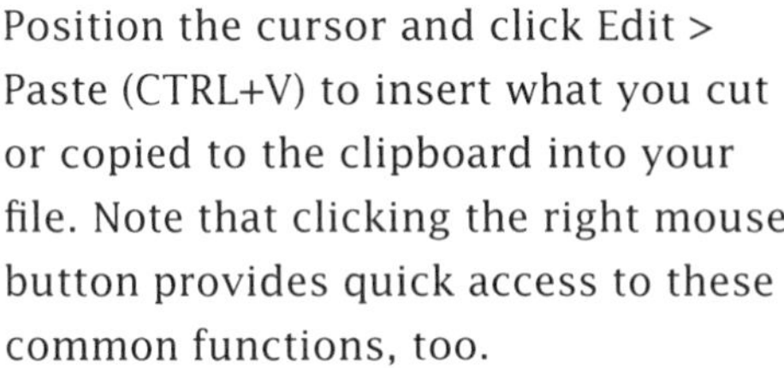

Position the cursor and click Edit > Paste (CTRL+V) to insert what you cut or copied to the clipboard into your file. Note that clicking the right mouse button provides quick access to these common functions, too.

Note the result of cutting and pasting "very" before "sweet" in this example.

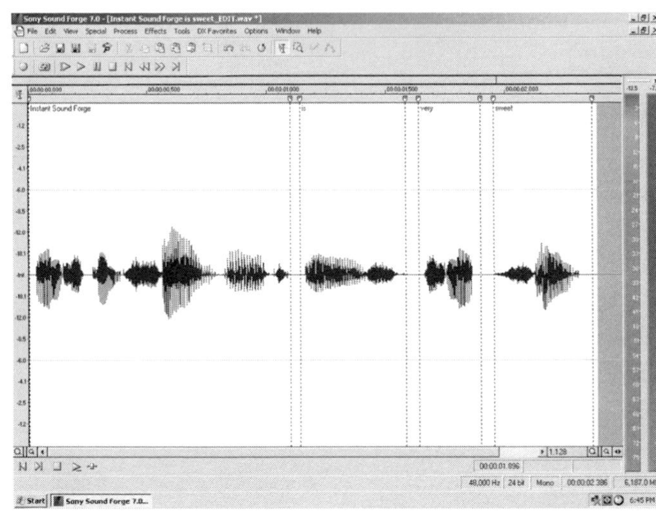

The cut, copy, and paste functions aren't limited to a single file either. You can insert content from another file or transfer data to another file at any time. Some people actually prefer to edit with multiple windows instead of just inside a single file. For example, you could grab only the best sections from a longer file and cut and paste them into another file to build a rough edit. Typically, on shorter pieces, I'll edit in the file, and use the build-up technique with a second file on longer editing projects. Your preferred working style is up to you.

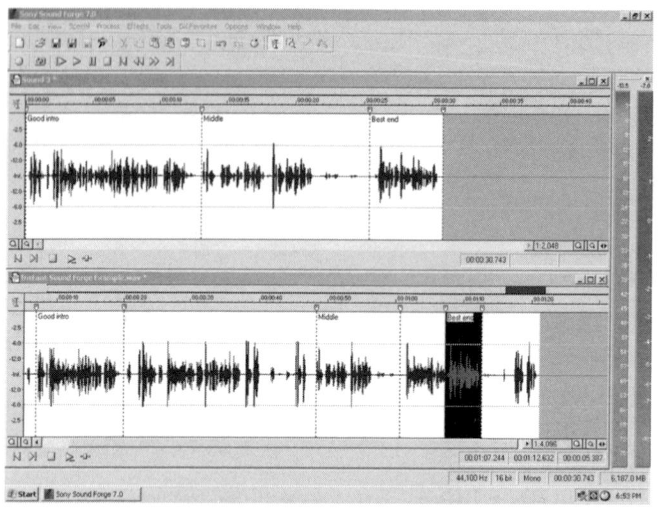

To create additional windows, click File > New. Make sure the new window matches the attributes of the source track (sample rate, bit depth, and channels). This way you can cut, copy, and paste between them with no problems.

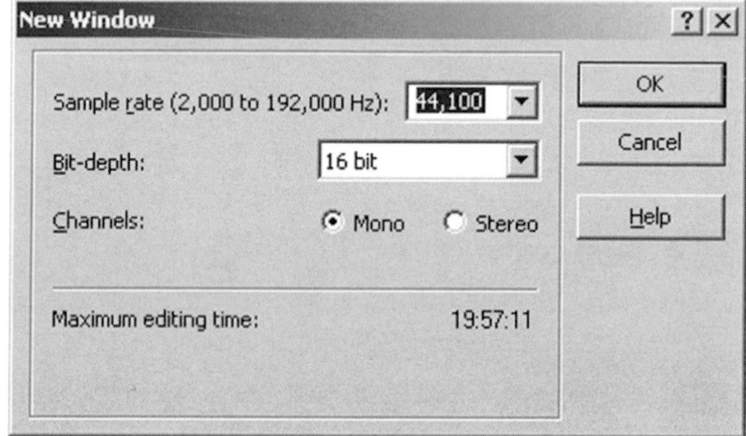

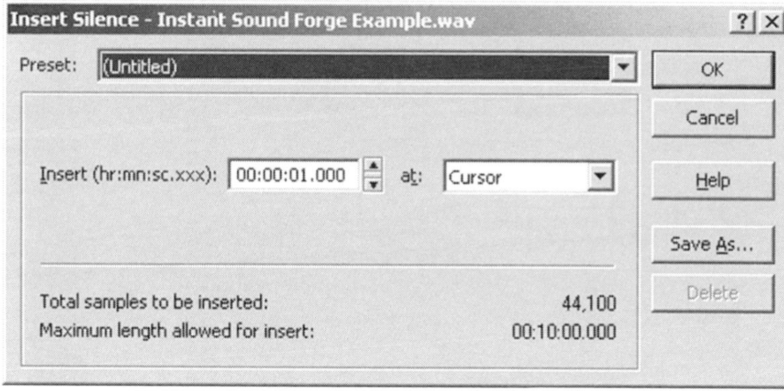

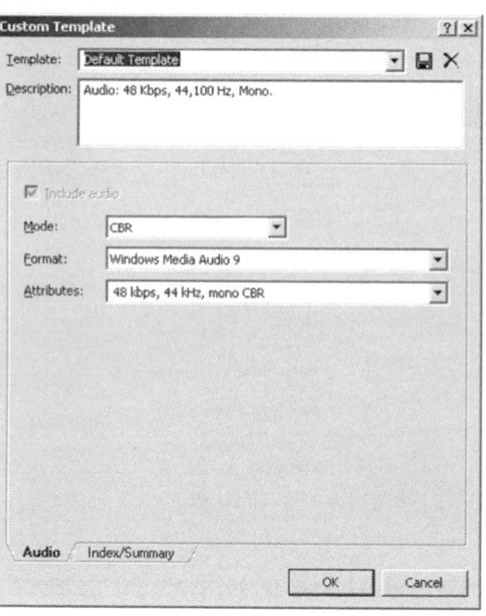

When editing you will often do a lot of cutting—removing parts of a file. On occasion, you may need to insert silence instead. Position the cursor where you want to insert the silence and click Process > Insert silence. Type in a value and click OK.

File conversions

Sound Forge lets you perform several file conversions.

If you need to convert from one file format to another (e.g. MP3 to .wav), open the file, click File > Save as, and choose the appropriate format from the File Types list. Each format has templates you can choose from or click the Custom button for additional settings.

If you work at higher bit-depths, such as 24-bit, you will need to convert to 16-bit if you will burn your work to a standard audio CD. The Sound Forge bit-depth tools include dither and noise shaping settings for optimizing the conversion. Dither is low-level noise added to the file to help mask any quantization error resulting from the conversion. Noise shaping gives you additional control. Experiment to find the best settings for your work. To change the bit-depth, click Process > Bit-depth converter and alter the settings as needed.

In addition to bit depth, you can change a file's sample rate. Files destined for audio CDs must be at 44.1kHz. You can either upsample or downsample depending on the original file. Do note that upsampling a low sample rate file will not increase its quality, though.

Downsampling requires the use of a low-pass, anti-aliasing filter to keep frequencies that are more that half the sample rate from introducing aliasing distortion into the file. To change the sample rate of a file, click Process > Resample.

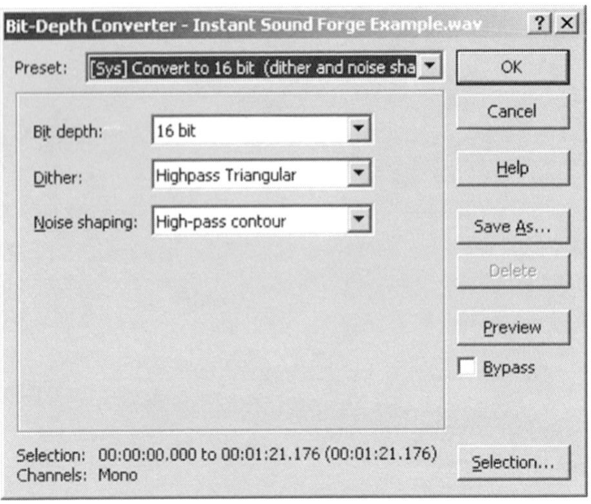

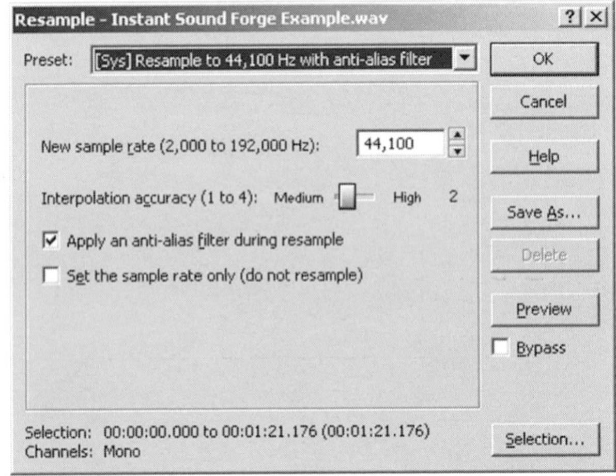

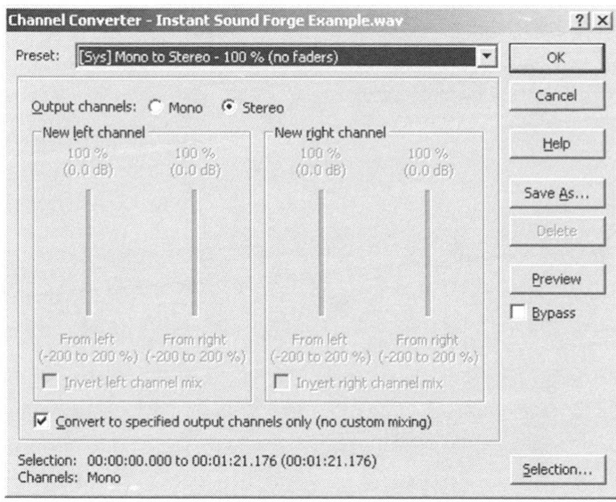

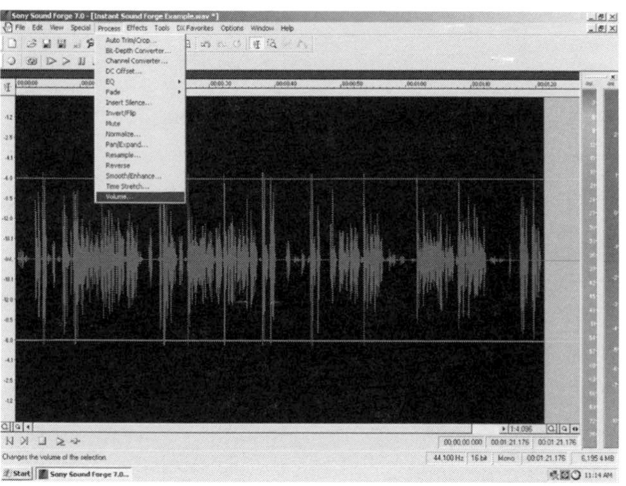

To change the channel configuration, click Process > Channel converter. You can convert a monaural file to stereo and vice versa. Note that converting a mono file to stereo does not make the file true stereo; it is still mono with equal energy in both channels. This is useful if you need to transfer a mono file to an audio CD as files must be two-channel, "stereo".

Volume

Although you should always strive to record the best levels, there may be times when you need to either boost or reduce the volume of an entire file or just a small portion.

To change the volume of the entire file, click Edit > Select All, use the keyboard shortcut CTRL+A, or double-click the waveform.

Next, click Process > Volume and make your adjustments. I usually boost or cut in 3dB increments. You can make finer adjustments to the control by clicking both the left and right mouse buttons and dragging the slider. Click the Preview button to hear how the change will sound.

To alter the volume of only a section of a file, select it, click Process > Volume, and make the change.

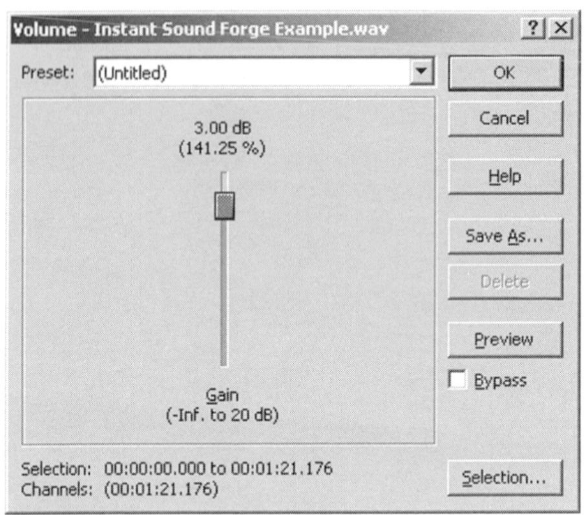

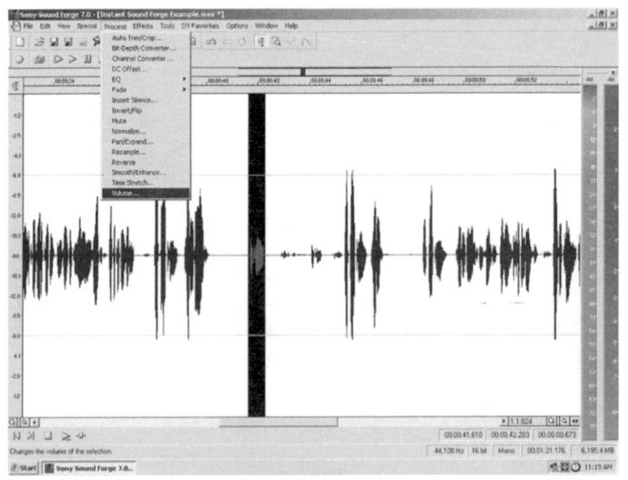

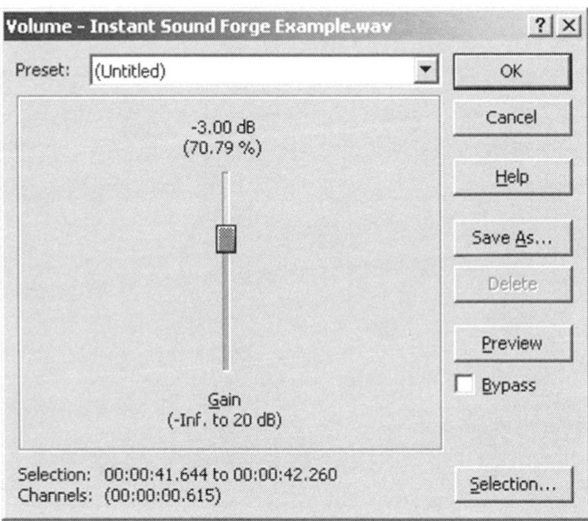

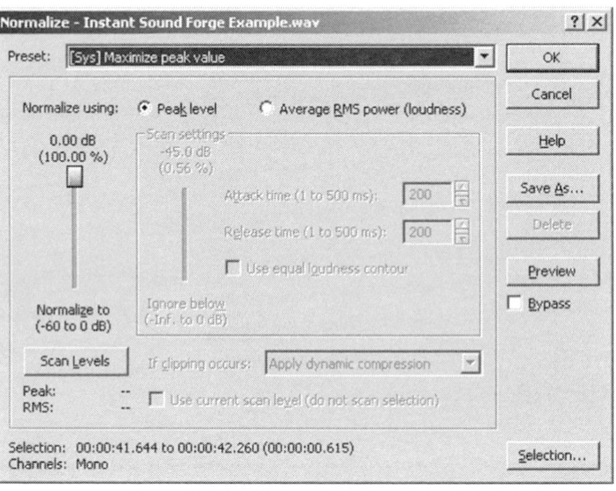

You can preview the volume change from the dialog box, but you will only hear the selection. A volume change may demand hearing the surrounding audio to see how the change fits. The best way to do this is to click OK to make the volume adjustment, then listen back to the file, including the surrounding audio. If the volume change it satisfactory, you're done. If not, Undo the change and start over or just boost or cut a little more until it sounds right. Again, boosting/cutting in smaller increments lets you fine tune the right level.

Still one more method for optimizing the level of a sound file is to normalize it. You can normalize either the whole file or a selection within it. Make the selection and then click Process > Normalize to display the dialog box.

You have the option to normalize either the peak level or the Average RMS power. Select the Peak level and Sound Forge scans the entire file (or the selection you made) looking for the loudest peak. The normalize function then boosts the volume of that peak to the level set by the slider and also increases the volume of the rest of the file by the same amount. You can also cut or decrease the peak level, if needed.

For example, if the loudest peak is at -3dB, normalize would bring its level to 0dB, a total increase of 3 dB. The rest of the file would be increased by 3dB, too. To make sure your file does not clip, I recommend peak normalizing to -0.03dB (99.66%) as a maximum.

Select Average RMS power and Sound Forge scans the entire file to determine its average level. The normalize function then boosts (or cuts) the volume based on the settings you indicate. RMS level is far different than peak level because the average level is overall much lower than any single or series of peaks. A file with an RMS of -10dB is VERY loud. Use caution when normalizing through this method. Start with the Presets and be prepared to experiment.

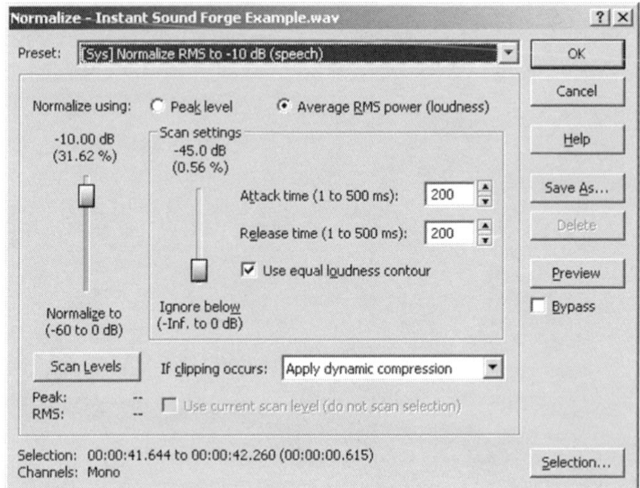

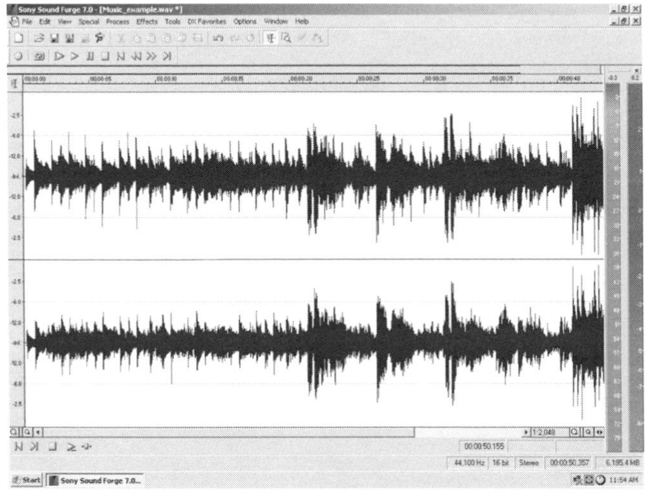

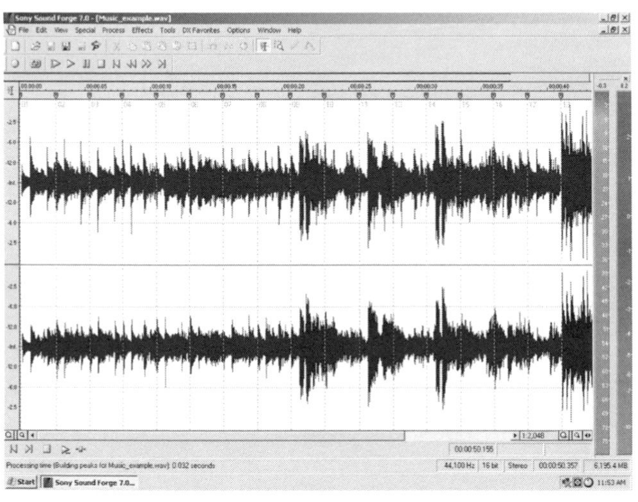

Editing music

Sound Forge is a great tool for editing and mastering music. Though most of the workflow is the same as detailed above, there are a few helpful shortcuts that make editing easier. As an example, you need to edit a full-length song into a 29 second piece to use in a radio commercial.

Open the song in the workspace and play it through once to get a feel for its rhythm. Play the song a second time and gently tap on your desk along with the rhythm. You may want to count the beats, too. As a rule, songs are either 4/4 (1-2-3-4) or waltz time, 3/4 (1-2-3).

Play the song a third time and count out the rhythm (1-2-3-4 or 1-2-3) while gently tapping the M key in time. Hit the M key hard enough to insert a marker on the downbeat only. Don't press the M key on every beat, just the 1. When finished your song will look something like this.

Inserting markers on the downbeats, the start of each measure, makes it a simple task to make edits that don't break the rhythm. Experiment with a few of your favorite songs.

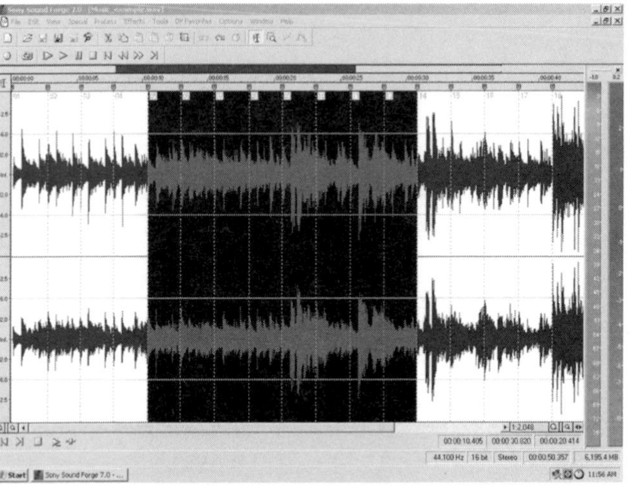

After the edit.

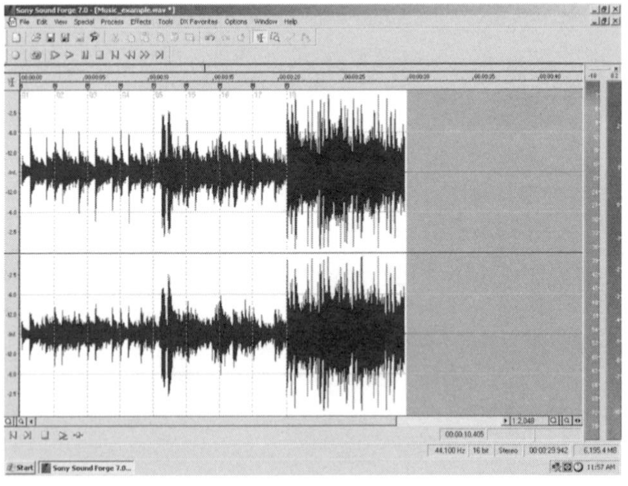

Chapter 6

Advanced Editing

With the basics down, time to introduce some more advanced ways to edit with Sound Forge®.

Mixing

Earlier it was mentioned that Sound Forge is not multi-track software, but it is possible to mix sounds together in one file. Use this sound-on-sound technique to combine multiple files in creative ways. The most obvious being adding music to a narration track.

After editing the voice track, open the music you wish to mix in a separate file. Since the music length may not match the voice track's duration, edit and trim the music track accordingly. Select the entire music file by clicking Edit > Select All or using CTRL+A and then copy the selection to the clipboard using Edit > Copy or CTRL+C.

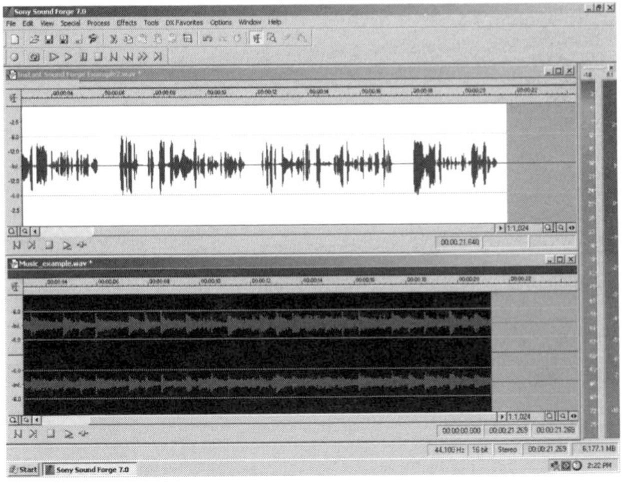

Switch to the narration track and position the cursor where you want the music to start. Click File > Paste Special > Mix or CTRL+M.

The Mix dialog gives you control over the volume level of the source track (in this case the music you copied to the clipboard) and the destination track (the narration). Adjust the volume to suit using the Preview button to monitor. With a busy music track I usually start about 12-15dB below 0. This keeps the music at a low enough level so the words are still easily understood. A quieter music track can be somewhat louder.

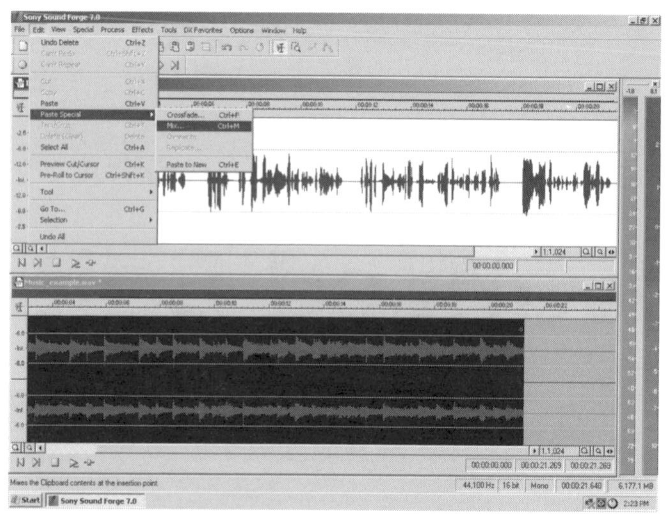

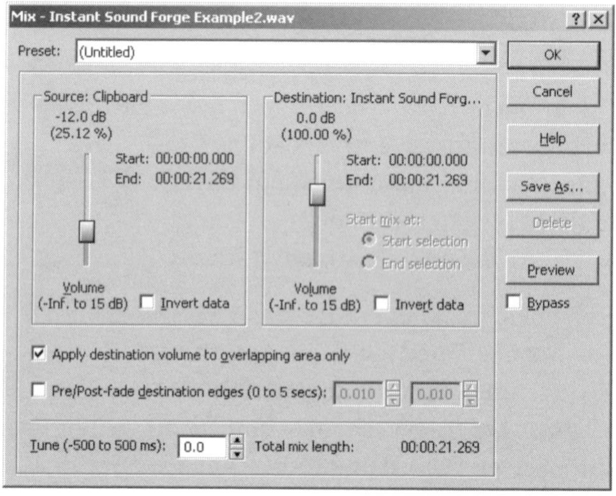

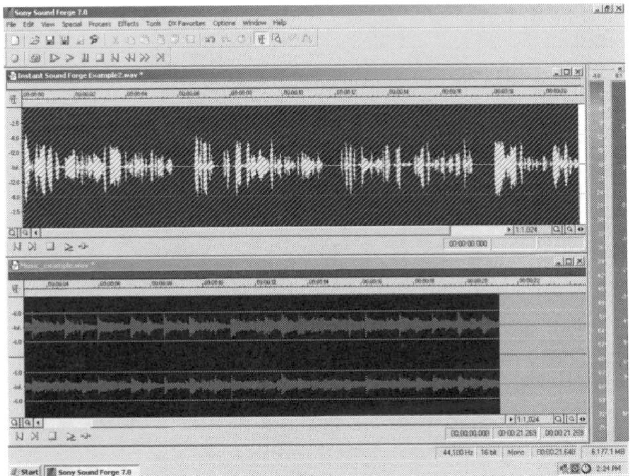

Important: adding waveforms together raises the overall volume of the file. Watch your levels so you do not introduce clipping distortion when mixing files together.

Sound Forge allows pasting a stereo file into a mono file. The program kept the mono attributes intact but automatically converts the stereo to mono during the mix paste special operation. If you prefer, you can convert your files yourself before performing the mix operation. Either make the music mono or convert the mono track to two-track (it won't be stereo, just equal energy in both channels i.e. dual mono). With the file attributes matching, perform the mix operation.

Another method for mixing sounds is to simply drag and drop one file onto another. Make a selection in one file and drag it to another.

The Mix dialog displays as before.

Alternately, drag a file from Explorer to another file. Sound Forge makes any necessary file conversions automatically. You can again make volume adjustments in the Mix dialog box.

For a project in my audio class, I have students tell a story using only sound effects such as getting out of bed and getting ready for work/school/date, cooking a meal, arriving at an airport, etc. It's a terrific exercise for learning all the basic Sound Forge editing functions along with the mixing techniques just discussed. Try it.

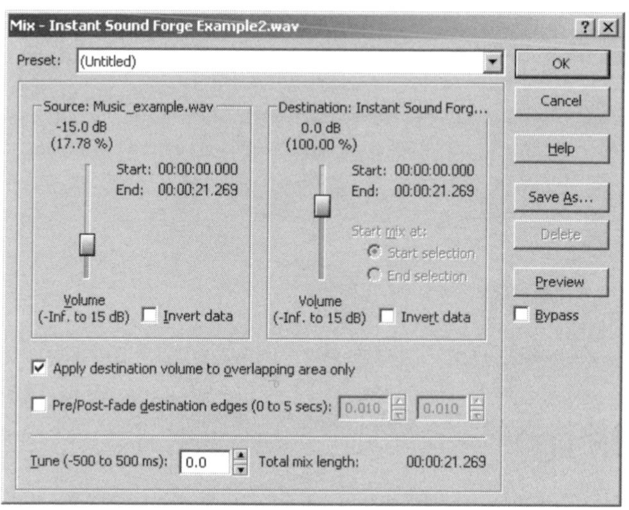

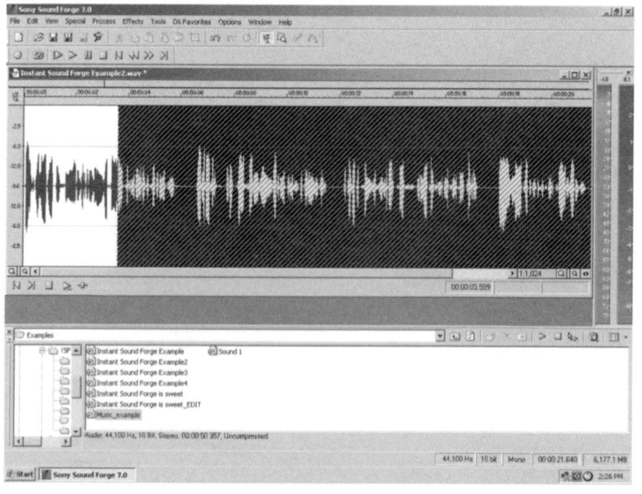

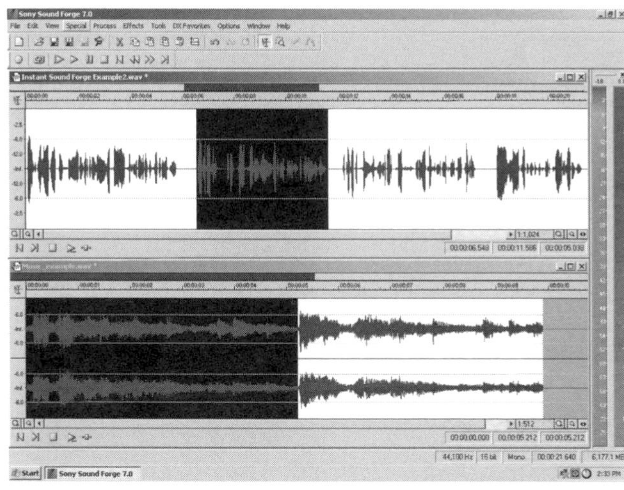

Instead of mixing sounds together, you can crossfade between them. Select the first file and copy what you need to the clipboard. Switch to the second file and make a time selection. This selection is the overlap or crossfade area.

Click Edit > Paste Special > Crossfade (or CTRL+F).

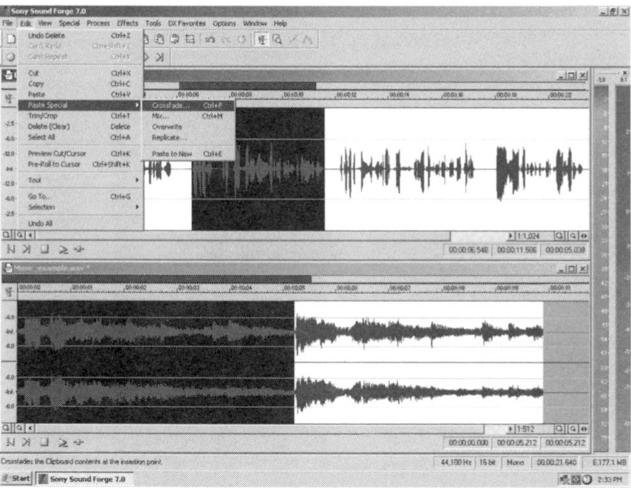

Use the settings in the Crossfade dialog to adjust the start and end level of the source (clipboard) audio with the start and end level of the destination track. Use Preview to monitor the settings.

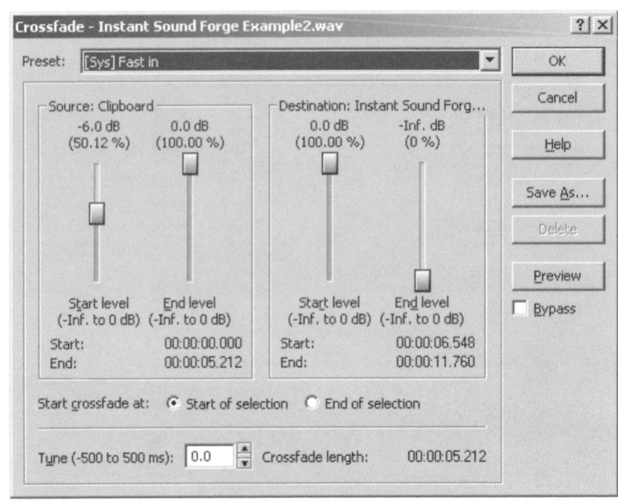

There are two other Mix options:

- Edit > Paste Special > Overwrite replaces the selection you make with audio from the clipboard.
- Edit > Paste Special > Replicate replaces as many copies of the clipboard audio needed to fill the selection in the destination file.

Timesavers

In addition to making selections with the mouse, you can mark in and out points with the keyboard. With the file playing, hit the I key to mark the in or start point. Hit the O key to mark the out or end point. Sound Forge automatically makes this a time selection. Hit the R key to turn this into a region or simply perform whatever operation you need.

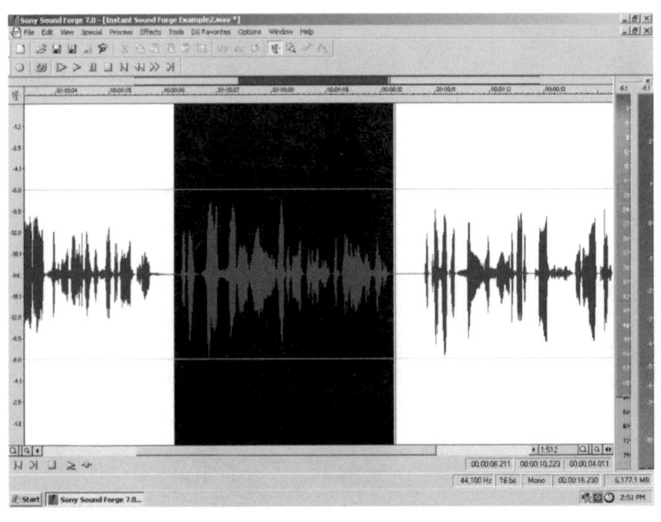

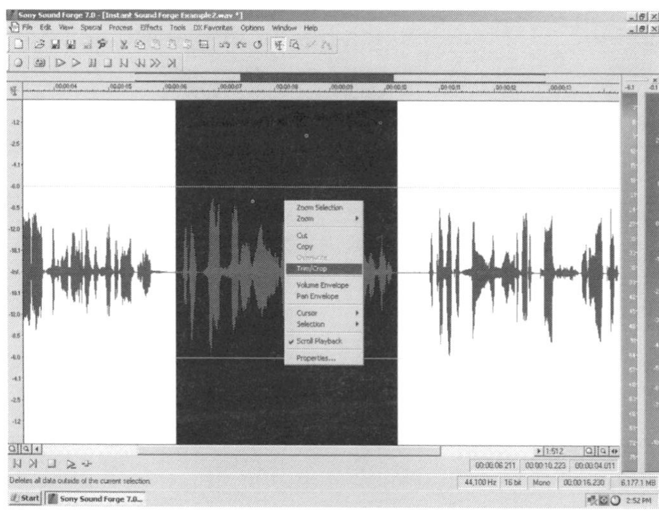

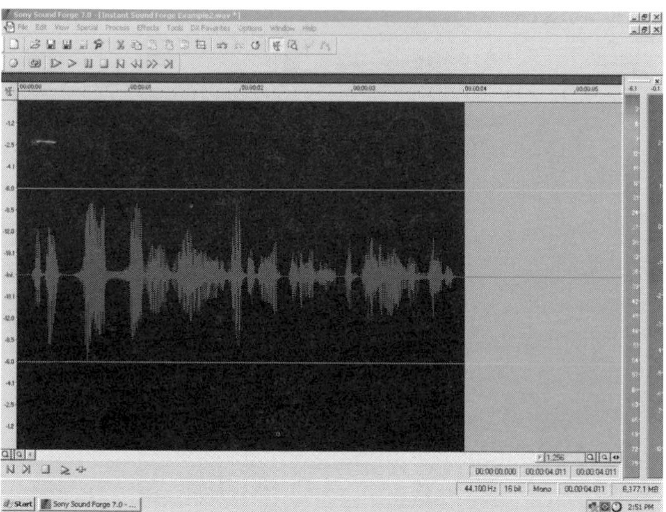

After making a selection, right click it and choose Trim/Crop to keep only what you selected and delete everything else outside the selection area.

You can also access this function using Edit > Trim/Crop or CTRL+T.

The Auto trim/crop tool is very handy for quickly eliminating silences leaving just the main material intact. It works by looking for silence, removing it, and moving nearby data together. Select the file and click Process > Auto Trim/Crop.

Use the attack threshold to set the initial level for the detection with -Inf as complete silence. The release threshold sets the end point. Data must fall between these two settings to be automatically detected and removed. Use the Fade in and Fade out settings to control how nearby data is affected by the trim.

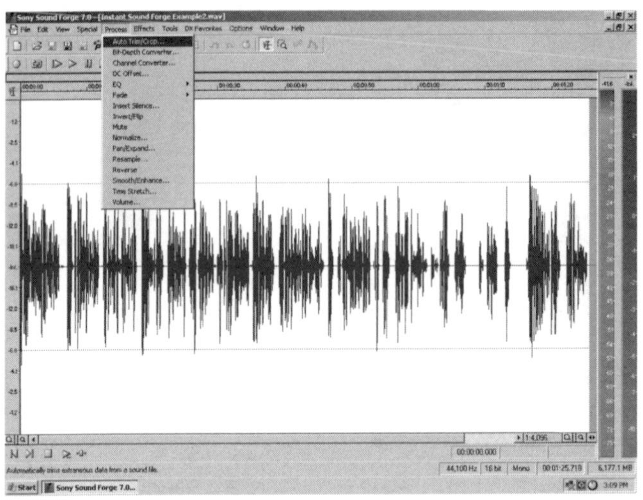

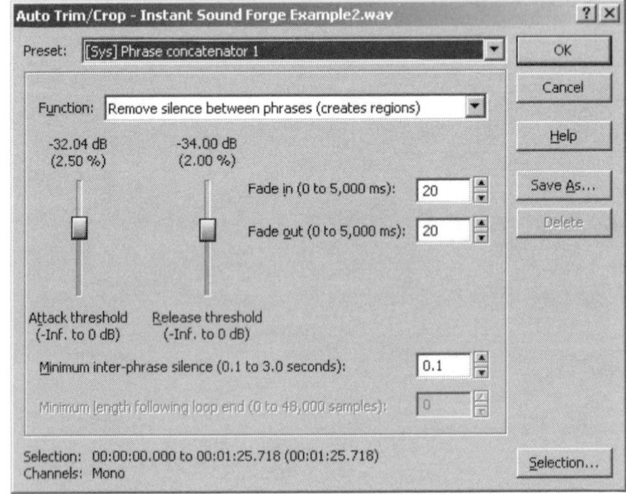

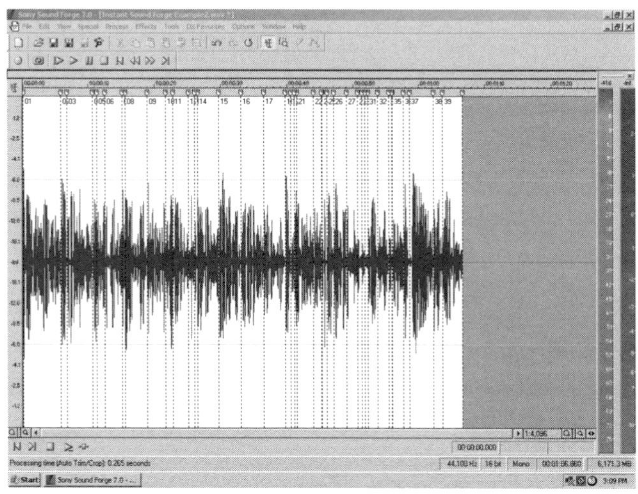

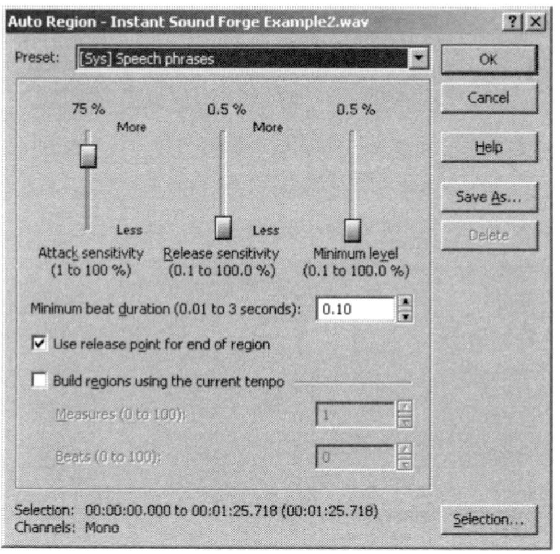

Choose a Preset and/or Function to see how this works with your file. For example, use the Phrase concatenator 1 preset with the Remove silence between phrases (creates regions) function to quickly eliminate all the silent pauses in a narration file and place regions around every phrase.

Closely related to this feature is Auto region. Click Tools > Auto Region and choose one of the Presets. For music, use the music presets. For voice, use the Speech phrases. Essentially, this utility detects the beats in music or the phrases in speech and automatically creates regions around them. Adjust the sliders to fine tune the process.

With regions in place, you can extract them to a series of files. For example, let's say you record the entire side of a vinyl album into one file in Sound Forge. Go through the file and place regions around each song. Use the Extract Regions tool to create several files from the one single file. Click Tools > Extract Regions. You can indicate which regions to extract, the destination for the new files, and a prefix for the file. Sound Forge appends the region name to this prefix.

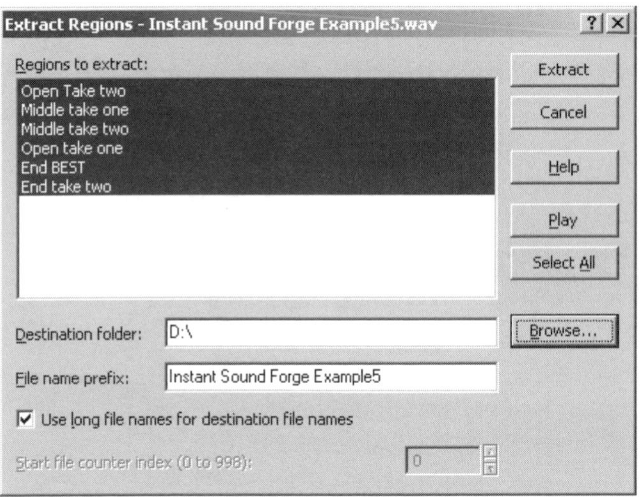

Playlist and cutlist

Regions can also make it easier to try out ideas quickly. With regions designating sections in a file already in place, click View > Playlist or use the ALT+3 shortcut.

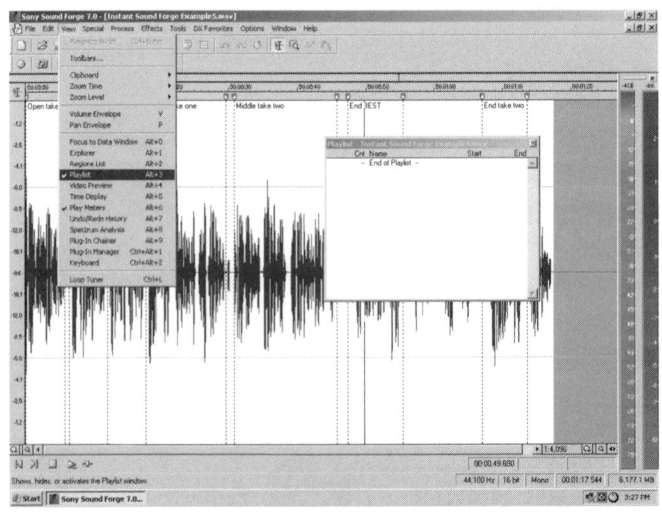

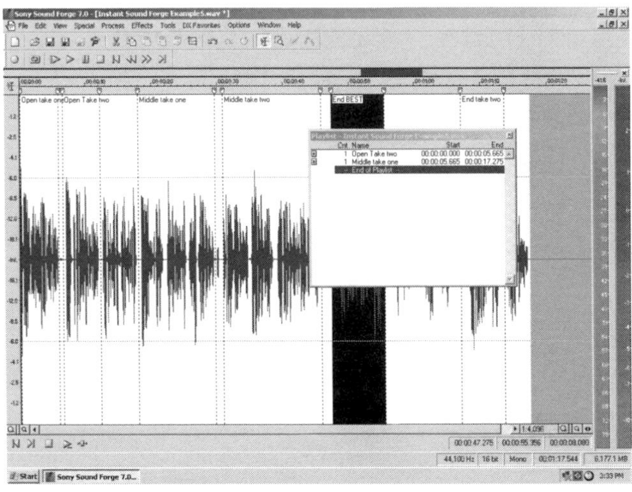

Select a region by double-clicking it and then drag and drop it on the Playlist. Add other regions to the Playlist, as needed.

To hear the Playlist, click one of the play buttons.

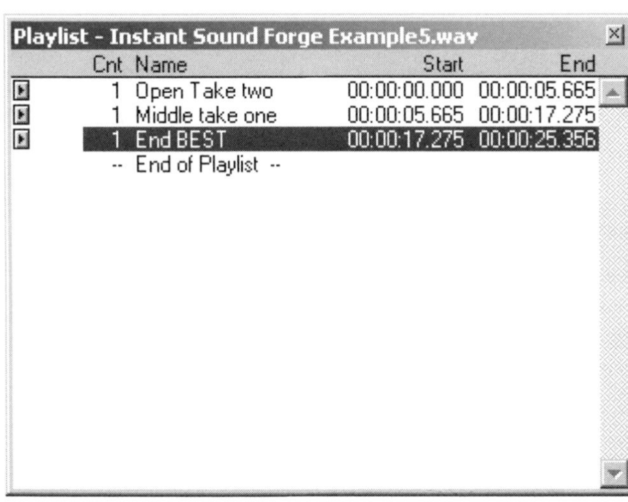

Rearrange the order, add, and delete regions until you arrive at the best final version. Adjust the region boundaries for further tweaking, too.

Once you are satisfied with the edit, right click the Playlist and choose Convert to New. You can also copy the data to the clipboard if you want.

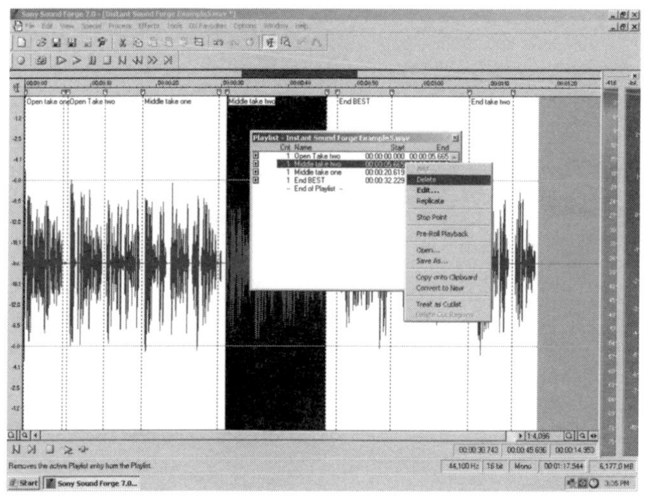

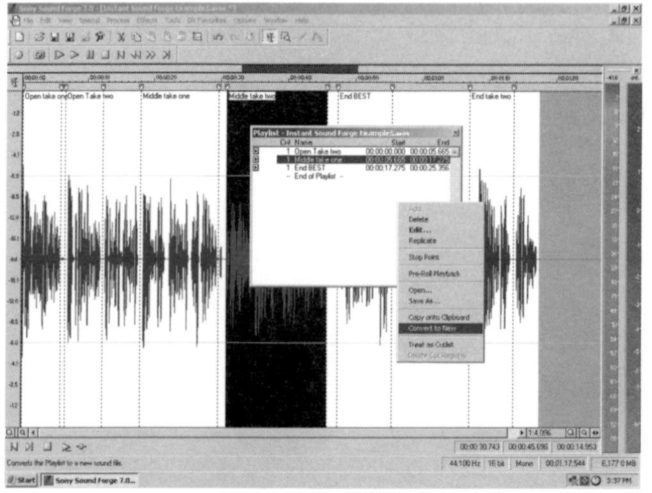

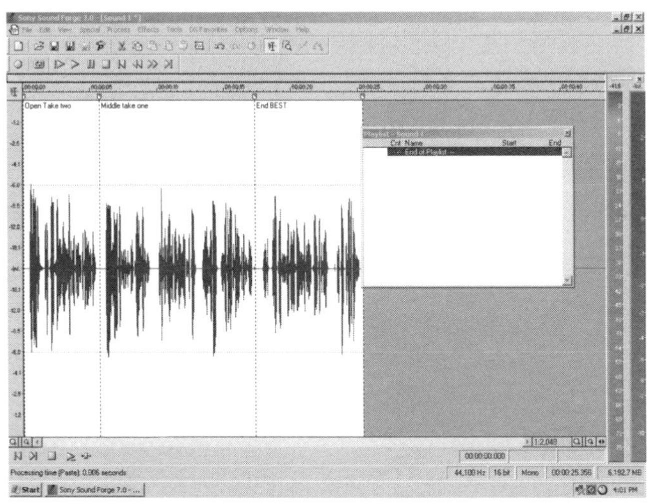

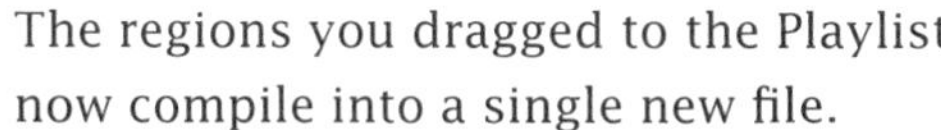

The regions you dragged to the Playlist now compile into a single new file.

To save a Playlist, right click it and choose Save as. Give it name and a place on your hard drive and click Save. You can open it later if needed.

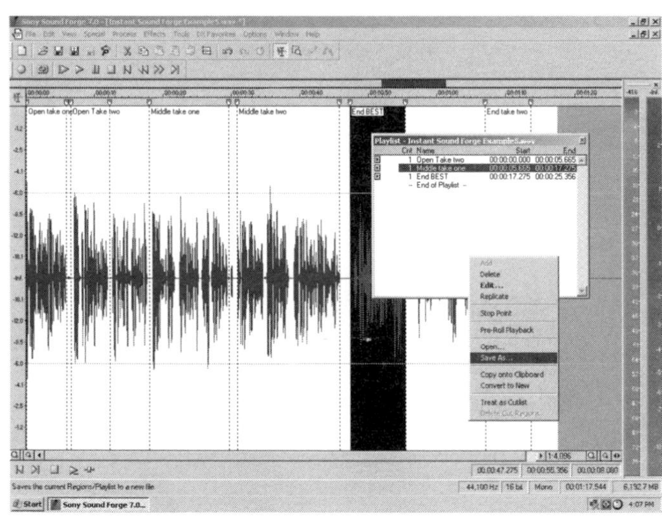

You can also choose to treat the Playlist as a cutlist instead. Any regions you add to the cutlist will be skipped when you play from the regular data window.

Working with video (audio for video)

Many of the techniques discussed so far apply when working with the audio portion of video files. Keep in mind that if you cut or delete audio, the video file is not affected. If you make such an edit during onscreen dialog, the subsequent sync will be lost. Instead be sure to mute instead of cut and use the Mix Paste Special features to add sounds. Of course, you'll be able to clean up the audio and sweeten it following the techniques still to come.

While thumbnails of the video appear across the top of the Sound Forge data window, you can also open the Video preview window. Click View > Video Preview or use ALT+4. If you have an OHCI-compliant 1394 DV interface, DV camcorder, or DV-to analog converter connected to your computer, you can preview the video on it. You'll also need a TV, obviously. Click the Ext.

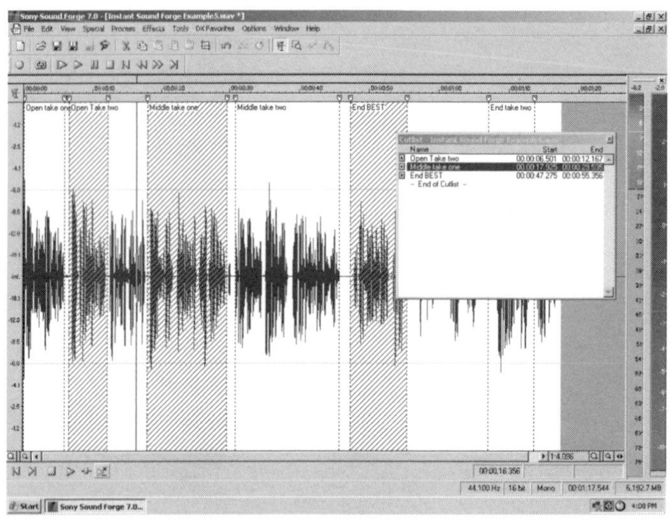

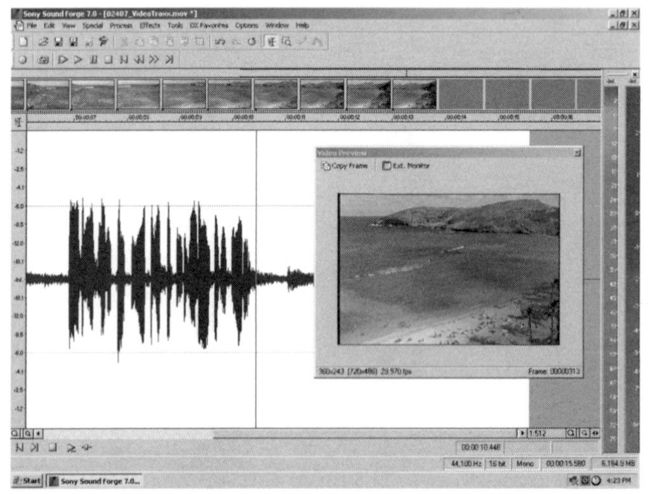

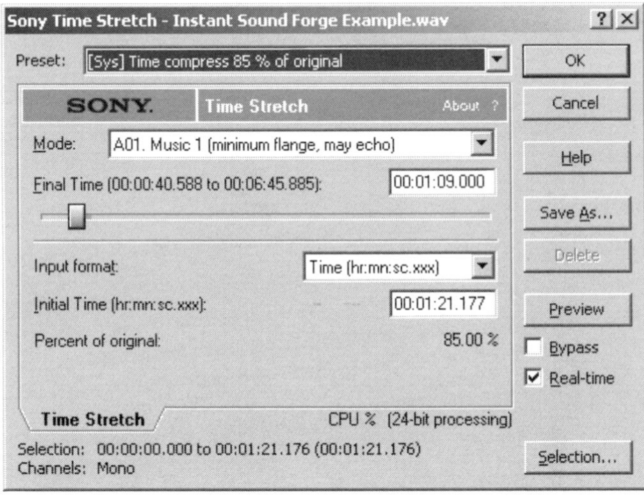

Monitor button to turn off the preview window and route the signal to the OHCI-compliant device.

Time

Sometimes you need to speed up or slow down an audio file. For example, you have 29 seconds for a radio commercial and the voice-over is 31 seconds. Through careful editing (cutting to save time or inserting silence to add length), you can often reach a target duration. Even just removing tiny slices at pauses and in between words can shorten the track considerably. I always recommend editing first before using the next tool.

To compress or expand time, click Process > Time Stretch. Start with the Presets and Modes to reach an acceptable solution. Choosing the proper Mode that works with your material is essential. Try several choices and listen carefully to how they affect your work. Adjust the slider to fine tune the duration. Click Preview to hear how the settings sound.

Cleaning up

Sound Forge makes it oh-so-easy to tweak your audio in minute detail. You can get rid of voice and dialog mistakes including breaths, lip smacks, and other vocal garbage, hunt down and eliminate or greatly reduce annoying hum and/ or background noise, and find and delete other unwanted sounds.

The Auto Trim/Crop process is fine for eliminating silence, but what if you need to eliminate background noise, too? Sure you can edit it out, but that can be tedious. Here's a better way. Open a file with a steady background noise, such as that produced by an air conditioner.

Click Effects > Noise Gate. Set the Threshold level first. Any audio above this level will be let through; the gate opens. When the signal falls below the threshold setting, the gates closes. This is a critical setting. If the level is too high, parts of words may be cut off. "Stop" becomes "tah". If the level is too low, the noise you don't want will still be heard.

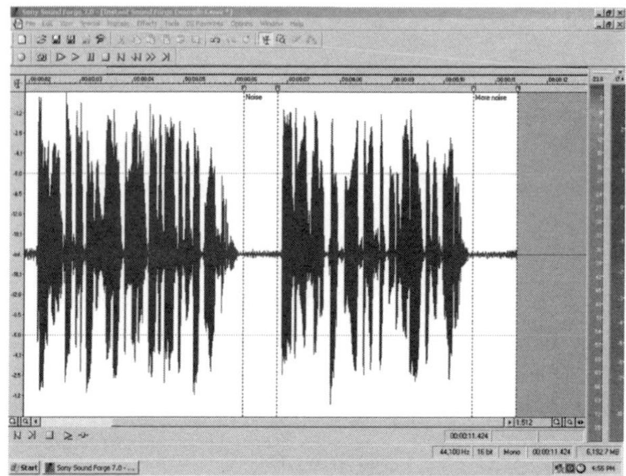

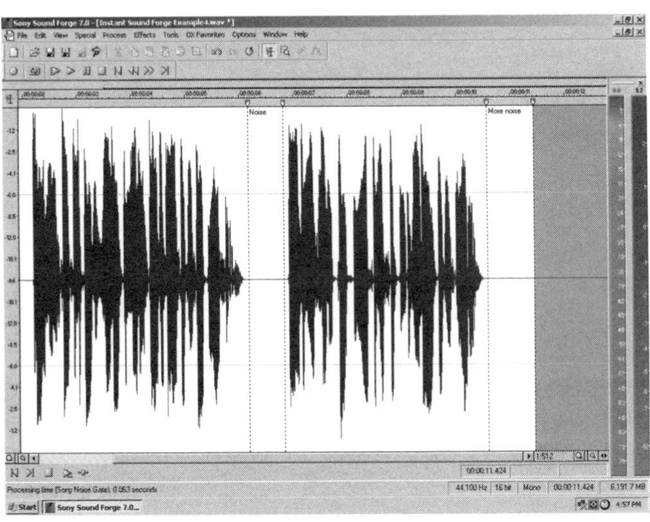

The Attack time sets how fast the gate works while the Release time sets how long it takes for the gate to close after the signal drops below the threshold. Think of it as a kind of fade. Longer release times can make sure the s and p in "stop" don't get cut off.

Even after you apply the process, make sure you listen back to the whole file before moving on to see if you chopped off any words or other important sounds. Also, note that the background sound, while missing during breaks, will still be present during the other parts of the file. The louder sounds should mask it sufficiently ...

... but not always. Using the noise gate may be more distracting as the background sound jumps in during speech and out during pauses. It may sound better to leave in the noise. The ear is pretty agile at focusing on the program and ignoring the background noises (if they are not too loud.). Listen critically to the before and after files before deciding the right version.

Is pesky 60Hz hum ruining your recording? Open the file and choose Process > EQ > Paragraphic EQ. From the Preset list choose 60Hz hum notch using four stacked filters. I find changing one of the filter's center frequency to 120Hz often works a little better.

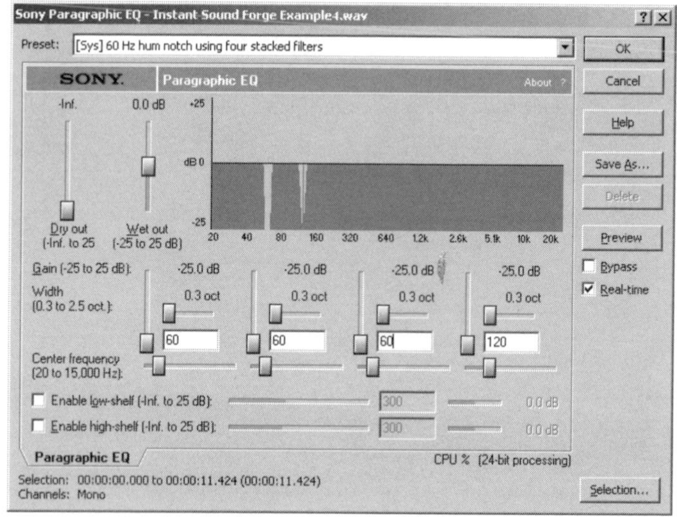

Two things bother me with voice-only recordings: excessive breaths and mouth noise, such as lip smacks. The noise gate process mentioned above can eliminate most of these, but frequently you need to edit them out manually. Since these are low level noises, time and amplitude zooms are often needed to really zero in on and delete the offending noises.

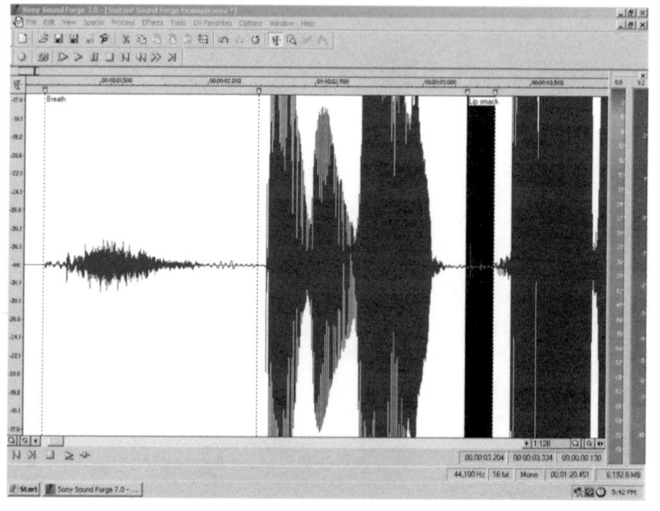

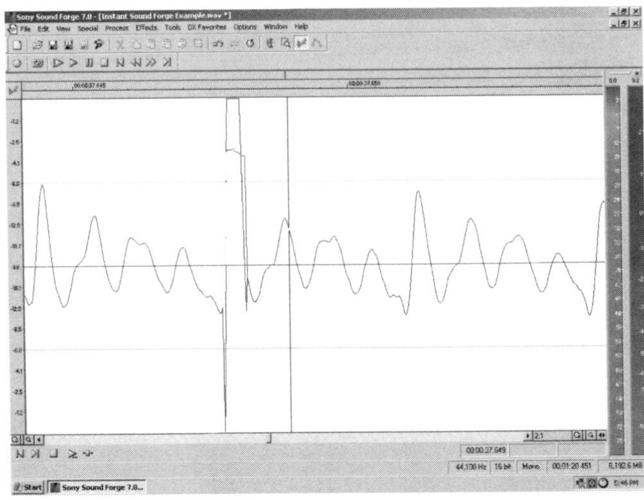

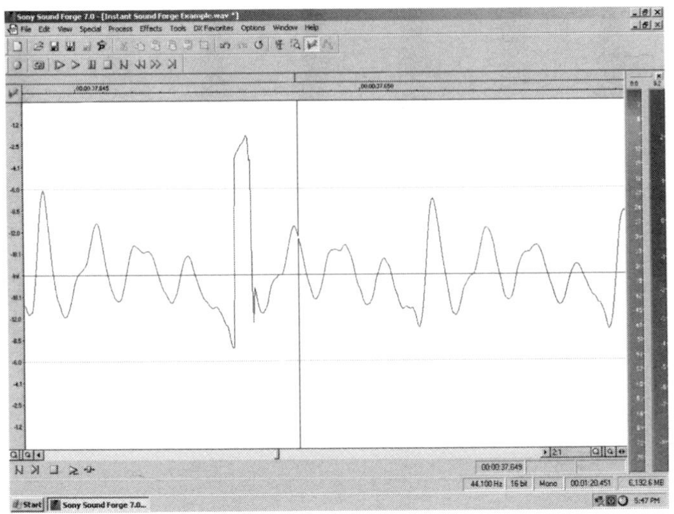

Repair options

The Draw tool can help you fix problems, such as restoring a single clip. Zoom in on the area to fix, click the draw tool on the main toolbar, and draw away.

Try to match the surrounding waveforms for the best match. Drawing is a bit hit or miss. Play the section back to hear how it worked (or didn't). Typically, drawing random waveforms is neat for sound design when you're trying to create something new, not fix a problem.

The repair tool is useful for fixing quick glitches and other short audio grunge. First, use the Tools > Find tool to locate the problem area.

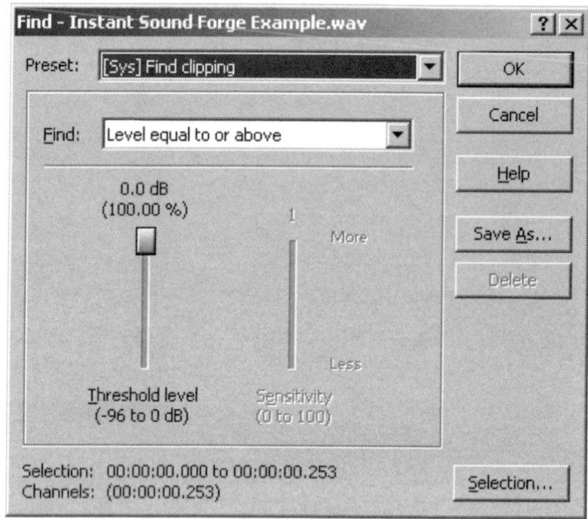

Sound Forge positions the cursor at the glitch. Zoom in tightly to the area.

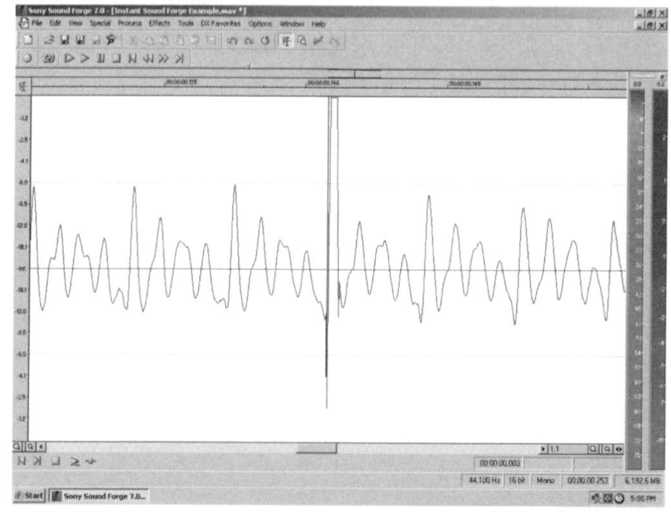

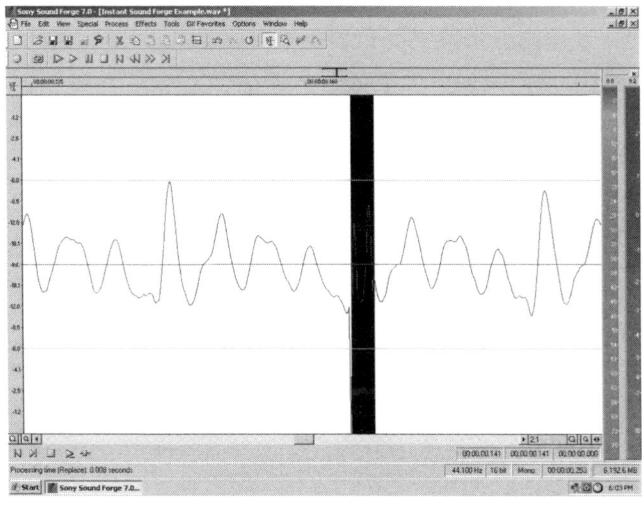

Next, select the problem carefully. Select the smallest portion possible and choose Tools > Repair > Interpolate or Tools > Repair > Replace. Interpolate may solve the problem or introduce another glitch while the Replace option takes a small amount of surrounding audio and copies it into the selection. If you are working with a stereo file, Tools > Repair > Copy other channel will fill in the selection with data from the opposite channel.

To search for clipped audio, use Tools > Detect Clipping. Choose the relevant settings in the dialog.

Detect Clipping - Instant Sound Forge Example.wav

Preset: [Sys] Detect all 0 dB clipping

OK

Cancel

Help

Save As...

Delete

Selection...

Threshold (-60 to 0 dB) 0.00 dB (100.00 %)

Clip Length (2 to 100 samples) 3

Selection: 00:00:00.000 to 00:00:00.253 (00:00:00.253)
Channels: Mono

Sound Forge places markers at any clips it finds. Now you can use the draw or repair tools to try to fix them. Even better: don't use the takes with clips; look for alternatives.

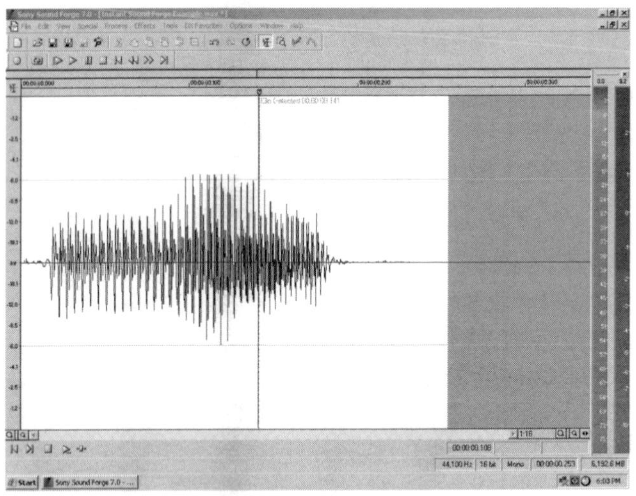

Chapter 7

Effects

Another area where Sound Forge truly shines is in the special audio effects department. There are over 40 effects and processes built-in, several automatable. Also, the program supports third-party DirectX plug-ins for even more creative power.

Effects divide into several categories.

- Tonal-based effects (EQ, Smooth/enhance) work on the frequency content of the audio.
- Time-based effects (reverb, delay) give a sense of space, such as the sound of a room, or add discreet repeats or echoes to the sound.
- Modulation-based effects (amplitude, flange, chorus, phase, wah) are time-based effects that include modulation or resonance settings that change the effect over time.
- Dynamics-based effects (compression, wave hammer) reduce the dynamic range -- the difference between the loudest and the softest parts -- of an audio file and/or maximize volume without clipping.
- Pitch-based effects (pitch bend, shift) allow altering the original frequency of a file.
- Other effects (distortion, gapper/snipper, vibrato, reverse) fall outside these categories but are just as useful.

The main effects listed under the Effect menu include:

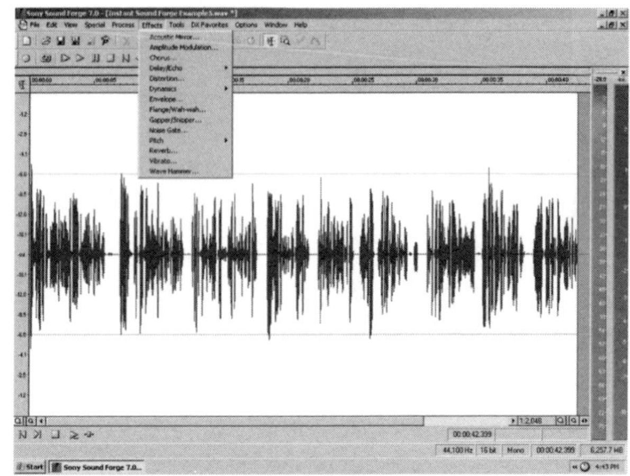

- Acoustic Mirror
- Amplitude Modulation
- Chorus
- Delay/Echo (Simple and Multi-Tap)
- Distortion
- Dynamics (Graphic and Multi-Band)
- Envelope
- Flange/Wah-Wah/Phaser
- Gapper/Snipper
- Noise Gate
- Pitch (Bend and Shift)
- Reverb
- Vibrato
- Wave Hammer

A few other basic effects are found under the Process menu:

- EQ (Graphic, Paragraphic, and Parametric)
- Reverse
- Fade (Graphic, In, and Out)
- Smooth/Enhance

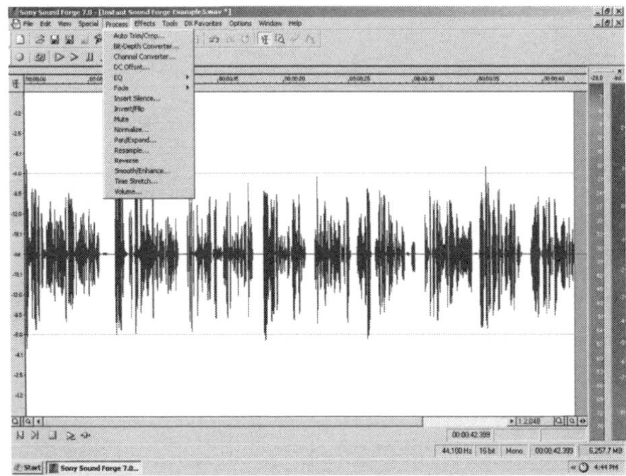

- Time Compress/Expand
- Volume

Several of these effects are automatable or programmable over time:

- Amplitude Modulation
- Chorus
- Distortion
- Flange/Wah-wah
- Graphic Dynamics
- Multi-Band Dynamics
- Reverb
- Simple Delay
- Smooth/Enhance
- Sound Forge Pan
- Sound Forge Volume
- Vibrato

Effects Workflow

The effects workflow is essentially the same as other editing tasks.

- Make a selection. You can apply effects to the entire file or just a section.
- Choose an effect
- Adjust its parameters to taste
- Alternately, choose a Preset from the list as a starting point
- Many effects provide separate control over the mix of Dry (original sound) and Wet (effected sound), too. Some have parameters you may change or automate over time.
- Preview as you make changes
- Tweak further
- Apply the final effect to the file
- Also, the Plug-in Chainer lets you string multiple effects together and process the audio through all the effects simultaneously.

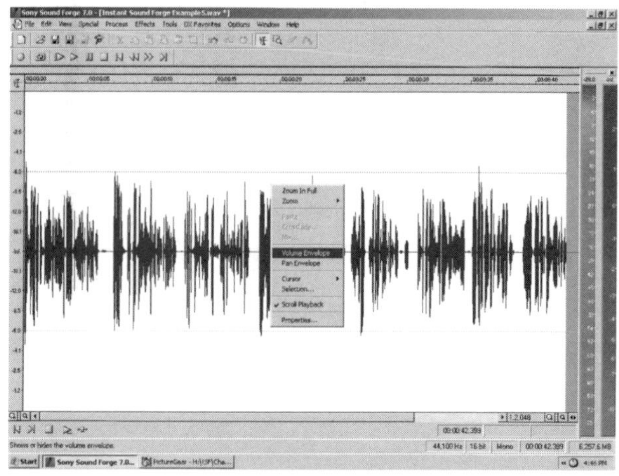

Volume and Pan

Change the volume by making a selection, clicking Process > Volume and adjusting accordingly. However, when you want to change volume over time, there's a better way. Open the file, right

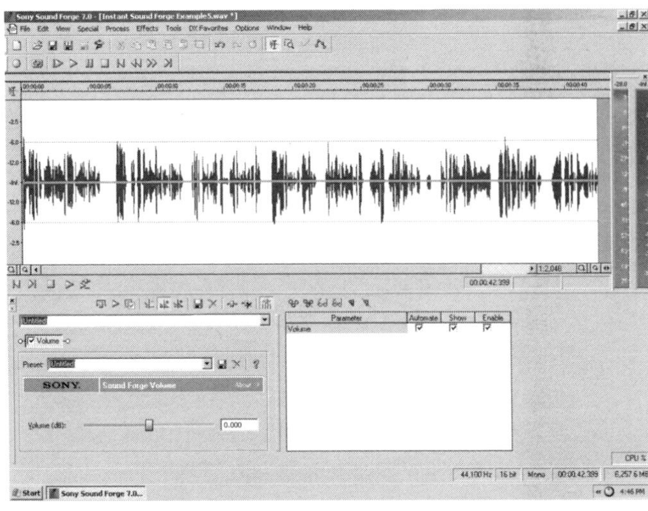

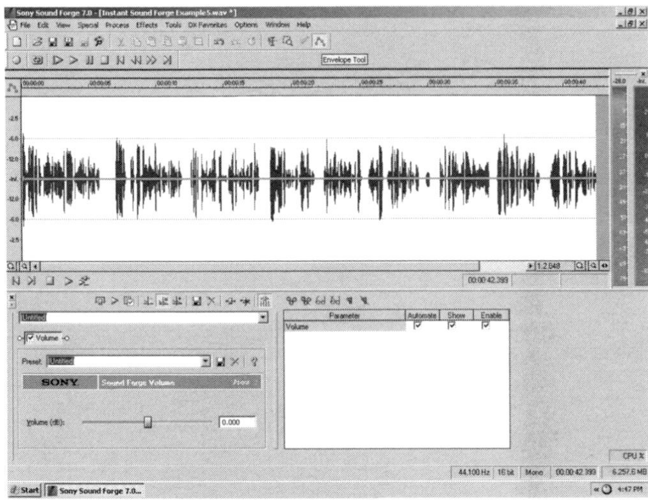

click, and choose Volume Envelope or type V, the keyboard shortcut. Typing V toggles showing and hiding the volume envelope. Close the Plug-in Chainer dialog to hide the envelope, too.

Sound Forge inserts a blue line through the file and also launches the Plug-in chainer which allows processing audio with multiple effects simultaneously.

Select the Envelope Tool from the main toolbar.

Position the cursor where you want to change the volume and adjust the Volume slider in the Plug-in chainer. Sound Forge adds a square box, or point, to the volume line and positions it corresponding to the volume change.

You can double-click on the volume line to add a point, too. Click and drag the point to adjust.

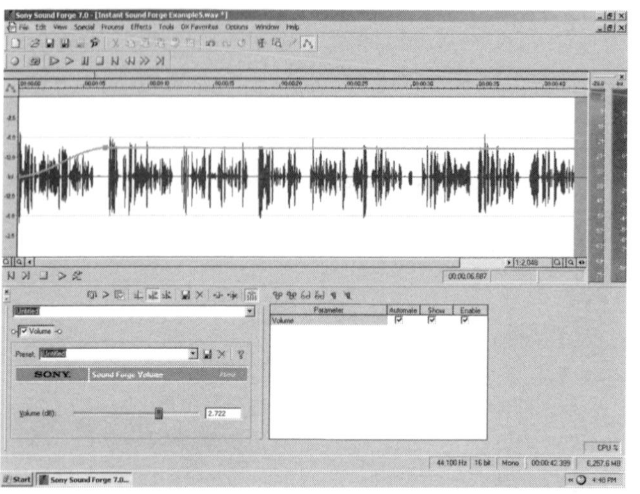

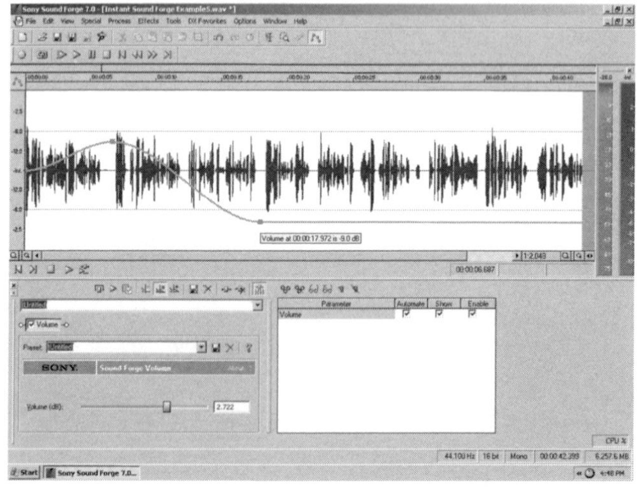

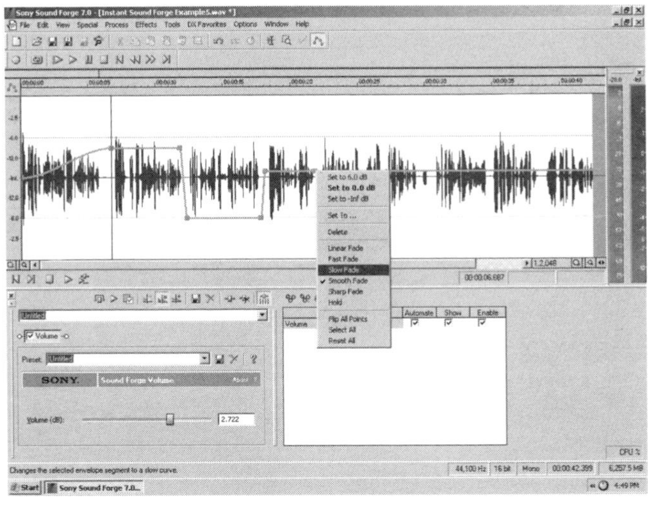

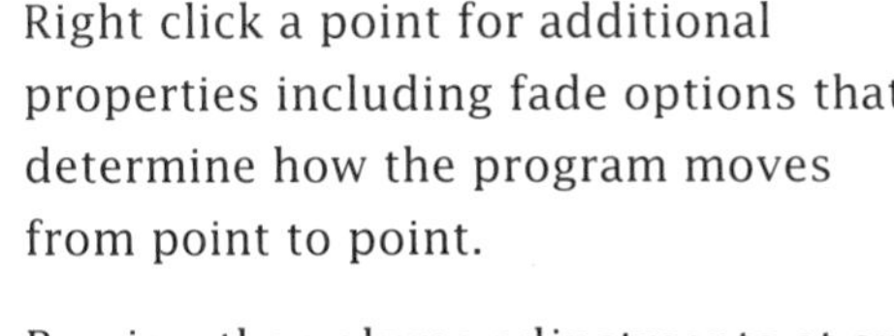

Right click a point for additional properties including fade options that determine how the program moves from point to point.

Preview the volume adjustments at any time using the Preview button in the Plug-in chainer or the regular transport controls.

When you are satisfied with the settings, click Process Selection to apply the volume change.

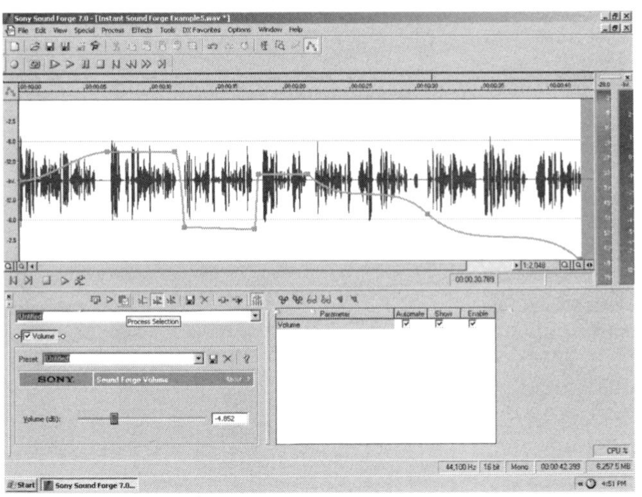

The volume envelope remains so you can make additional changes or Undo and tweak further.

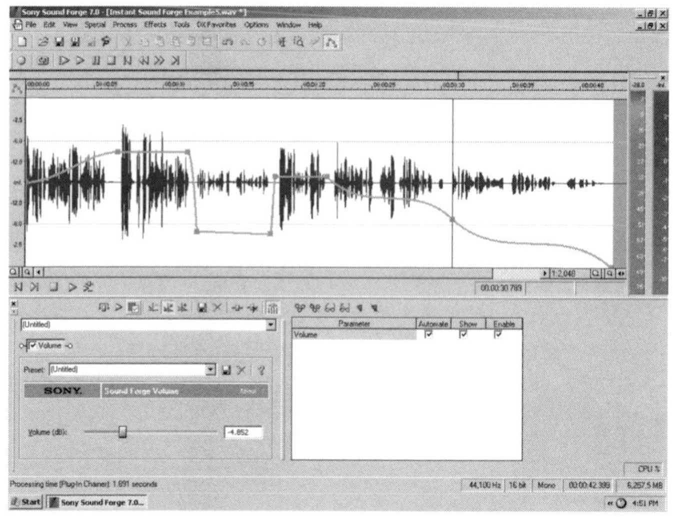

Automate Pan over time, too. Panning is adjusting the balance and/or moving a stereo file between the left and right speakers. Open a stereo file, right click, and choose Pan Envelope or type P, the keyboard shortcut. Also, P toggles showing and hiding the Pan envelope. Add points and make adjustments using the same techniques described for the volume envelope above.

Click Process Selection to finish the effect.

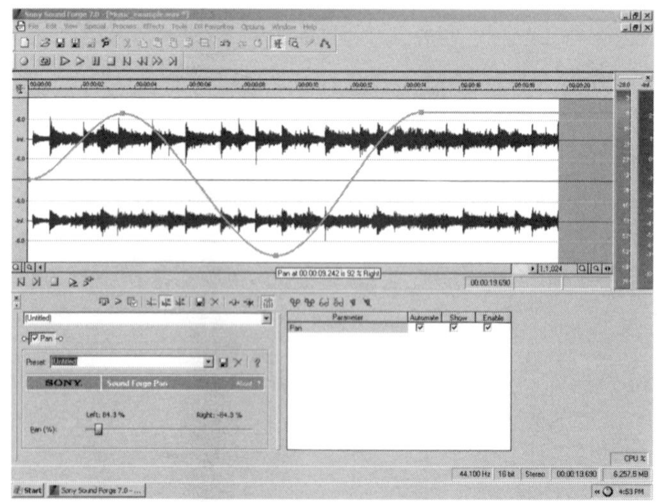

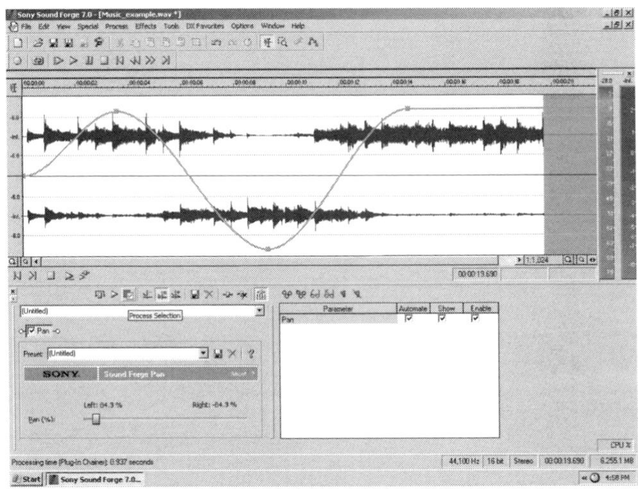

EQ

Equalization, or EQ for short, let's you adjust the tonal qualities of a sound. The bass and treble controls on your car or home stereo are a form of EQ. Sound Forge has far more sophisticated EQ tools, though.

Click Process > EQ > Graphic, then click the 10 Band tab. If you've ever used a graphic equalizer, this should look familiar. The sliders represent specific frequency bands that you can boost (increase volume) or cut (decrease volume) to shape how a file sounds.

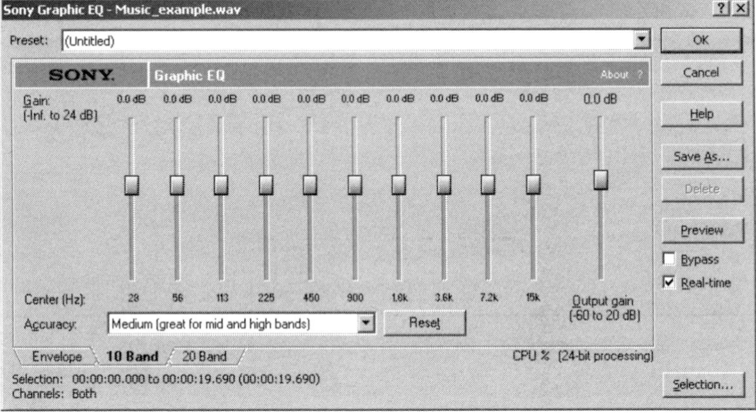

Many people use the "smile" curve to boost the bass and treble of a file to make it sound better in the cars or on home speakers. This is not the only use for EQ.

Instead, use the controls to reduce annoying frequency bands, such as hum, and/or accentuate certain frequencies, such as making a thin guitar sound warmer or a dull snare drum sound brighter. Don't forget that EQ can be CUT to affect tonal quality, not just boosted. EQ will change volume levels, so watch those meters and compensate accordingly.

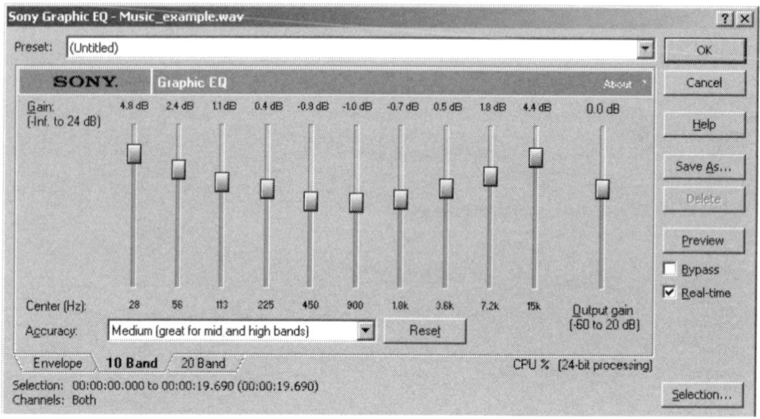

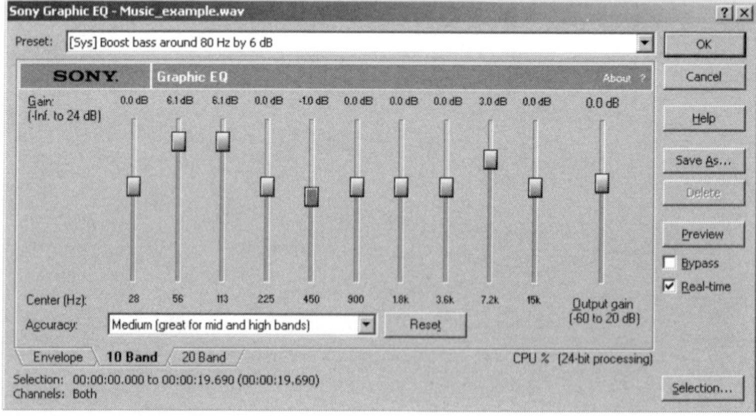

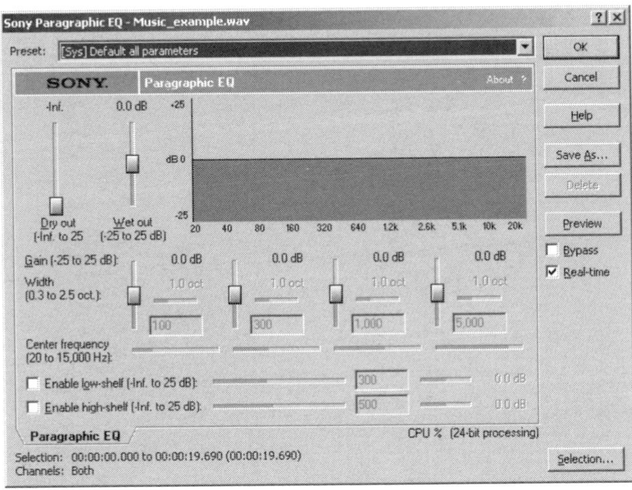

Click Process > EQ > Paragraphic for a powerful EQ tool.

Here you can control the Gain, Width, and Center Frequency of four separate bands. There is also a low-shelf and high-shelf filter with adjustable frequency and gain. What's especially helpful is seeing the EQ adjustment in the display. Note the output gain control. Using EQ will affect volume; you still want to avoid clipping.

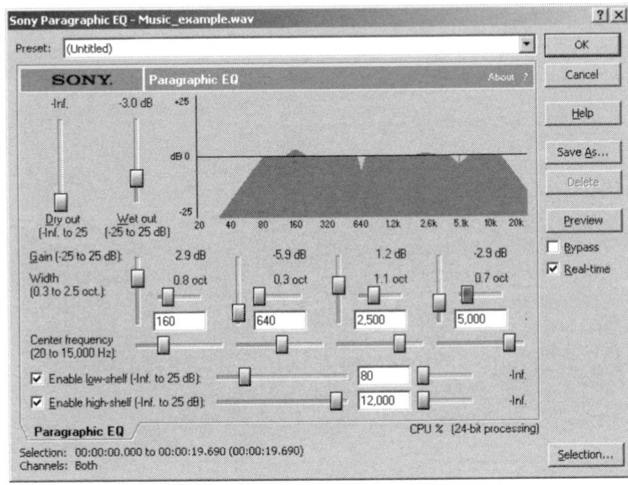

Click Process > EQ > Parametric gives you control over a Center frequency and Band width along with Amount and Output Gain.

The four filter types include low- and high-frequency shelf, band-pass, and band-notch/boost.

Choose the Preset: Phone line effect to make a file sound like it's playing over a telephone. All the effects built-in to Sound Forge have Presets. Use them as a starting point or to learn how a particular effect works.

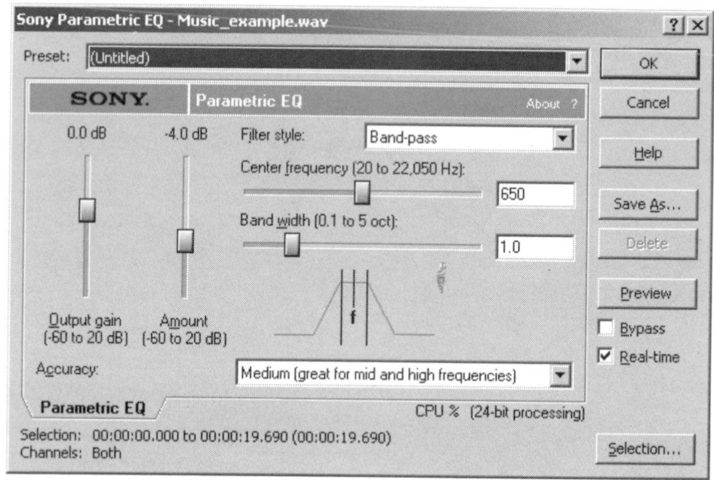

Compression

The difference between the loudest part of a sound file and its softest is called dynamic range. Audio files can have tremendous dynamic range. Keeping the soft parts intelligible without risking sending the loud section into clipping distortion is no easy task. Gratefully, compression is the tool that can:

- Decrease overall dynamic range of recordings
- Reduce peaks that can distort recordings

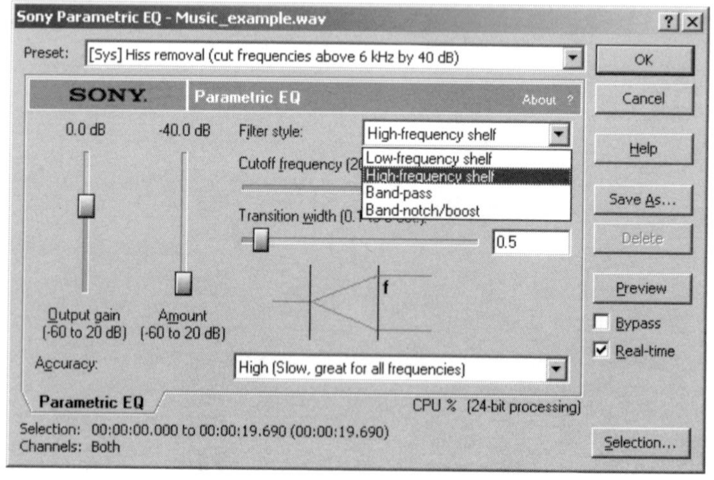

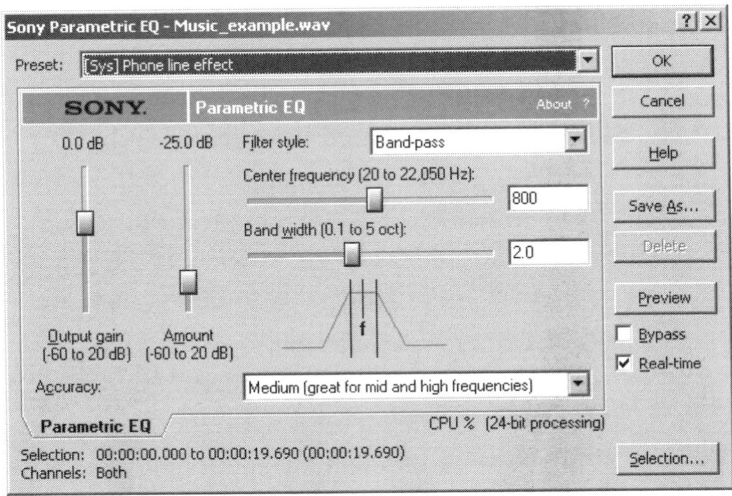

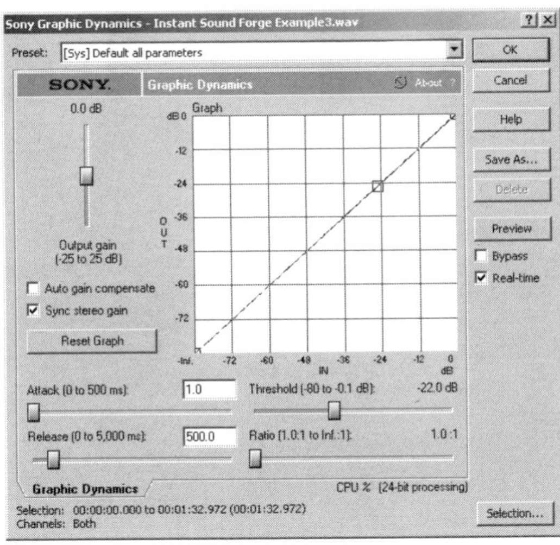

- Smooth dynamics on instruments and voice
- Increase punch to individual sounds and whole recordings
- Reduce plosives and sibilance on sung vocals and spoken word recordings

A funnel is the metaphor for how compression works. It lowers the volume of louder parts while raising the volume on softer parts, essentially squeezing the audio into a smaller pipe.

Open up a file and then click Effects > Dynamics > Graphic. The compressor has several interactive sections. Read the explanations below to understand how the settings work together.

Threshold. When a signal (and for purposes of simplicity, any audio) reaches and/or exceeds this specific threshold level, the compressor starts working to reduce the level. Any audio below the threshold setting is unaffected.

Ratio. This determines how the output is compressed. Ratios can be set at unity (1:1) up to infinity to one. In other words, at a 1:1 ratio, a 1dB signal change results in a 1dB output (no or unity gain). At other ratios, the output is reduced by relative amounts. At 4:1, a 4dB increase in input level results in only a 1dB output level gain. Any ratio above 10:1 is called limiting. With heavy limiting, no matter how much the input level increases, the output is restricted (limited) to only a small range.

The Graph makes it easier to see the interactive nature of Threshold and Ratio. Click and drag the box in the graph. The dotted line simulates the original audio; the solid line shows the effect the compression has on the file.

Attack sets the time it takes before audio above the threshold setting gets compressed. Essentially, use this control to either clamp transients (fast settings) or let transients get through before the compressor kicks in (longer or slow settings)

Release is the opposite of attack. This control determines how long it takes for the compressor to stop affecting the audio after the signal drops below the threshold. Again, vary the time from very short to very long. Short times act on the signal constantly producing some unnatural staccato effects while long times are smooth and more forgiving.

Output gain. This control helps you add level back into the signal that is often lost during the other processing steps. Check Auto gain compensate to force the program to automatically make up any volume loss. Keep an eye on the meters, though, or you risk clipping the audio.

If you've never used a compressor before, load up a drum loop and put Sound Forge into loop playback mode (keyboard shortcut Q). Next, use the sliders to experiment with the settings. Start with some of the Presets and tweak from there. Use the Preview with Bypass to hear the before and after changes.

There are two different kinds of compression known as hard and soft knee. Hard knee compression affects the signal immediately when

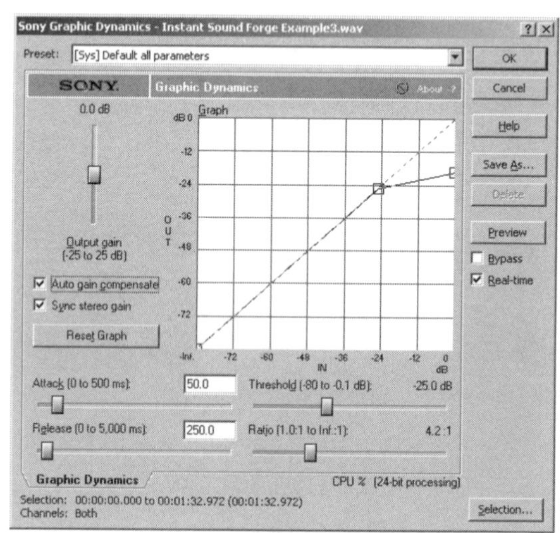

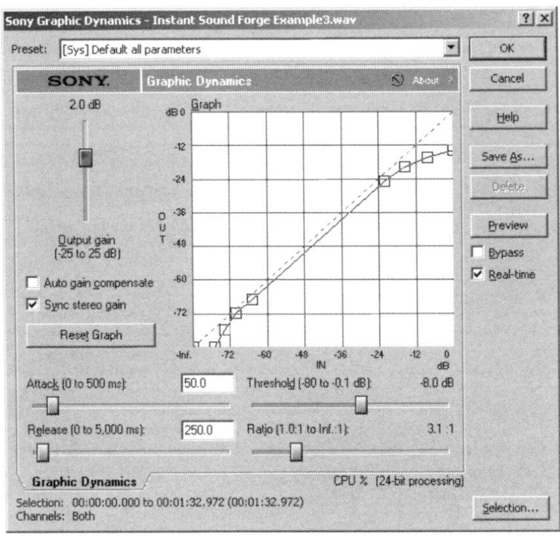

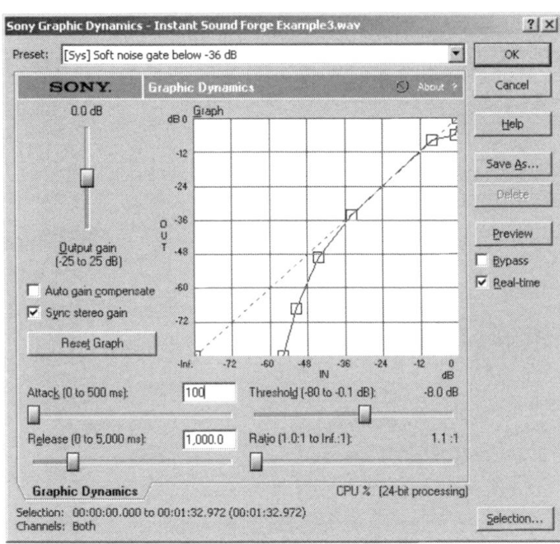

it exceeds the threshold. Soft knee compression affects the signal slowly and gently. Click the line in the Graph to add points and drag them to shape the knee of the compressor. Right click a point to delete it.

You can also use the Graphic compressor as a noise gate by adding points to the bottom of the graph. Audio below these settings is effectively turned off.

Pitch

Click Effects > Pitch > Shift to change the pitch of a sound. Lower or raise the pitch using the slider. The settings are musical so you have a coarse adjustment (Semitones) and a fine adjustment (Cents).

Changing the pitch also effects the length or duration of the audio. Click Preserve duration to maintain the file's time during the pitch shift processing. Choose from the Mode settings until the audio sounds best.

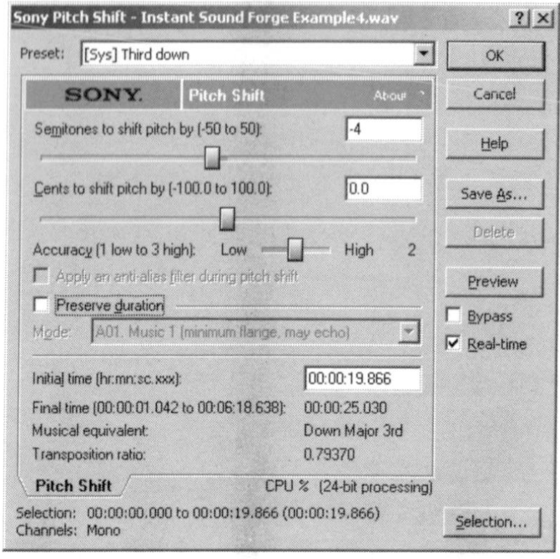

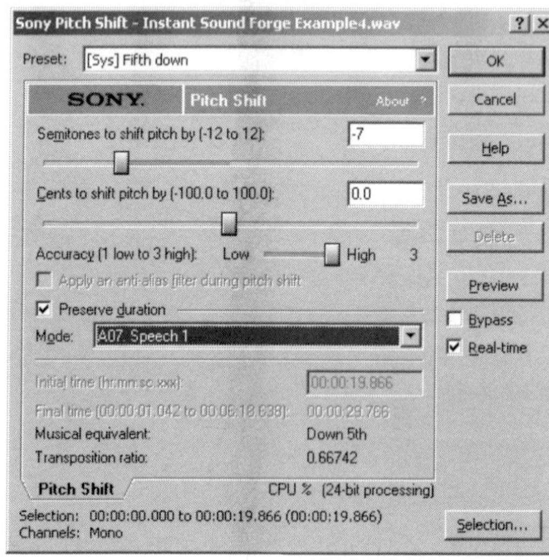

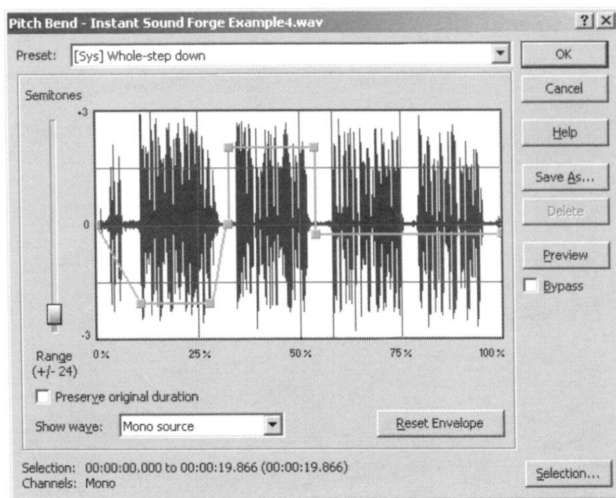

This pitch change affects the selection or the entire file as a whole. To vary the pitch shifting over time, click Effects > Pitch > Bend. Set a Range for the Graph and then add points to the envelope by double-clicking and then dragging them as desired. There are additional right-click options when using the envelope.

Use this to create some crazy (Whammy bar) or realistic effects (Doppler).

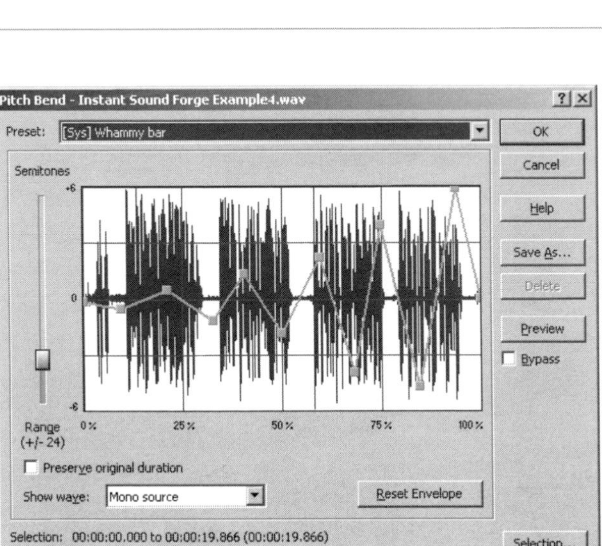

Delay/Echo

Ever been to a canyon and yell "Hello!" only to hear your voice return a short time later? Sound Forge can emulate that phenomenon. To add distinct repeats to a sound, click Effects > Delay/ Echo > Simple.

There is control over the Dry (original audio) and the Delay Out (sometimes called wet). Adjust the delay time to hear the effect. Open a voice or guitar file, click the Preset > Slap-back echo for a recognizable sound.

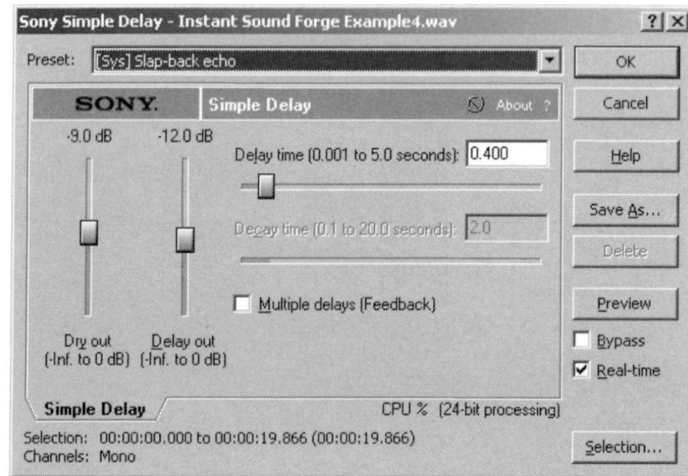

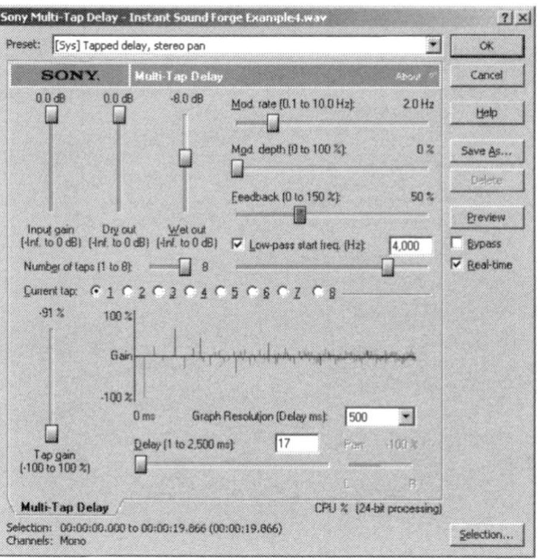

Click Multiple delays to feed the repeat back through the original delay. This creates a series of repeats over time. Adjust the Decay time slider to taste, but be careful that high time values can build up a very loud file quickly (enough to ruin headphones or speakers). Try just under a second to create a vocal twitter reminiscent of John Lennon's Beatles recordings.

For a more sophisticated delay experience, with modulation and control over up to eight distinct delays, click Effects > Delay/Echo > Multi-tap. With a simple voice file loaded, click Preset > Tapped delay, stereo pan and adjust the Feedback to 50%.

Use the Number of taps slider to specify up to eight individual delays. Click Current tap and make adjustments for the Tap gain, delay time, and stereo panning. There is no stereo panning adjustment for a monaural file.

Use the Mod. rate, Mod. depth, and Feedback controls to modulate or change the quality of the delay over time. Try the Presets and experiment to find how the tools interact to change the sound.

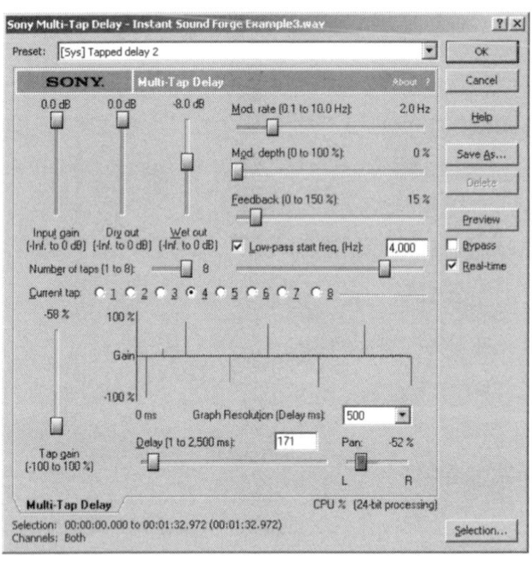

Reverb

Reverb differs from delay in that instead of separate echoes, the repeats blend together into a wash and trail away. Next time you are in a large parking garage, yell hello or clap your hands to hear how the sound bounces around the open space, slowly decaying away. Reverb is, in essence, the result of sound interacting with a room. Larger rooms tend to have greater reverb times, while sound in a smaller room goes away faster. Sound Forge can emulate a variety of these spaces.

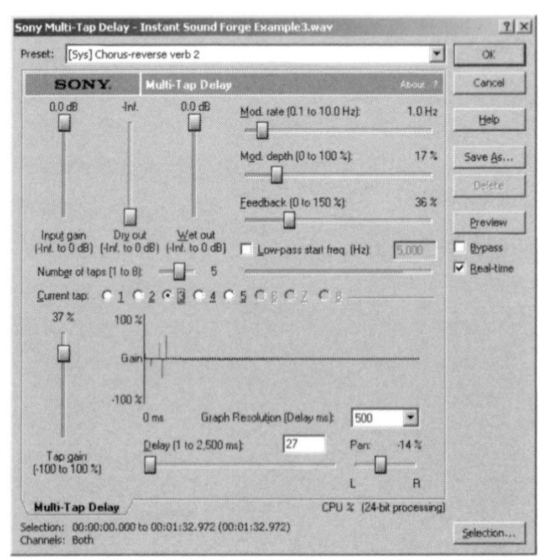

Open a file and click Effects > Reverb. Choose the Preset > Very long hall and

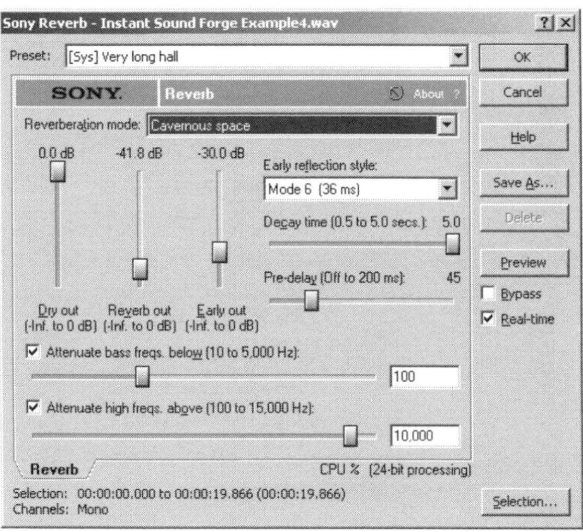

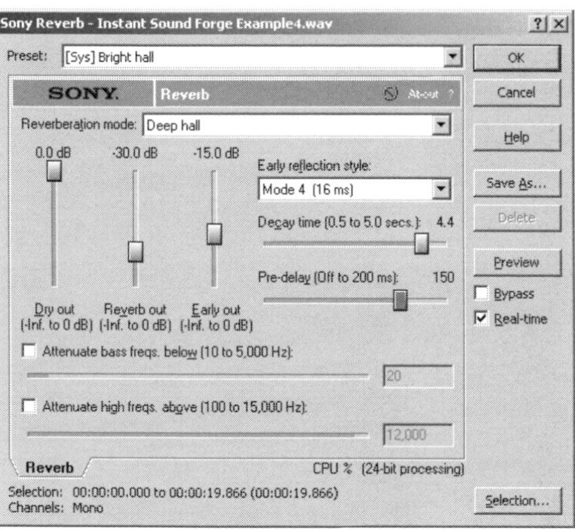

then change the Reverberation mode to Cavernous space. Click Preview to hear your audio file played back in a very large space.

Select from the Reverberation mode to find the right space. Control the balance of Dry out, Reverb out, and Early out with the sliders. Dry is the original sound, Reverb the effect level, and Early out the first reflections heard as sound strikes nearby walls and other surfaces (remember reverb is an emulation of an acoustic space). Choose the Early reflection style from the adjacent list.

Adjust the Decay time to find the right room size. The Pre-delay setting determines the time between the original sound and the start of its reverb tail. These settings help indicate the room's apparent size.

Select and adjust Attenuate bass freqs. and/or Attenuate high freqs. to control the frequency curve of space's reverb. High frequency sounds decay faster than low frequencies; this setting helps you parallel this. Reducing the amount of bass energy in the reverb can keep the resulting effect from sounding too cluttered or muddy.

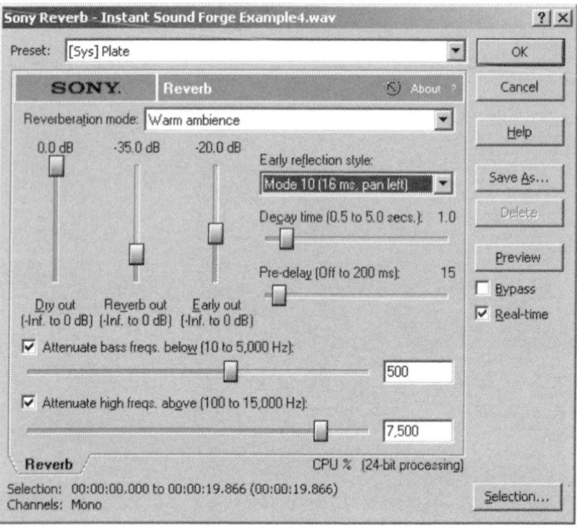

Acoustic Mirror is a tool that uses "samples" of real spaces in which to place your sounds. It's discussed in another chapter.

Other effects

Rather than go into detail about all the effects available, give them a listen yourself. Open up some sample files, launch the effects, and try the Presets to hear how they change your work.

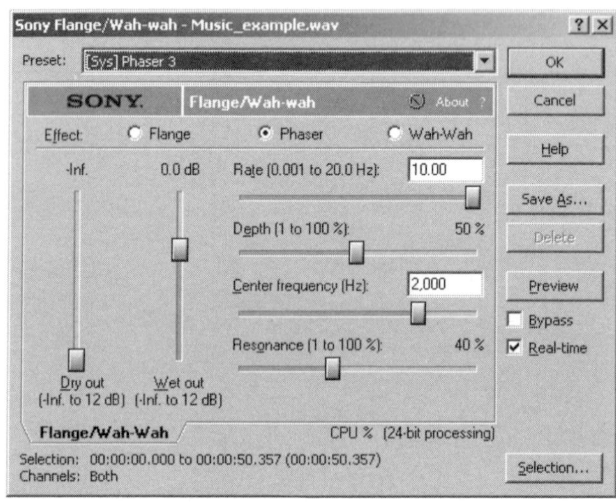

Save your settings / recall (Save as)

Sound Forge includes a lot of effects Presets to get you started. You can also save your own settings and recall them later. After you've made suitable adjustments to an effect, click Save as. Give the setting a name and click OK.

You can recall your Presets from the list at any time. To delete a Preset, select it from the list and then click Delete.

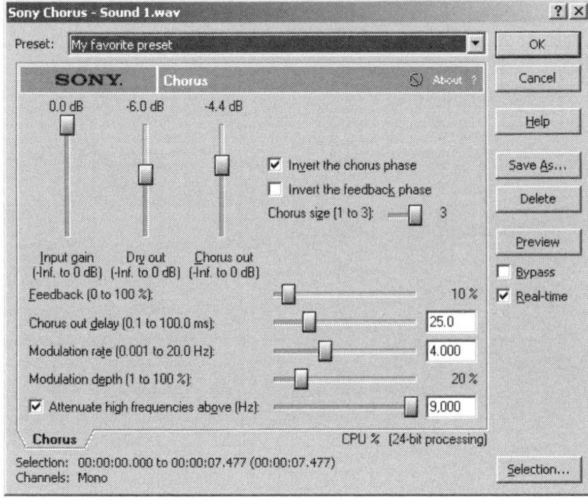

Plug-in chainer

It's possible to string together multiple effects into a chain and process the audio through several different effects at the same time. Click View > Plug-In Chainer. This window can dock along the bottom or float freely.

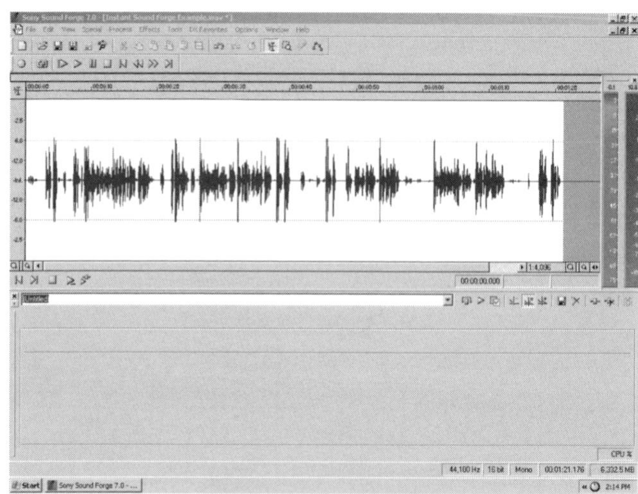

Click Add Plug-Ins to chain.

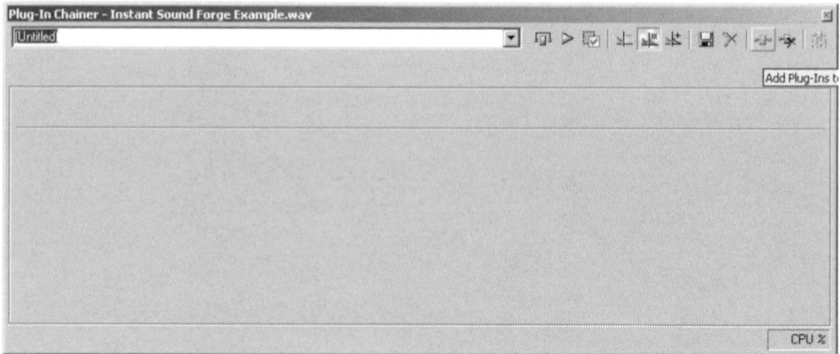

Use the Plug-in Chooser to select effects. Notice the order of all the DirectX Plug-Ins on your computer. Click a folder to navigate through the alternatives.

- All lists every plug-in available.
- Automatable lists only those plug-ins with automatable parameters
- Sony lists the effects that shipped with Sound Forge (and any other Sony plug-ins)
- Third Party lists any plug-ins from other sources
- Packaged Chains lists any effects chains you created and saved
- DX Favorites lists the effects added to the DX Favorites menu.

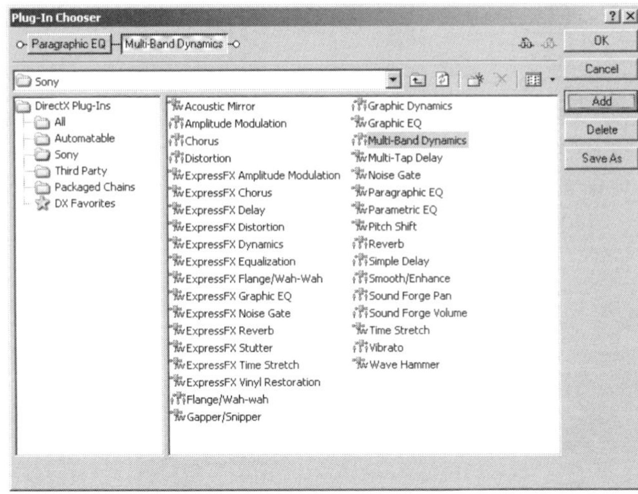

Select and effect then click Add to start your chain. Double-clicking the effect name also appends it to the chain. Continue to add effects as needed, then click OK. Select an effect from the chain and click Delete to remove it from the chain.

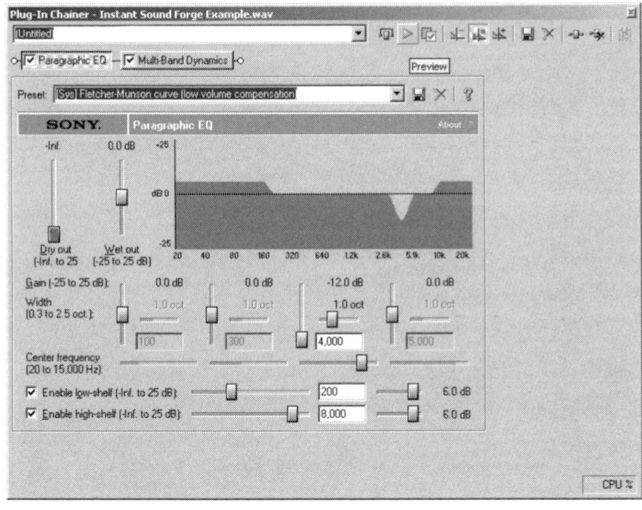

Click an effect to display its parameters. Click the Play button to Preview and Bypass to monitor the before and after.

Rearrange the order of the chain by clicking and dragging an effect tab to the desired location. You can save the Preset chain, recall it or any others you create, and delete chains, too. Click the disc and/or X icon respectively.

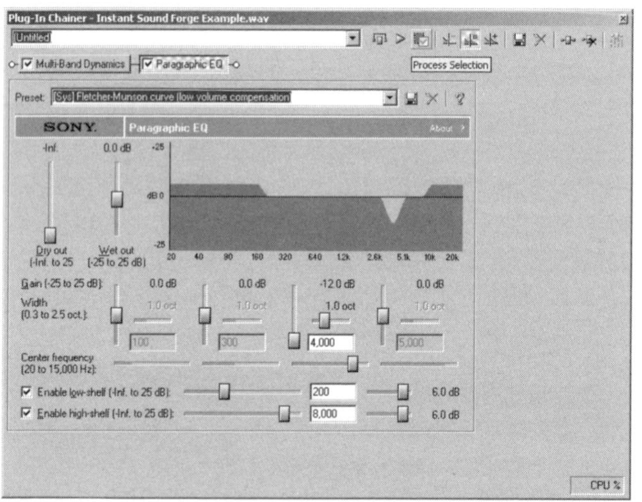

To process the selection with the chain, click Process Selection. Note that the Tail Data setting is important. If the Plug-In Chain adds a tail when processing, such a when adding delay or reverb, choose from the three available options.

- Ignore tail will not extend any tail beyond the end of the file.
- Mix tail combines the tail with any existing audio data and extends the time, if necessary
- Insert tail adds the tail to the file's end.

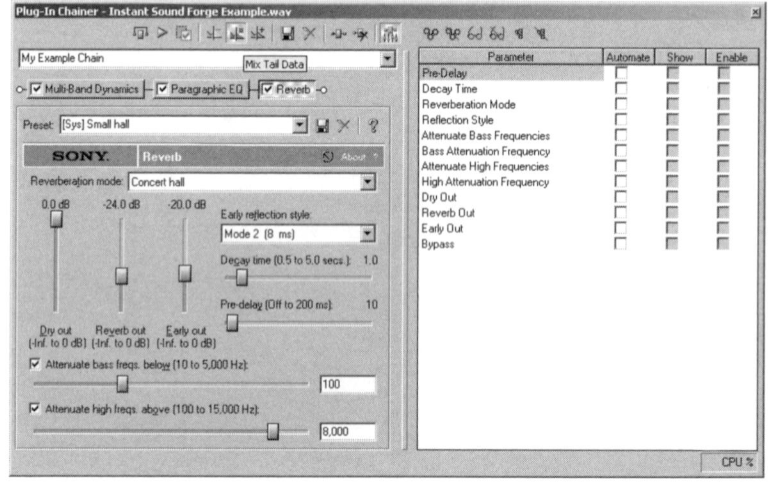

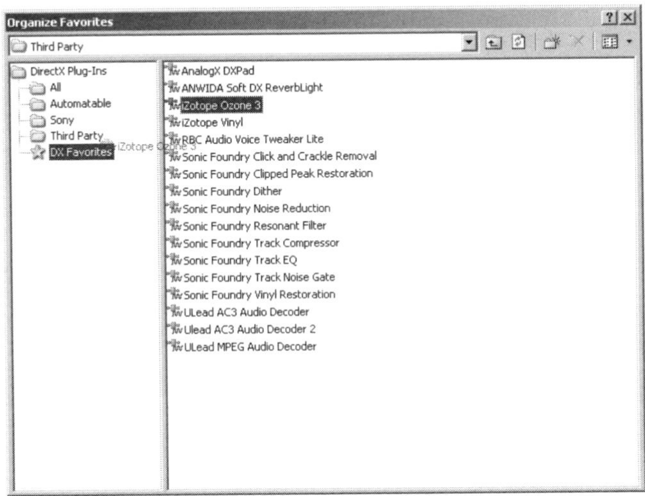

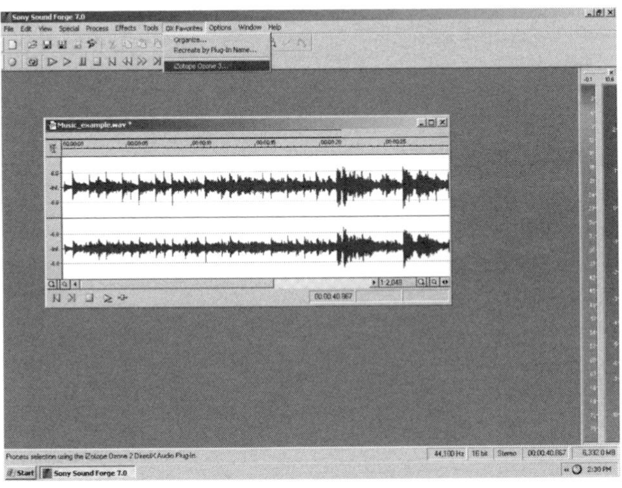

Add to DX Favorites

To add plug-ins to the DX Favorites menu, click DX Favorites > Organize. Navigate to the plug-in, select it, and either drag it to the DX Favorites icon (star) or right click and choose Add to DX Favorites.

Third party plug-ins

Sound Forge supports any third-party DirectX plug-in available. Several manufacturers offer tools to shape your sound as freeware, shareware, and commercial options. Many are offered as demos so you can try before you buy. For a list of what's available, go to:

www.directxfiles.com.

After installing a third-party plug-in, use Add to DX Favorites to put it only a click away.

Effects automation

Several effects included with Sound Forge are automatable or changeable over time. Effects automation works just like the volume and pan automation discussed earlier.

To access the automatable effects, click View > Plug-In Chainer and then click Add Plug-Ins to chain.

Navigate to the Automatable effects, select one, add it to the chain, and click OK.

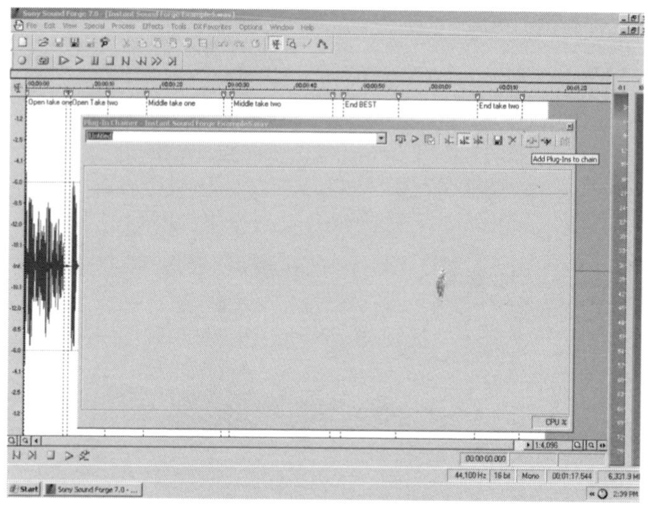

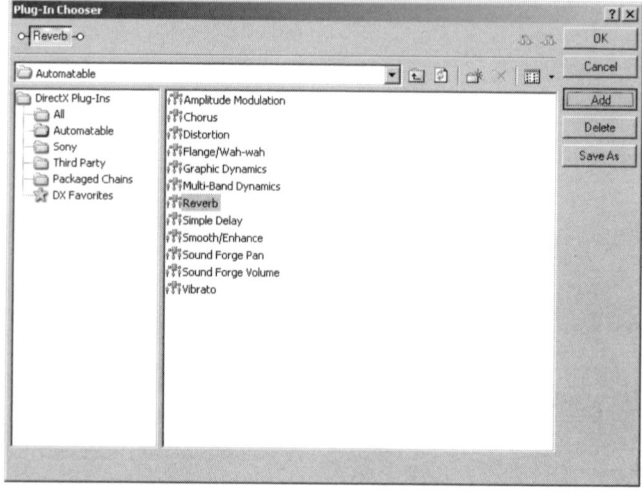

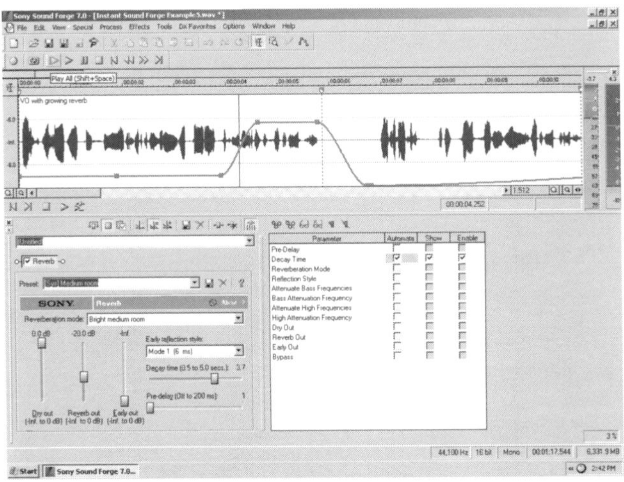

Select any parameter(s) to adjust by clicking its checkbox. An envelope appears on your file. Add points and adjust the envelope as needed. Click Preview to monitor the progress.

A useful feature is to show and hide the automatable envelopes, especially if you are changing multiple parameters and the screen gets rather busy.

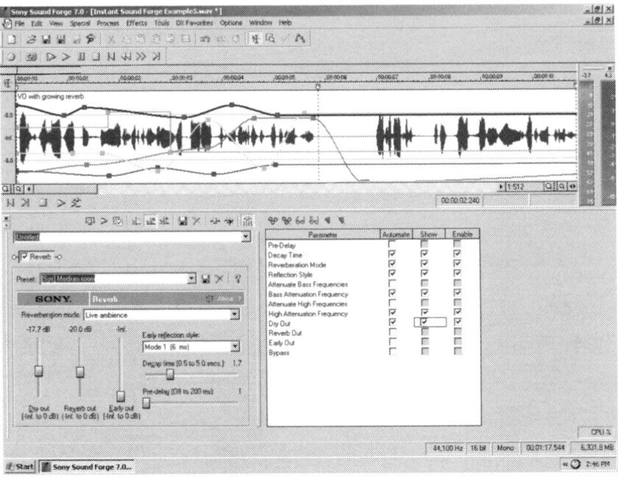

Preset Manager

Manage your personal Presets and Chains, even share them with other Sound Forge users by using the Preset Manager. Click Tools > Preset Manager.

This is your personal Presets list. Select and drag any or all Presets from the lower window to the upper window. To name and save your Preset Package, click File > Save as. You can then back this up, transfer the settings to another computer, and/or send them to another person.

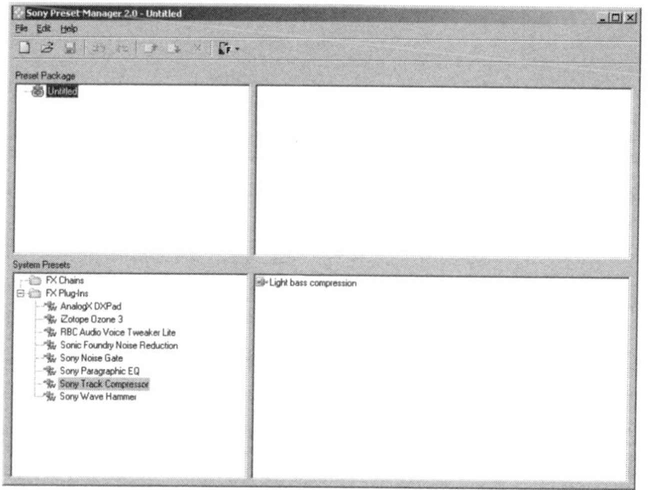

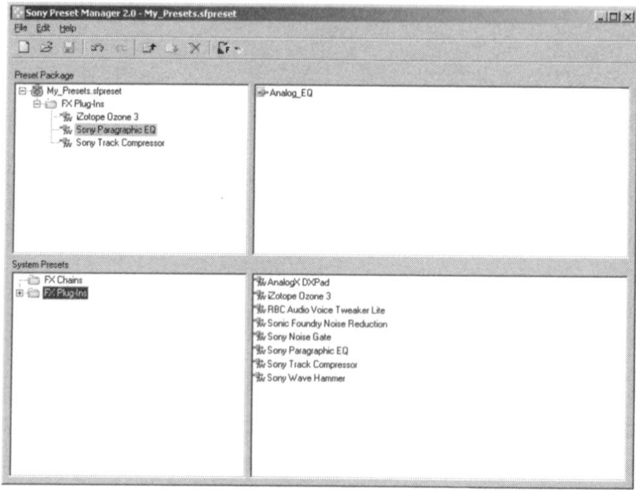

Chapter 8

Restoration

Though many of the tools and techniques discussed so far are useful for both fixing and sweetening your audio projects, there are other problems that Sound Forge handles with power and speed.

De-essing

Is excessive sibilance ruining your recordings? If you hear a predominant "ess" sound, you can reduce its annoying effect with Sound Forge. Use EQ first. Click Process > EQ > Parametric. Set the Filter style to Band-notch/boost, the Center frequency 4.75 kHz, and the Band width to 1 octave. Experiment with the Amount to reduce the sibilance.

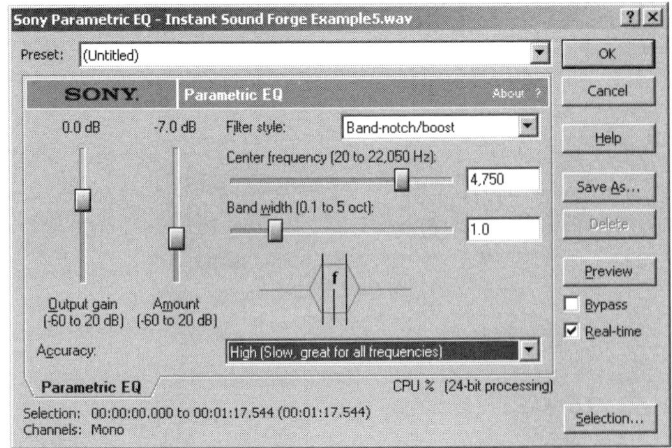

If that doesn't do the trick, try a little frequency dependent compression, called de-essing. Click Effects > Dynamics > Multi-band. This compressor has additional control over particular frequency ranges. From the Presets list, choose Reduce loud sibilants (de-esser). The multi-band compressor can also help recover from excessive plosives such as popped Ps and Ts.

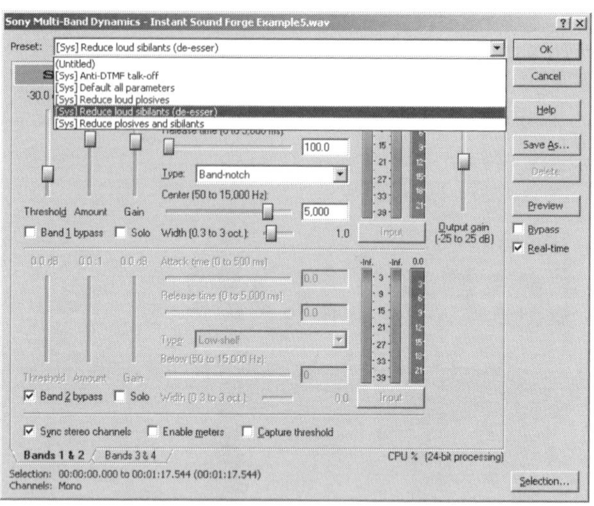

Instead of compressing the entire frequency range, this compressor focuses on a specific, narrow range. Sibilance resides around 5kHz. With this Preset, when the sound level in that range exceeds the threshold, the compressor turns down the volume to reduce the sibilance.

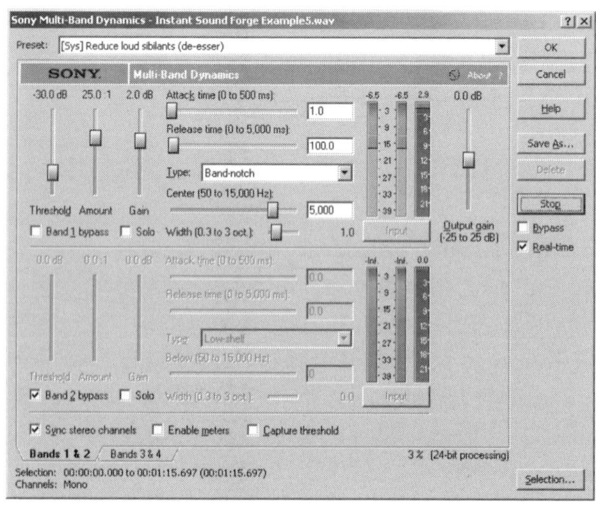

Vinyl restoration

A wonderful benefit to digital recordings is their lack of extraneous mechanical noise. The same thing can't be said for old vinyl. Surface noise, clicks, scratches, and so forth can really interfere with a pleasurable listening experience. After recording into Sound Forge®, use the tools to clean up the sound before saving the file to your the format of choice (CD, MP3, etc.).

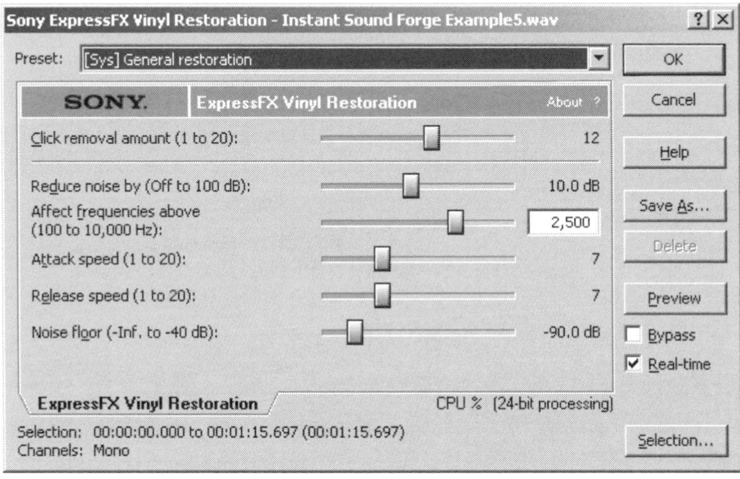

Click Tools > Vinyl Restoration to use this multi-function tool. Click removal amount scans the file for ticks and removes them. The Reduce Noise by, Affect frequencies above, attack, and release work together just like the multi-band compressor discussed above. The Noise floor is a general purpose noise gate, cutting off sound below the setting.

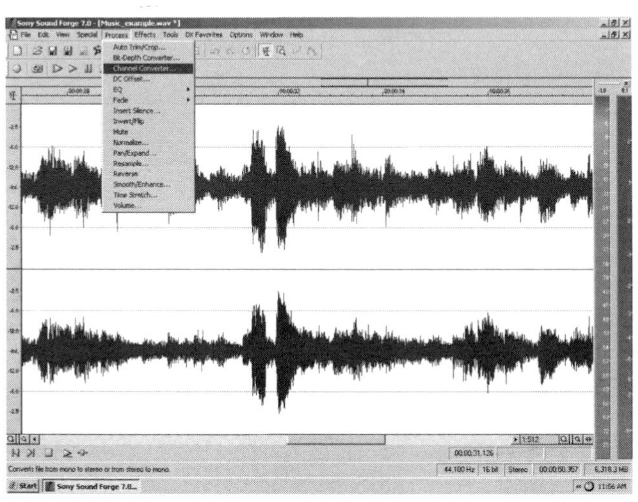

Vocal elimination

This tip is not just for the Karaoke crowd. To eliminate a vocal from a stereo recording, such as removing the lead singer from a song, click Process > Channel Converter.

From the Presets list, choose Stereo to Stereo-Vocal Cut (remove center material). This setting eliminates any material centered in the stereo image. That may be more than vocals, though, so this technique greatly impacts the resulting sound; you might not care for the effect.

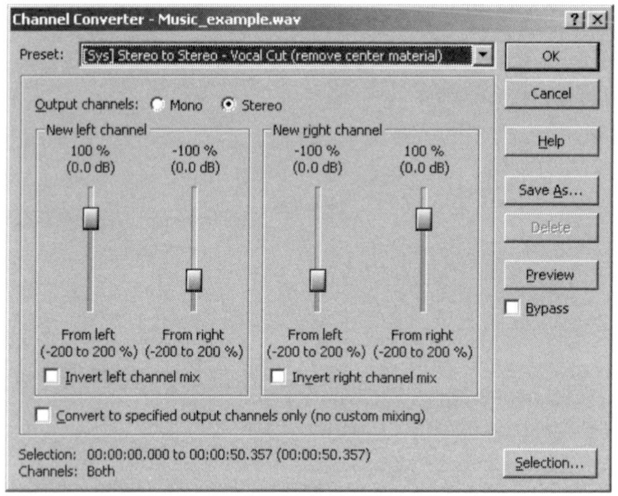

Stereo simulation

Turn a mono file into pseudo-stereo by clicking Process > Channel Converter and choosing the Preset Mono to Stereo - Invert phase pseudo-stereo.

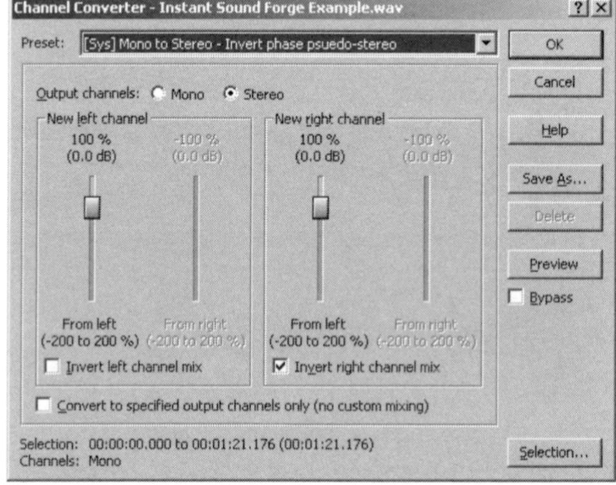

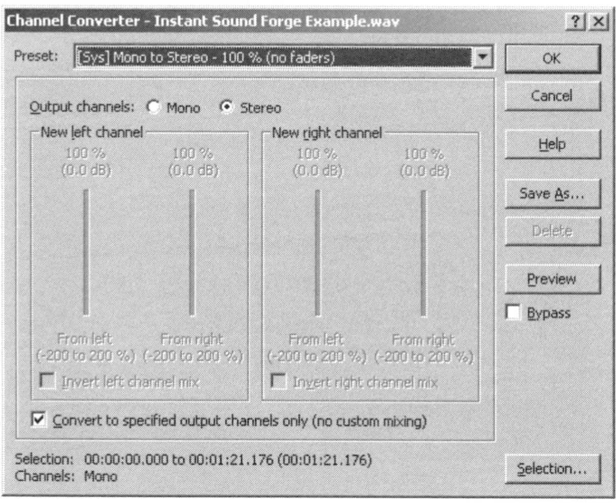

Alternately, convert a mono file to two-channel by using Process > Channel Converter and the Preset Mono to Stereo-100%. It will not be stereo at this point, just dual mono.

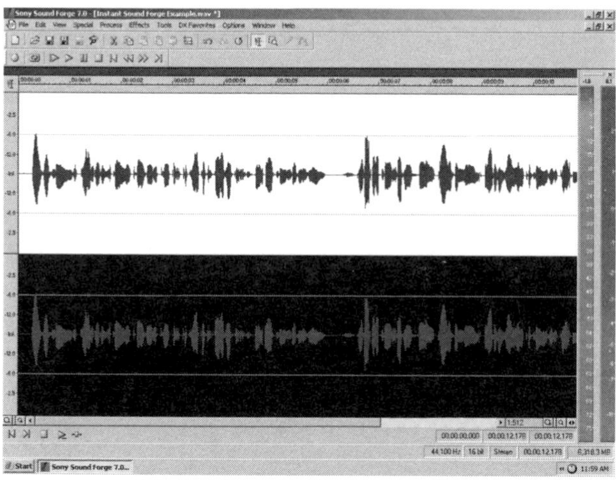

Select only one channel.

Click Effects > Pitch > Shift, adjust only the Cents a small amount, and click OK. This will add a subtle pitch shift to the file giving the illusion of stereo.

Reducing excessive room ambience

Have a recording with the hollow sound of a mic too far away from the sound source? Or a file with too much room and not enough of the good stuff? Try to prevent this from happening by placing mics closer to the subject to pick up more direct sound. But if that's too late, these techniques may salvage the recording. It will never be perfect, but hopefully it will be better.

Click Process > EQ > Paragraphic. First, enable both the low- and high- shelf. Set the low-shelf to 100 Hz and the amount to -inf. Set the high-shelf to 10,000 Hz and its amount to -inf, too. These settings clean up the extreme highs and lows from the track.

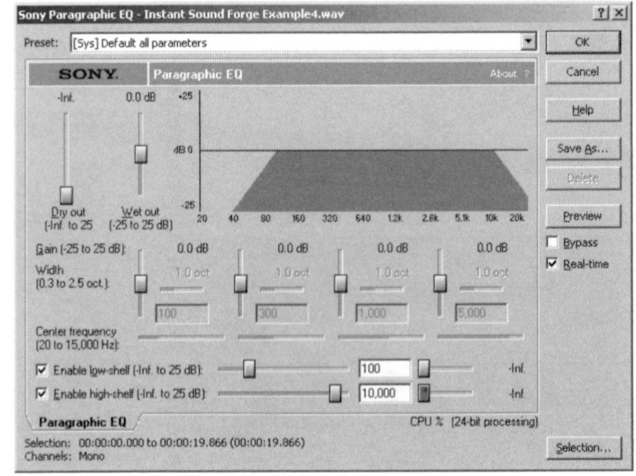

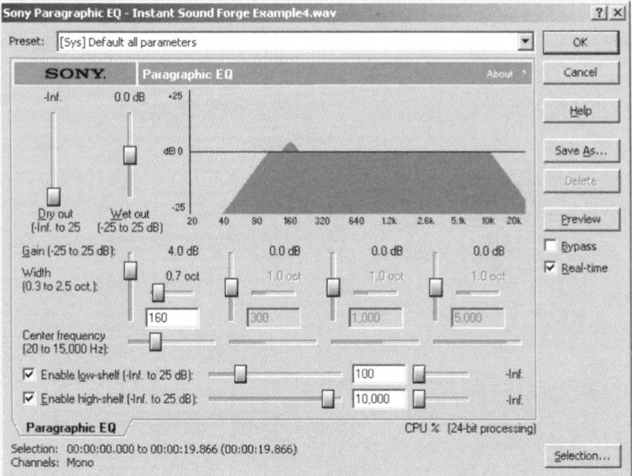

Next, add some bass to the thin-sounding recording. With the same Paragraphic EQ open, set the first slider Gain between 4-6dB, Width to 0.7 oct, and the Center frequency to 160Hz for male voice, 320Hz for female.

Use the adjacent slider to add intelligibility to speech. Try 4-6dB, Width 1.0 oct, and Center frequency at either 1,750Hz or 3,500 Hz (not both).

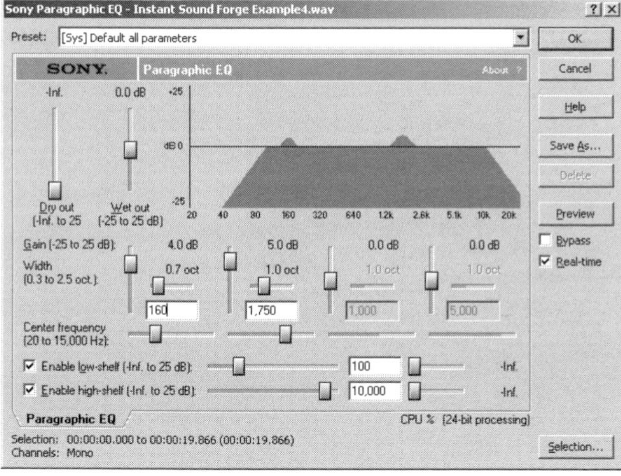

Now locate and reduce the room's resonance. This is the "sound" of the room. Use the third slider to booth a single frequency band significantly, say 10dB, with a Width .5. With the file playing, sweep the Center frequency until the sound of the room is rather pronounced.

Once you locate this magic frequency, cut the band significantly to reduce. Set the Gain to -25. Use Bypass to check the before and after. Tweak until you find the most improved sound, then click OK to process the file.

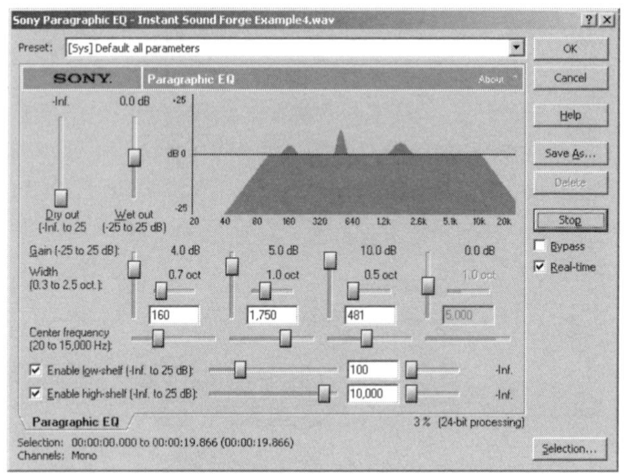

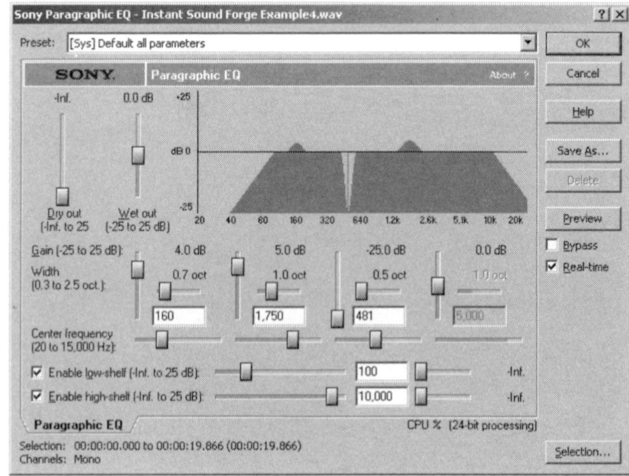

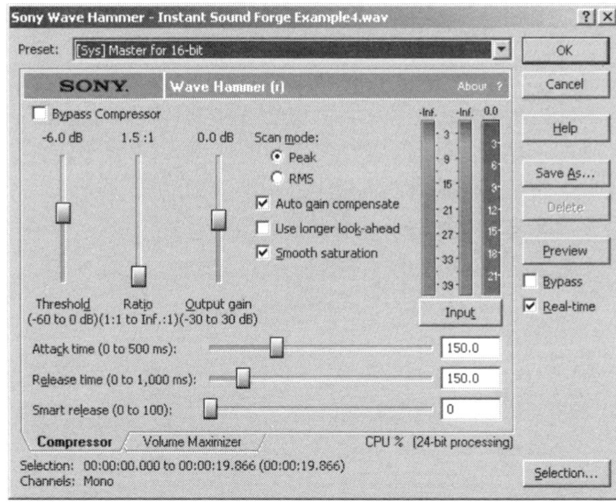

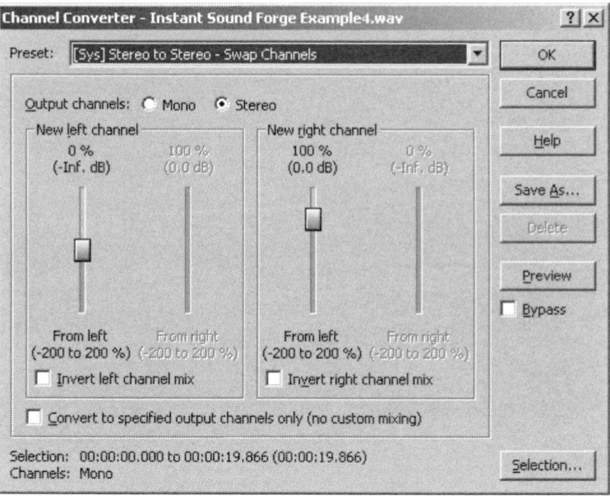

Finally, a little gentle compression may help bring everything together. Click Effects > Wavehammer and experiment with the Master for 16-bit Preset until it all sounds good.

Processing Mid-Side Recordings

There is a stereo miking technique called Mid-Side that provides additional control over the stereo information after the recording is finished. Use these techniques to process M-S recordings.

Open the file. The Mid channel must be in the left. If not, click Process > Channel Converter and use the Stereo to Stereo - Swap Channels Preset.

Next, click Process > Pan/Expand and choose Mix Mid-Side from the Presets and/or Process. Adjust the envelop until reaching the desired stereo effect.

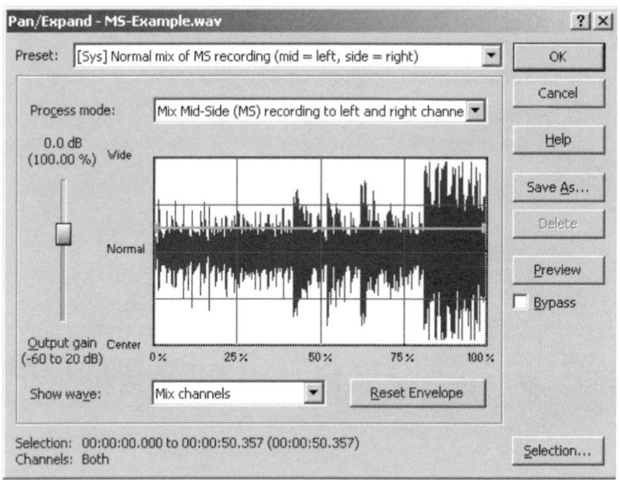

Handling severe noise problems

If a recording has excessive hum, air conditioner sound, or other annoying noise, consider adding the Sony Noise Reduction DirectX plug-in to your toolset. This remarkable plug-in is not included with Sound Forge and must be purchased separately. Noise Reduction is actually a four plug-in package.

Noise Reduction. If you work with noisy recordings, especially if you record in the field, this plug-in alone is well worth the extra expense. Recordings you thought were beyond repair can get a new life with the careful application of noise reduction. I'm consistently amazed by how well it works.

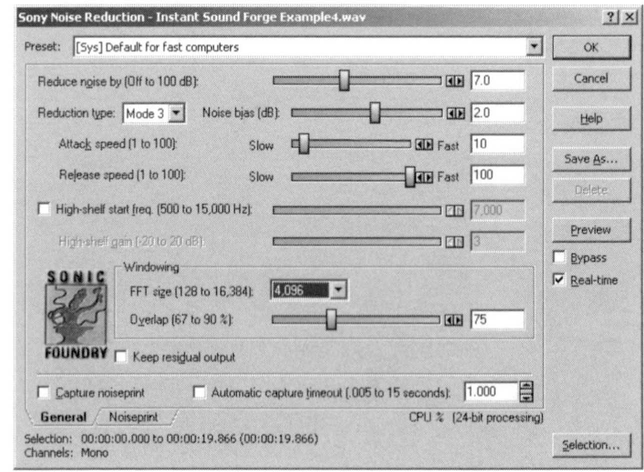

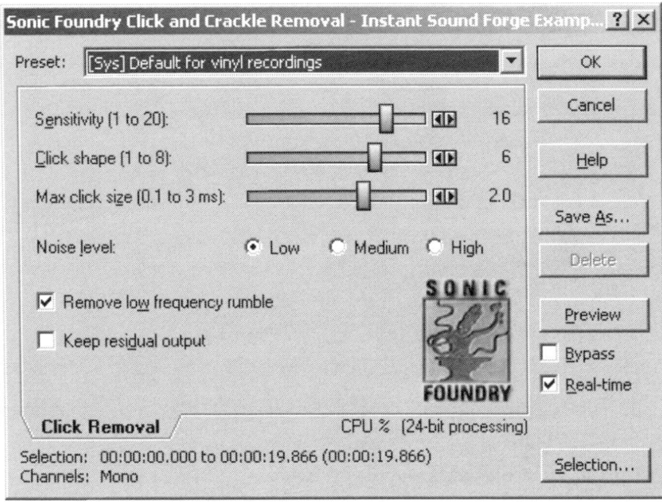

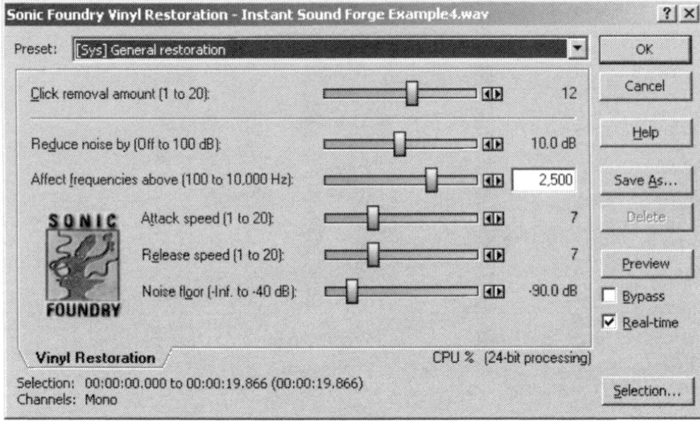

Click and Crackle Removal and Vinyl Restoration. If you're heavy into vinyl, the additional features go beyond what's included with Sound Forge. Refer to that section above for details on using these tools.

Clipped Peak Restoration works well recovering information lost by recording above digital zero (O dBFS).

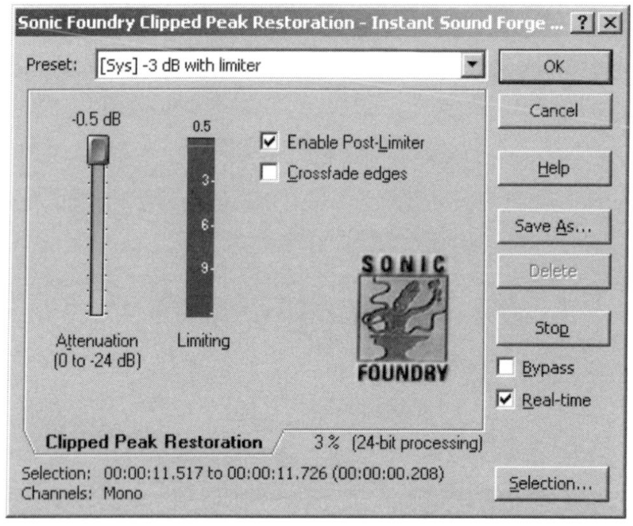

Perform any other sweetening first before using noise reduction. Use EQ, tweak the volume, add a tiny amount of compression, and generally make the recording sound as good as possible. Ignore the noise during this phase.

Then, start working on the noise. Zoom in on your waveform and select a small slice of just the noise. Look for pauses and/or between words and phrases for a sample.

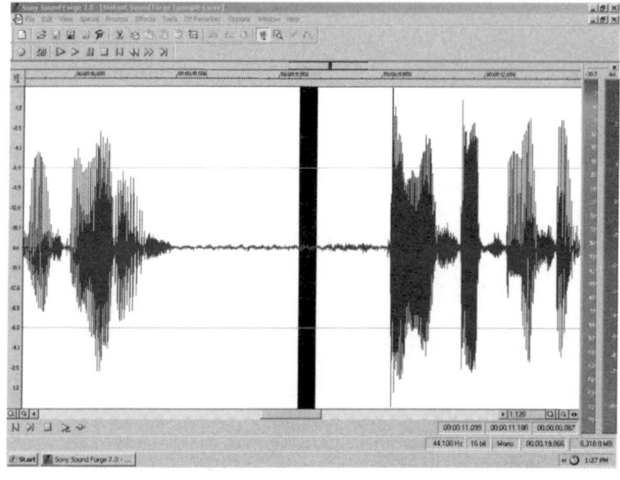

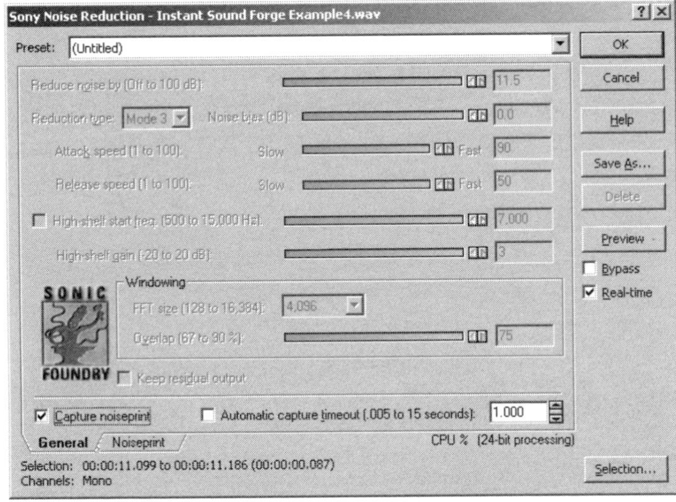

Launch the Sony Noise Reduction. If you haven't added it to your DX Favorites, do that first. Call up the Preset Default for fast computers. Click the Capture noiseprint checkbox and then click Preview.

The plug-in samples the noise then reduces it based on the settings. Experiment with the Reduce noise by, Reduction type, and Noise bias to find the optimum settings for the material. If the noise is high frequency, such as hiss, enable the High-shelf and use this EQ to further tweak the sound.

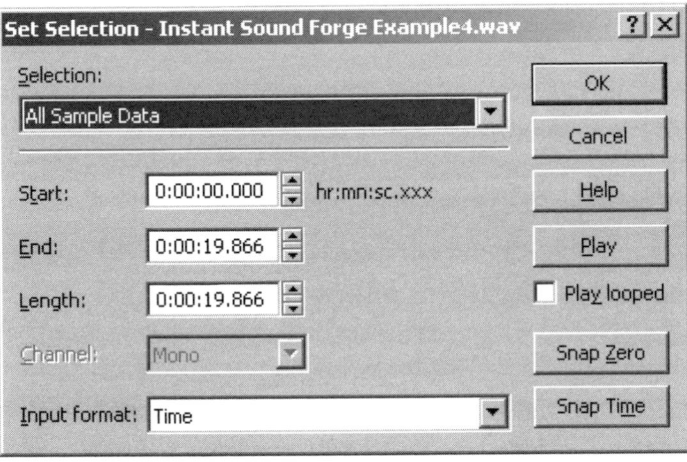

To listen to more than the selection and/or to apply the noise reduction to the entire file, click the Selection. button. Choose All Sample Data from the selection list and click OK.

Now Preview the effect on the entire file. You may get better results by making smaller noise selections, using lesser amounts of noise reduction, and instead applying the plug-in process a few times in succession.

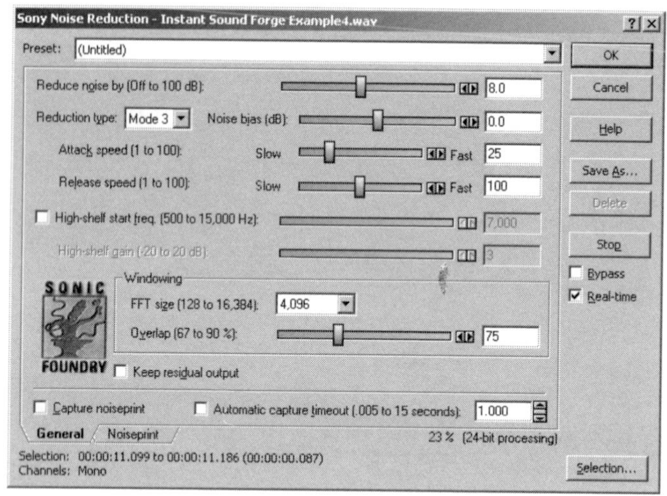

After noise reduction, try using the noise gate to further kill the noise during quiet sections in the file. It may or may not work, depending on the material, but might be worth a try. Click Effects > Noise Gate and set it to shut off any remaining noise without cutting off the sound you want to keep.

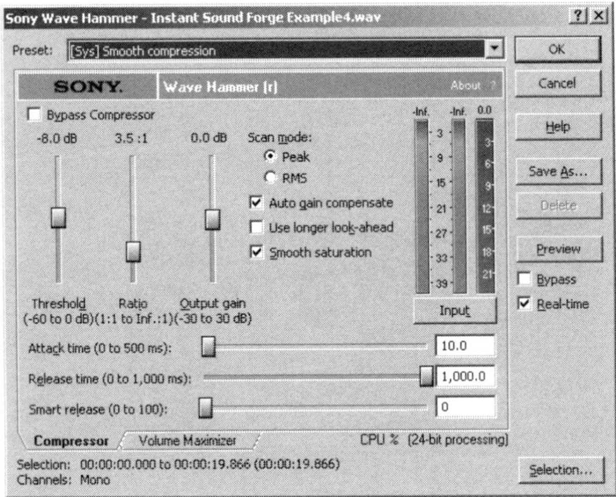

Finally, add a little compression, such as the Wave Hammer, to finalize the sound.

Clipped peak restoration

No matter how hard you tried, you still clipped the audio in a few places. There is a tool that can help recover the lost audio information. First, scan the file to locate any clips. Use Tools > Detect Clipping.

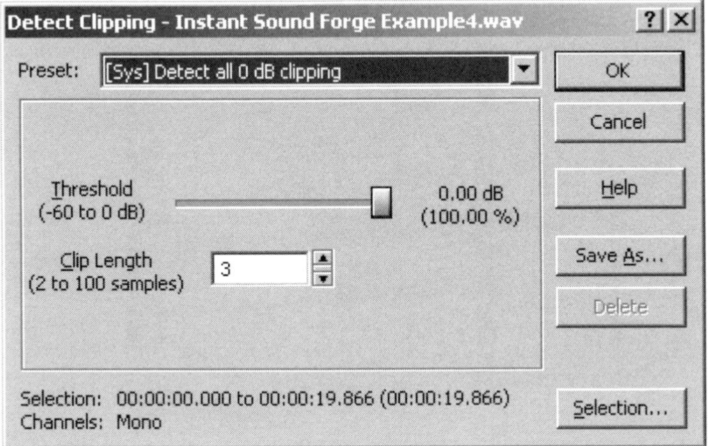

Sound Forge places markers at any clips.

Zoom in and carefully and select the clipped waveform.

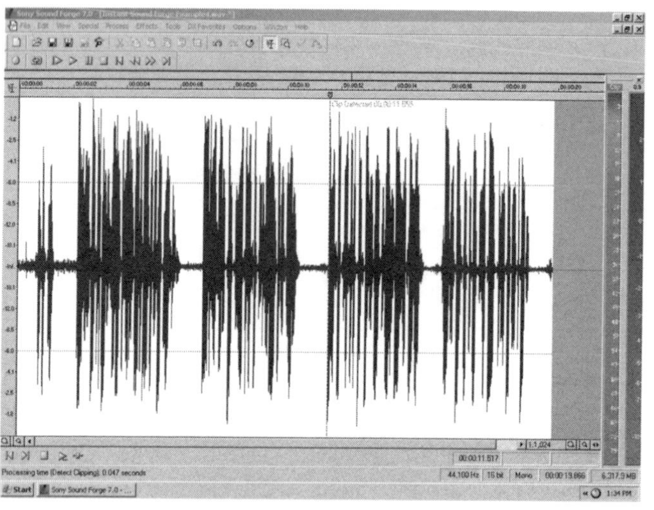

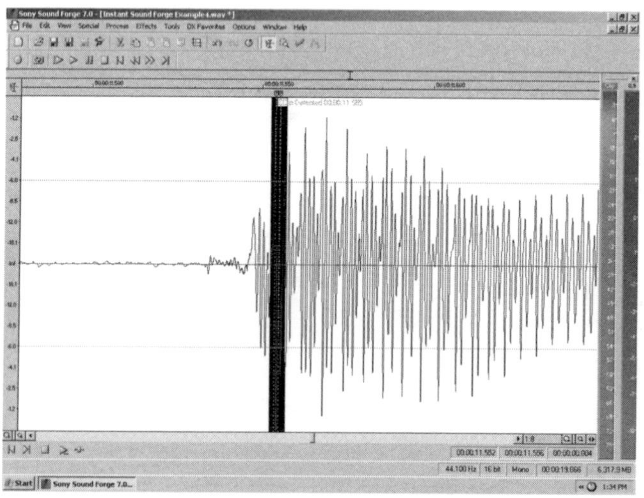

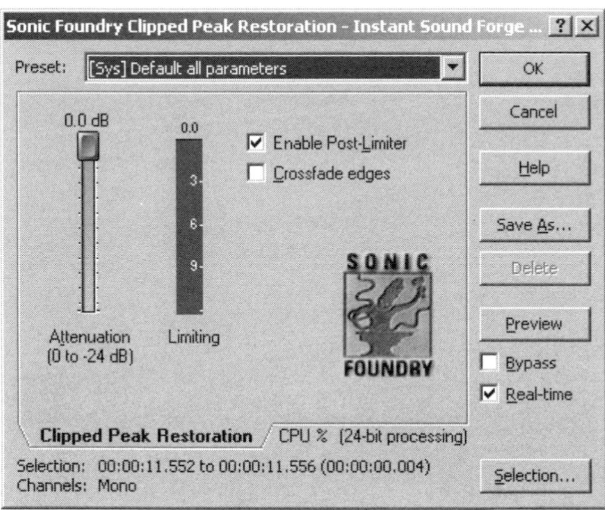

Open the Sony Clipped Peak Restoration tools. Experiment with the Presets to hear how they improve the final sound. The plug-in is only marginally successful on hard clipped material, but works well on occasional, less severe clipping.

Chapter 9

Finishing Secrets

What makes for good audio? Refer to this list as you work on your projects:

- Make sure you can understand what people say whether for sung vocals or spoken word. Listeners want to hear and comprehend other people. Clarity it vital. Voice rules! All other sounds are secondary.
- Paint a picture in the listener's mind's eye through appropriate sound choices.
- Fix obvious mistakes or mask them through other means.
- Keep distracting noise to a minimum or eliminate it altogether.
- Keep your volume level consistent.
- If possible, put your personal stamp or "sound" on your work. Sometimes, though, you just need to keep it real (because that's what a client wants).
- If mixing music or sweetening sound for a video, be sure to fill the entire frequency spectrum with a diverse mix of low, mid range, and high frequency sounds.
- For visual (film/video) and aural (radio) projects, layer the soundscape with voice, hard sound effects, soft or ear candy sound effects, ambient backgrounds, and music. Make sure your choices are suitable for the message being delivered, too.

- Always make room for sound and prevent background elements from stepping on or masking important material. Use the stereo image (Left, center, right) and the "virtual" stage (front to back). Louder sounds appear closer to the listener than softer ones. Wetter sounds (such a sound with an effect applied) appear farther away than a dry (unaffected) sound. Don't forget about time: first this, than that, then something else.

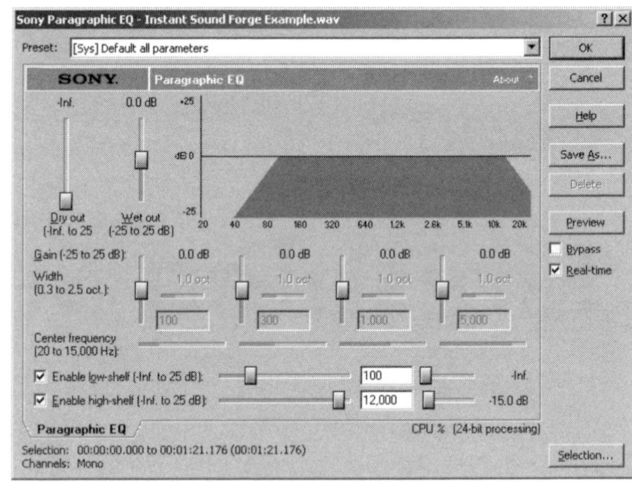

Spoken word finishing

Working from an edited voice-over and/or dialog track, start with these basic settings. Obviously, you need to experiment to find what works for your material.

First, apply some EQ. Click Process > EQ > Paragraphic. Enable the low-shelf, enter 100 for the frequency, and set the slider at -inf to roll off the extreme low bass. There's very little energy down there for human voice anyway. If there's a lot of hiss or "air", enable the high-shelf and roll off starting at 12,000 Hz, too.

Add a slight bump (1-3dB) at 160Hz for male vocals and an octave higher (320Hz) for females. This adds some warmth to the sound. Drop the mid range between 500-800Hz by a few dB and add a little sparkle in the 7-8kHz area. Listen for sibilance and back off a little if necessary.

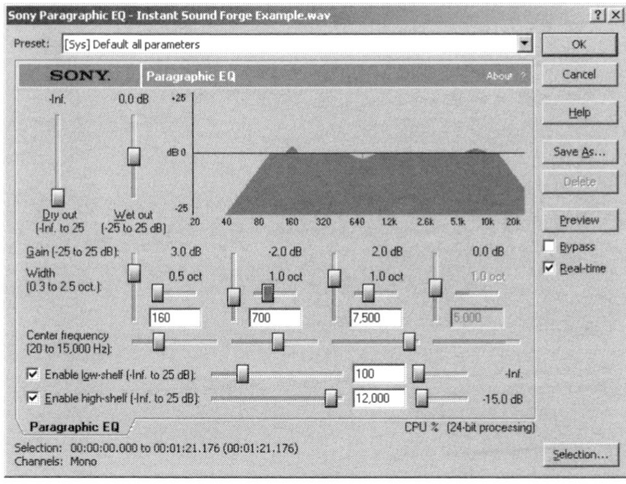

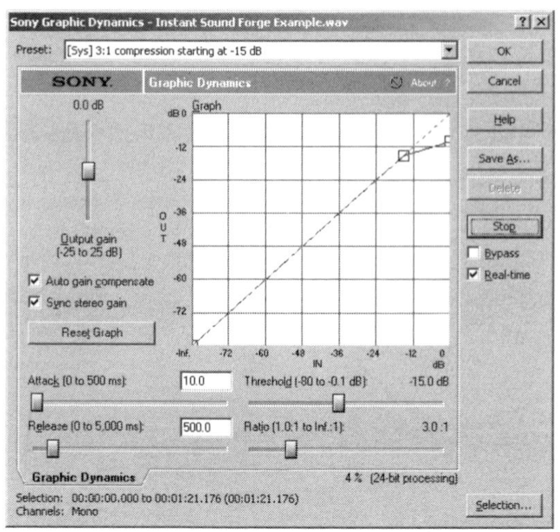

Next, add a little gentle compression (always after applying EQ). Click Effects > Dynamics > Graphic and start with the 3:1 compression starting at -15dB Preset. Adjust the settings to smooth out the vocal. If you hear pumping or other unusual artifacts, you're applying too much effect. Listen for a smooth, gentle sound with a more consistent level.

If you prefer, use the Plug-in Chainer to tweak both EQ and Compression at the same time and preview the results in real time.

Mastering music for CD

After recording and mixing music, the final step before duplication and distribution is mastering. Many people use Sound Forge® to add that final mastering sheen to their recordings. It has the tools most used by today's top mastering engineers.

Unfortunately, there are so many factors involved with music mastering that the subject demands in-depth treatment far beyond the confines of this book. There are no rules as to which EQ to use, what compression settings sound best, and so forth. It's all about opinion and personal preference. It's all about what sounds best to your ears! So, here are some general guidelines to get you started.

- Make sure you have an accurate monitoring system in a listening environment that isn't negatively impacting the sound you hear. If your speakers and room are deficient, you may compensate for these shortcoming while mastering. When you listen elsewhere, the mix may not sound as intended.
- Even with a monitoring system you can trust, play your works-in-progress on a variety of systems in several different environments. Compare what you hear to what you did. Take your notes back to your studio and use what you discovered to tweak the master.
- Listen to music that is similar to the style you are mastering before you begin. This gives you a solid reference.

Before mastering, clean up the tracks by editing out count-ins, intro and/or outro chatter, and other elements. Put one-third second of silence at the start of the track. Click Process > Insert Silence and add .33 at the Start.

Also, check the end for noise and make sure you aren't cutting off a reverb tail. Add silence (a second or two) to the end if needed.

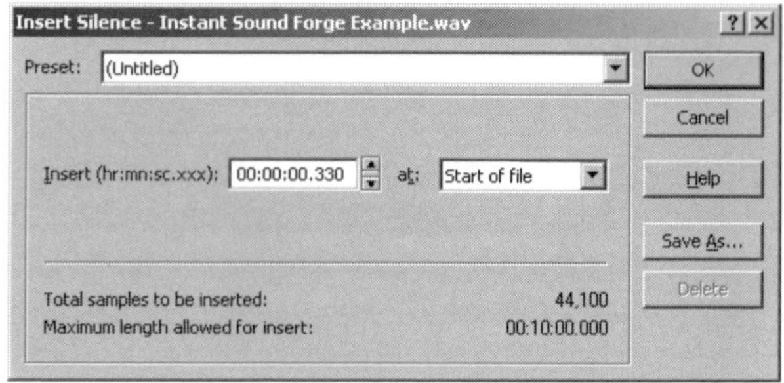

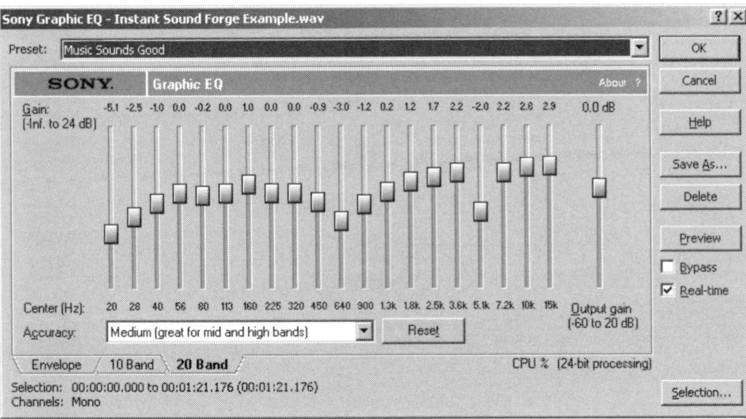

Next, use EQ to bring out the frequencies that make the music sound better and/or to cut out frequencies that are too loud.

De-essing might be needed to tame an overly bright vocal.

After EQ, consider using compression on the entire mix. Either try the Wave Hammer or consider Effects > Dynamics > Multi-Band. By working on specific bands, the mastering session

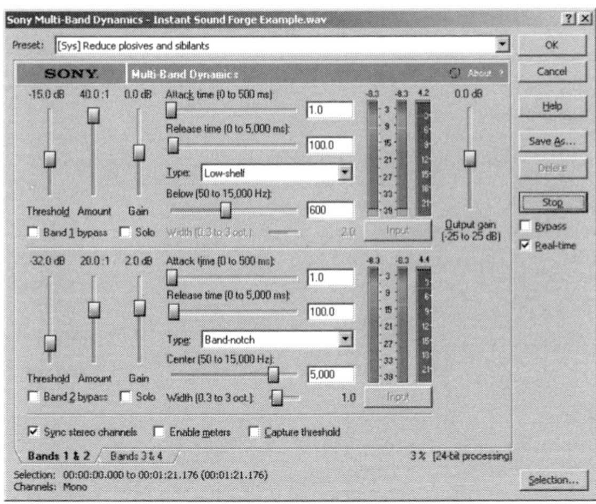

can either accentuate or diminish the level in specific frequency ranges. For example, compress the bass to make it more predominant without affecting the mid-range.

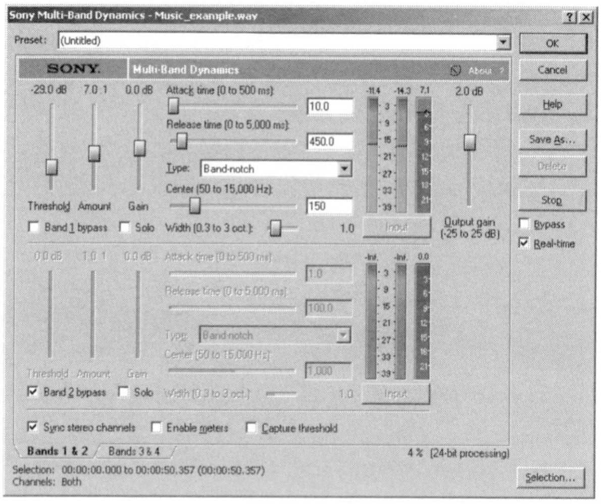

After multi-band compression, or instead of using it, click Effects > Wave Hammer to launch this finishing tool. The Wave Hammer is both a Compressor and a Volume Maximizer. The Compressor settings are similar to Sound Forge's other compressors with the additional options of compressing either the Peak or RMS level and a Smooth saturation setting for warming up the sound when adding a lot of compression. Try the Presets for an idea of the versatility of this tool or start with the Master for 16-bit Preset.

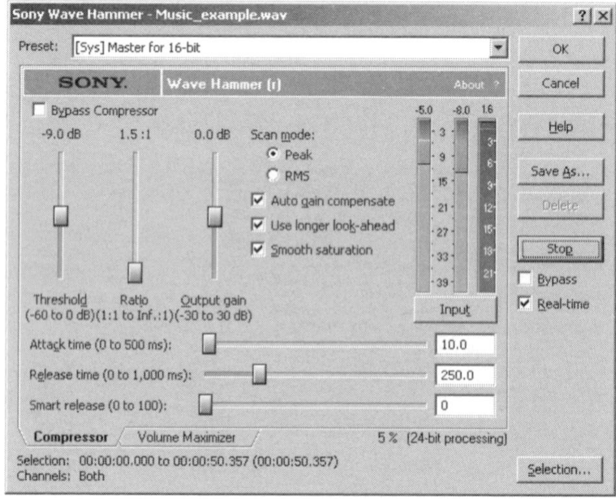

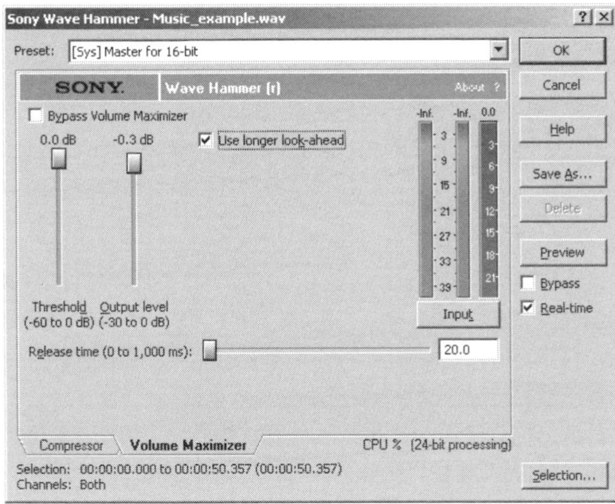

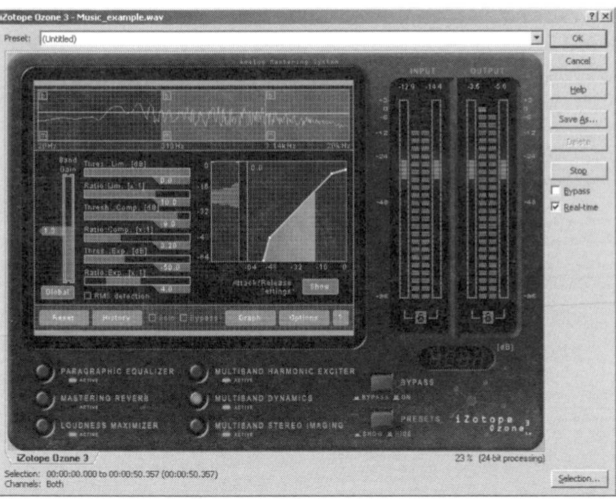

Click the tab to display the Volume Maximizer. This is a sort of smart or dynamic normalization that raises the level to the maximum level based on the Output level setting. I caution you to keep this setting at -0.1 or -0.2 as a maximum. As the name implies, this tool is a way to make your music sound louder.

There are third-party DirectX plug-ins available for audio mastering. One such tool, Izotope Ozone 3, includes a Paragraphic Equalizer, Mastering Reverb, Loudness maximizer, Multi-band Harmonic Exciter, Multi-band dynamics (compressor), and Multi-band stereo imaging in one complete package. Ozone provides a bevy of controls to tweak your audio and ships with dozens of Presets to get you started. Find out more at ww.izotope.com.

If you work at higher sample rates and larger bit depths, you need to downsample and reduce the bit-depth before your files can be used for an audio CD. If your files are already 44.1kHz/16-bit, ignore these two steps.

To downsample, click Process > Resample and choose Resample to 44,100 Hz with anti-alias filter (the sample rate for audio CDs).

To reduce bit depth, click Process > Bit-Depth Converter and use the Convert to 16-bit (dither and noise shaping) Preset to convert to the 16-bit depth for audio CDs.

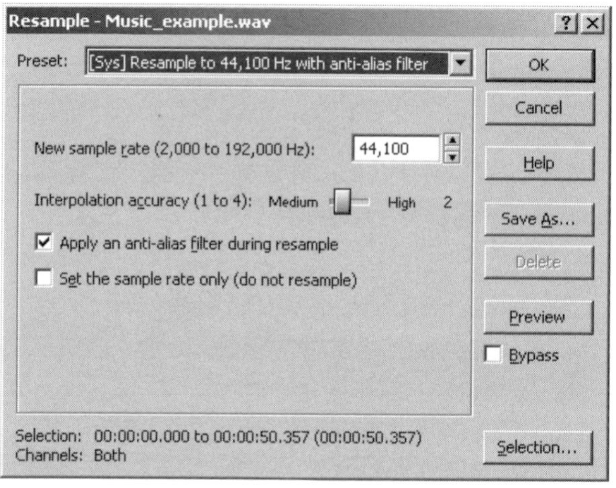

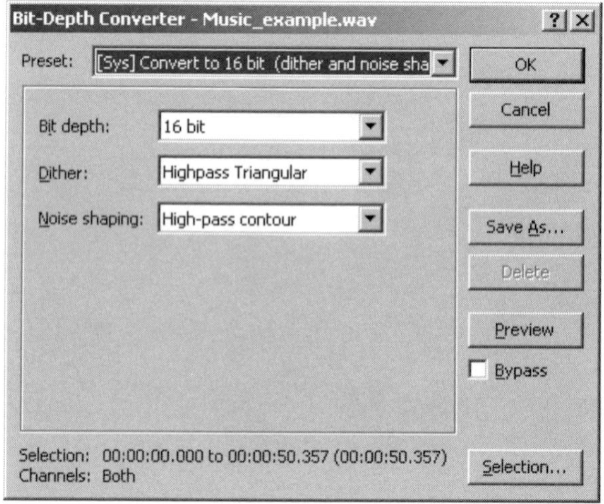

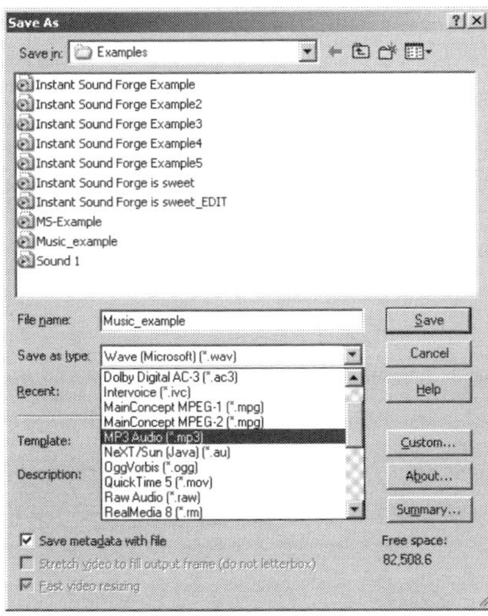

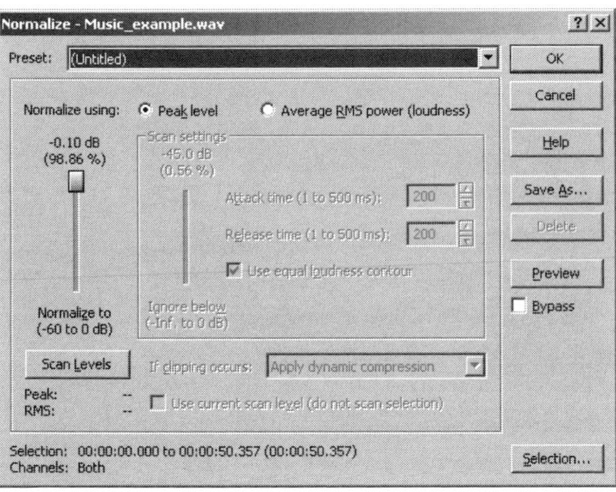

MP3s (and other compression formats)

Converting to MP3, Real, and Windows Media is as simple as clicking File > Save As and choosing the format from the Save as Type list.

For better results, treat your final file as follows: Use the Paragraphic EQ and enable both the low- and high-shelf at 100Hz and 10,000Hz respectively and gain set to -inf. Process the file. Next, compress the EQ'd file slightly, 3:1 or less, to just tame the peaks and reduce the overall dynamic range somewhat. After compressing, normalize the file to 98% using the peak method.

Finally, encode the file to the format(s) of choice.

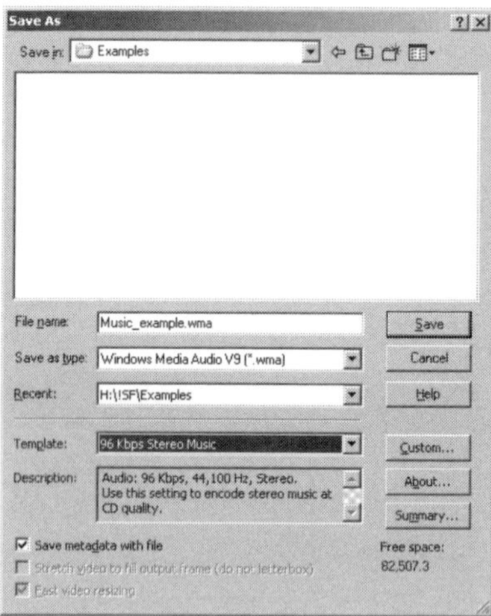

You can insert Command markers in your file prior to encoding. These markers can display messages and launch Web URLs. For instance, a band could imbed a command into a Windows Media file. As a listener plays the song, their Web browser would automatically take them to the band's Website.

Position the cursor in the file to place the Command marker and click Special > Insert Command or use the C shortcut key.

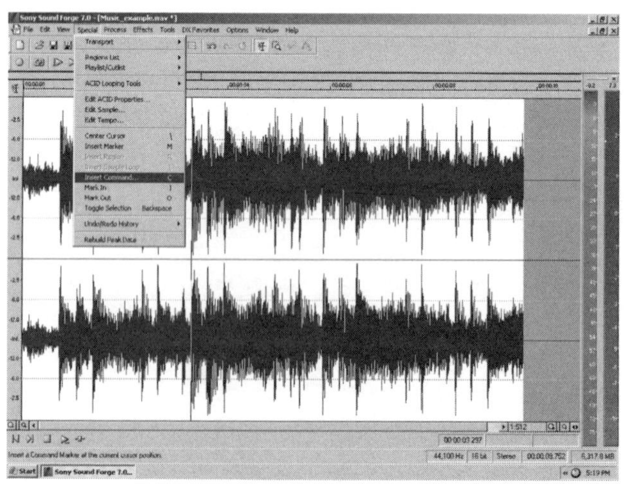

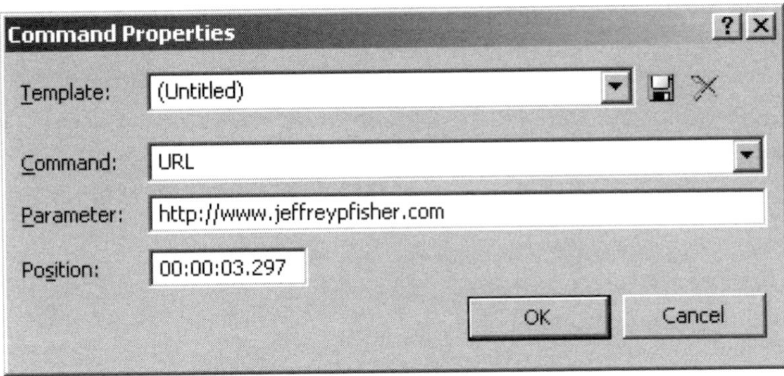

Choose a command from the box and enter the proper parameter. When you encode the file, the command will be encoded, too. Note: command support varies by format.

Burning a CD

To make a CD directly from Sound Forge, insert a blank or appendable CD into your CD burner. Open the file and click Tools > Burn Track-at-Once audio CD. You can only add one track at a time.

Select from the options and click Start to begin. You can continue to add files to the disc until it is either full or you check Close disc when done burning. Important: to play the CD in any audio player, you must close the disc, though.

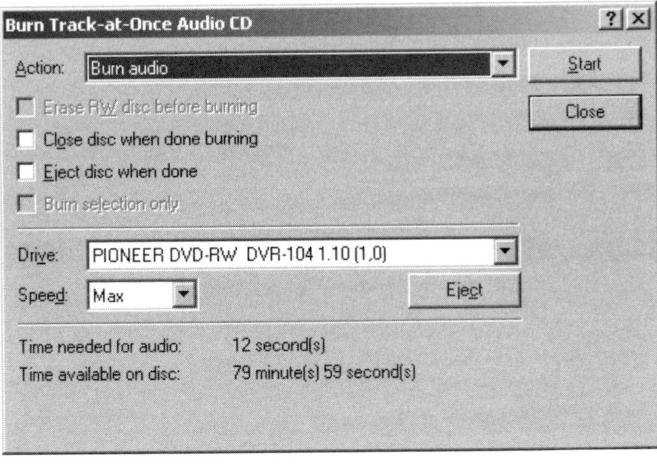

For more sophisticated CD authoring tools, consider buying the separate CD Architect software also available from Sony.

Chapter 10

Other Sound Forge Jobs

By now you realize that Sound Forge is a powerful and indispensable recording, editing, fixing, sweetening, and finishing tool. Its versatile and feature-rich tools will help you both overcome nearly any audio problem and turn your music and sound projects into something special. Well, guess what? Sound Forge has a few more goodies under the hood.

Sound design

Sound Forge is ideal for music, games, radio, film, and TV sound design duties. You can edit and generally finagle audio in a myriad of ways. When Ben Burtt devised the ground-breaking soundtrack for the original Star Wars (Episode Four: a New Hope) he had few tools at his disposal. Armed with some high-quality mics and analog recorders, he captured many sounds from the real world. Back in the studio Burtt manipulated those sounds using varispeed, reverse, EQ, filters, flanging, delay, and stacking. It took time, creativity, and ingenuity to craft the sonic world of this sci-fi classic.

Today, Sound Forge alone gives you more tools and flexibility than Burtt had nearly three decades ago. You can work easier, faster, and at the highest fidelity in ways he could only dream about. Of course, Mr. Burtt has all the new tools now as he continues his role as sound designer for the Star Wars saga.

Start with high quality recordings either you create yourself or from other sources, such as sound effects libraries. Use the Process and Effects tools to change, shape, distort, filter, improve, lo-fi, and otherwise create entirely new sounds.

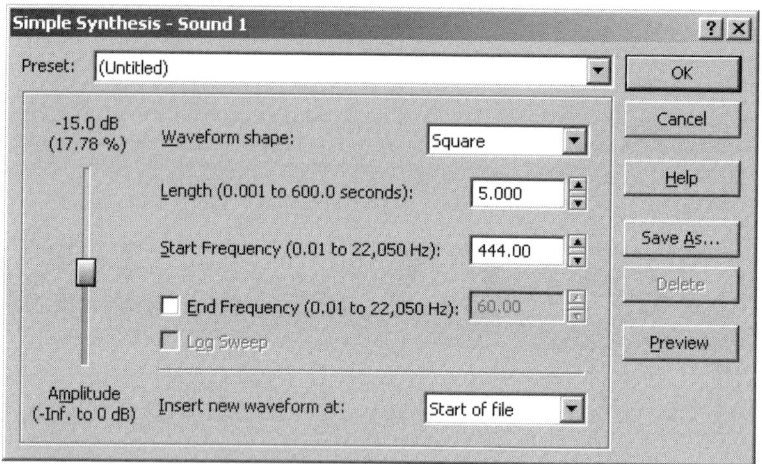

Sound Effects Library Resources

- The Hollywood Edge, www.hollywoodedge.com
- Sonomic, www.sonomic.com
- Sony Sound Effects Series, www.sony.com/mediasoftware
- SoundDogs.com, www.sounddogs.com
- Sound Effects Library.com, www.sound-effects-library.com

Click File > New to create an empty file, then use Tools > Synthesis > Simple to create a basic waveform that you can then turn into something new. There are several Waveform shapes, including noises, from which to choose.

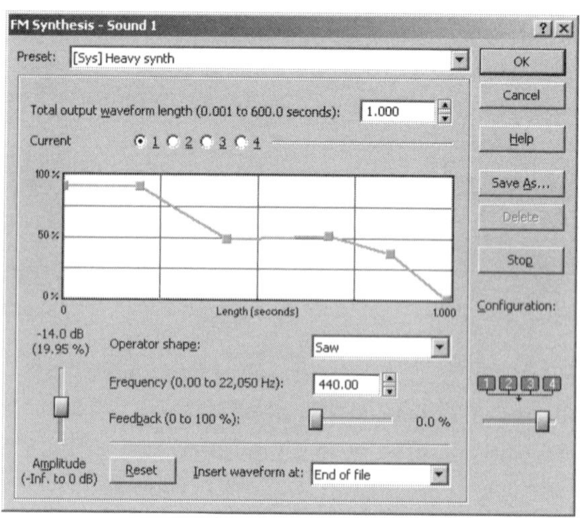

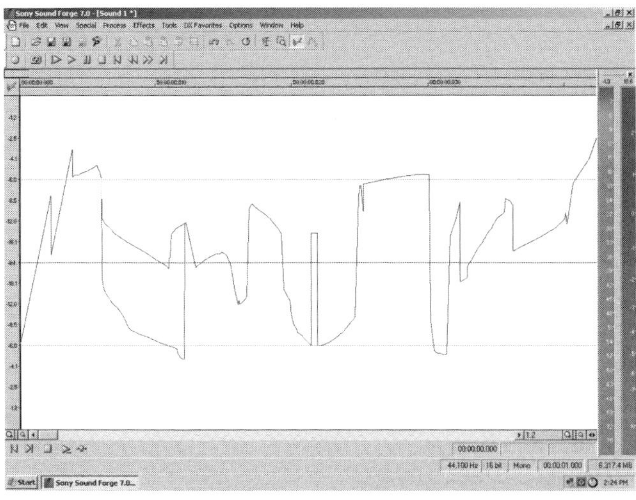

Use Tools > Synthesis > FM to create more complex waveforms. Go through the Preset list as a starting reference and let your creativity flow from there.

Also, try drawing waveforms with the Draw tool. Start with something, draw randomly, and hear the result.

Sound Forge can also create DTMF/MF tones used by telephone companies at Tools > Synthesis > DTMF/MF.

Acoustic Mirror

Acoustic Mirror is another terrific tool for sound design. At first, it may seem that this tool is only good for adding the sampled reverb from real spaces to your recordings. While that is one purpose for which this effect excels, you can do a lot more with it. Acoustic Mirror lets you superimpose the characteristics of one sound on top of the other.

Sony provides a variety of impulse files to use with Acoustic Mirror. These impulse files are primarily acoustic spaces and microphone responses to

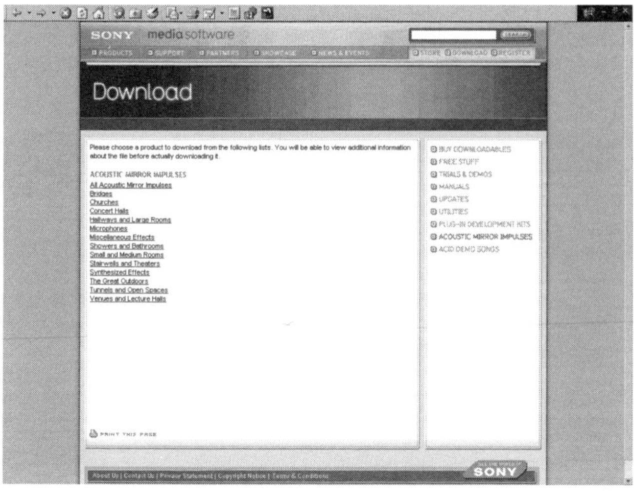

use to treat your recordings. Find them on the Sound Forge application disc or download them from the Sony Web site at mediasoftware.sony.com

With a sound file open, click Effects > Acoustic Mirror and Browse to find an Impulse. Preview the result. Tweak the settings to taste. Notice the Convert mono to stereo checkbox. This setting can create a lush stereo sound from a mono source depending on the material and impulse.

Click the Envelope tab to adjust the impulse volume and length. For ex-

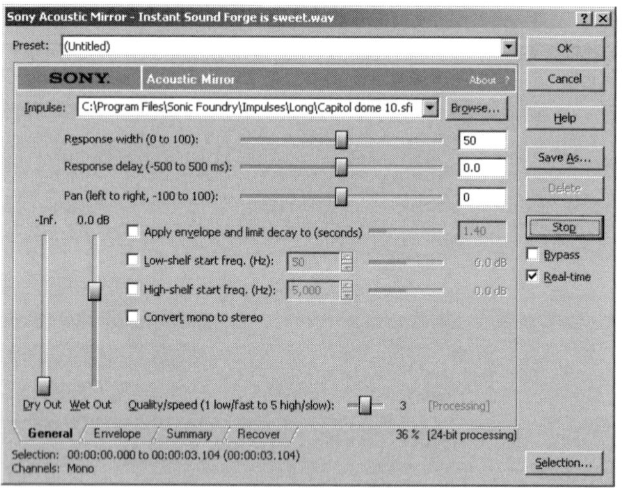

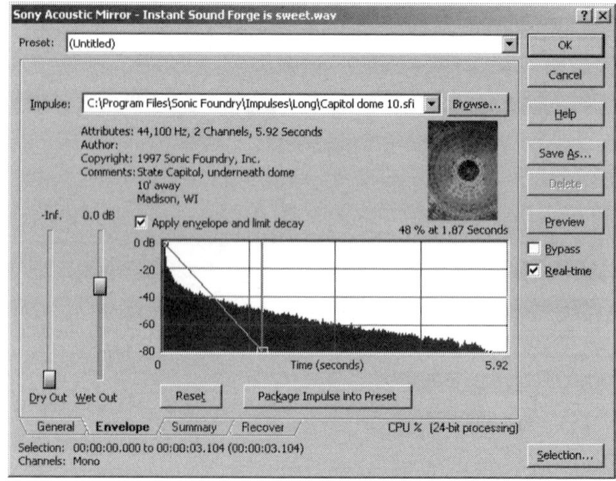

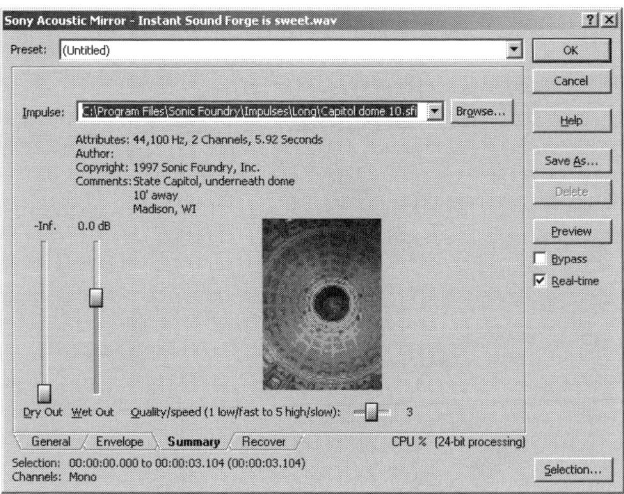

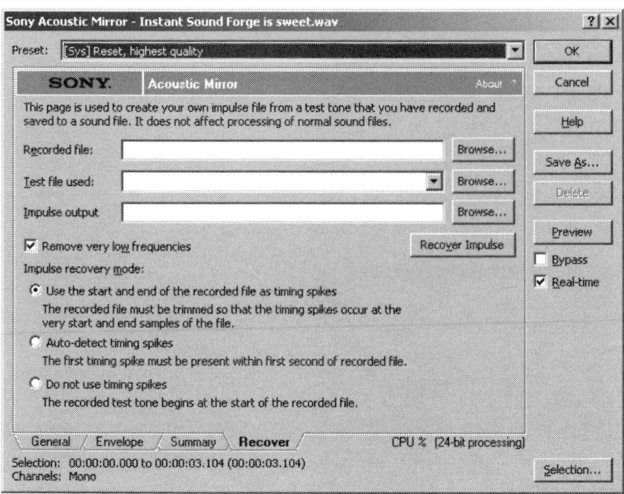

ample, you could shorten the decay time of a long reverb tail. Enable Apply envelope and limit decay and make adjustments.

The Summary tab shows information about the impulse.

Use the Recover tab to create your own impulse files. The basic process is to play the special test tones in the environment (or through a device) and record the result. Using the Recover tools, Sound Forge listens to the recording, extracts the test tones, leaving a "sample" of the space or device. Then, use the new impulse to impart its characteristics on other sounds.

Use this powerful feature to create impulses of your favorite acoustic spaces and/or analog gear. I've "sampled" some of the sounds from my favorite effects devices, created impulses from them, and now use them via Acoustic Mirror. Download the test tones from the Sony website.

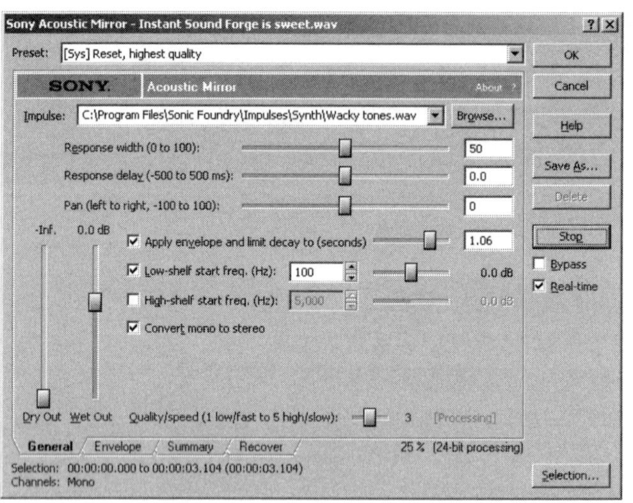

Acoustic Mirror isn't limited to using impulse files, though. It accepts any .wav file to use as the superimposed sound. When treating an existing recording, you'll hear the effect of the superimposed sound, but not the sound itself. Instead, you get an entirely new sound. Try some of the files included or use your own.

Acid tools

Do you use Sony's popular loop-based production software Acid®? Sound Forge includes tools for recording, editing, processing, and adding special Acid® effects to loops that contain provide special tempo, beat, and musical key information used by the Acid software.

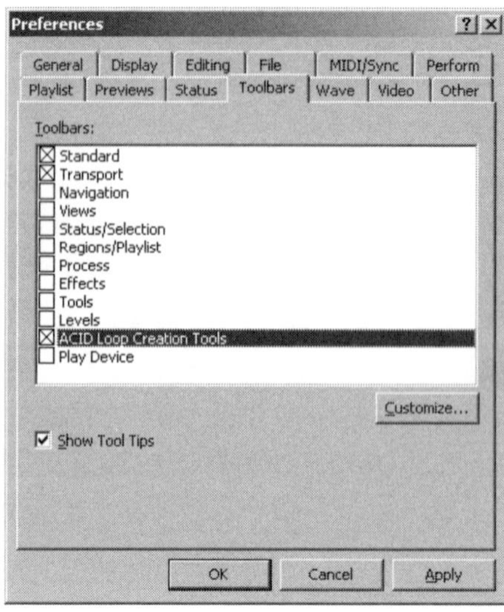

Click View > Toolbars and check the Acid Loop Creation Tools checkbox to add the Acid tools to the Toolbar.

The toolbar can dock or float freely and gives access to a variety of Acid tools (from left to right):

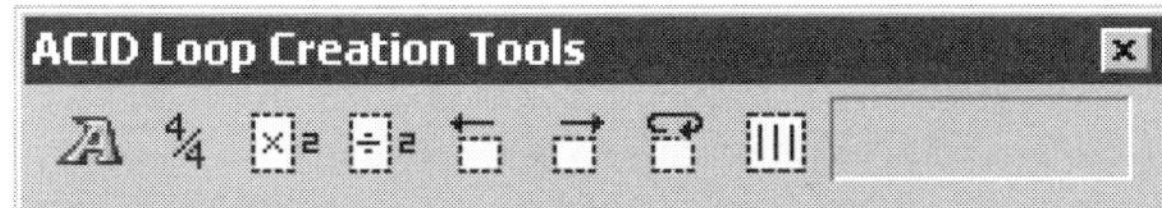

- Edit Acid Properties
- Edit Tempo
- Double Selection
- Halve Selection
- Shift Selection Left
- Shift Selection Right
- Rotate Audio

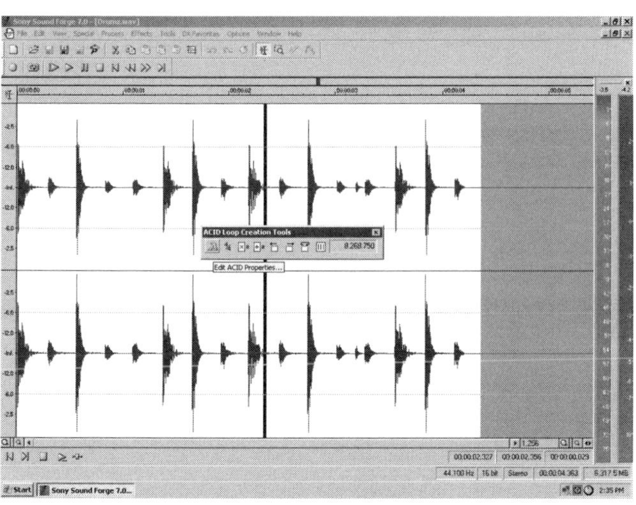

- Selection Gridlines

Click the Acid logo on the toolbar to Edit Acid properties or click Special > Edit Acid Properties.

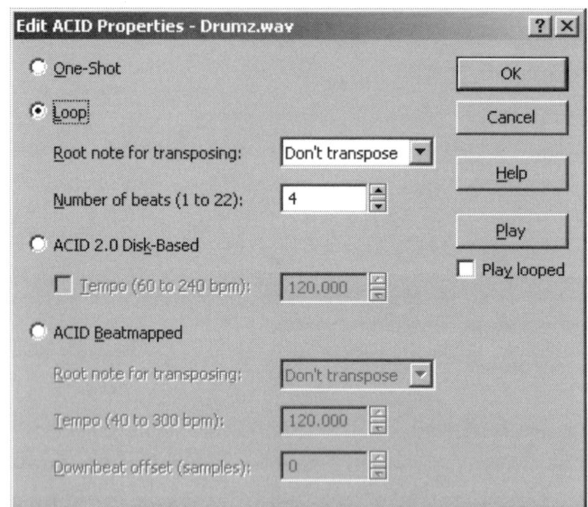

Indicate how Acid should treat the file

- One-shot plays the file once, such as a single drum hit.
- Loop plays the file as a circle with the end returning to the beginning seamlessly. This is the primary format used by Acid. Indicate the Root note of the loops. Use Don't transpose for drum beats or other non-pitched sounds. Type the Number of beats, too.
- Acid 2.0 Disk-Based is a legacy setting for older Acid versions.
- Acid Beatmapped adds key and tempo information to longer files.

After "Acidizing" the file, click File > Save as and save the file as a Wave (Microsoft) (*.wav) file. Make sure the Save metadata with file checkbox is enabled. This saves the special information needed by Acid with the file.

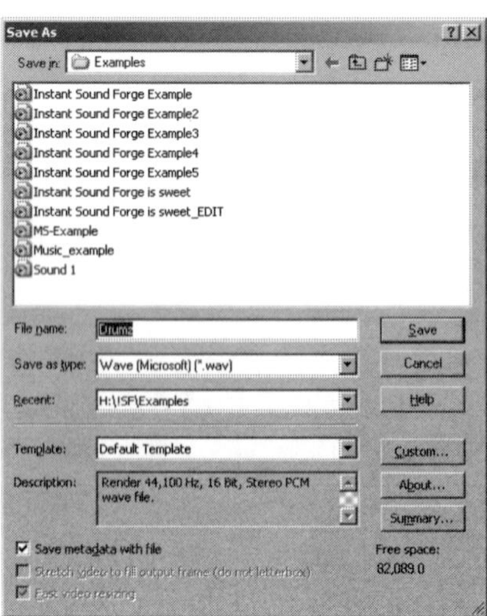

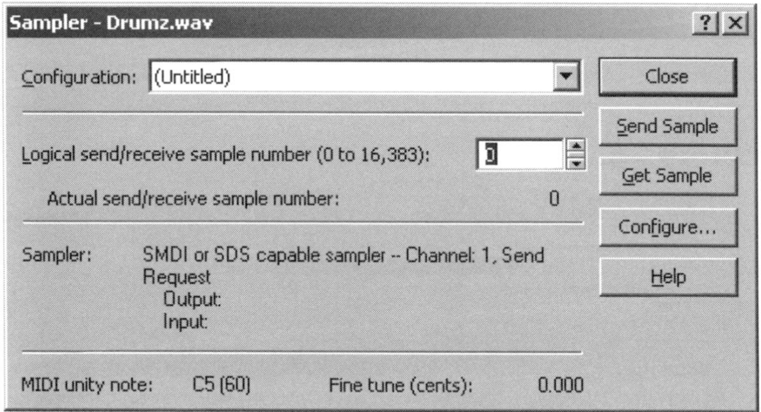

The Spectrum Analysis tool is useful for finding the fundamental note of a file as you prepare loops (see below).

MIDI and Sampler tools

Sound Forge also has tools available to prepare samples to work with an external sampler. You will need a MIDI connection between the Sound Forge computer and the hardware sampler to both send and get samples. Click Tools > Sampler to setup the connection.

Click the Configure button for even more options.

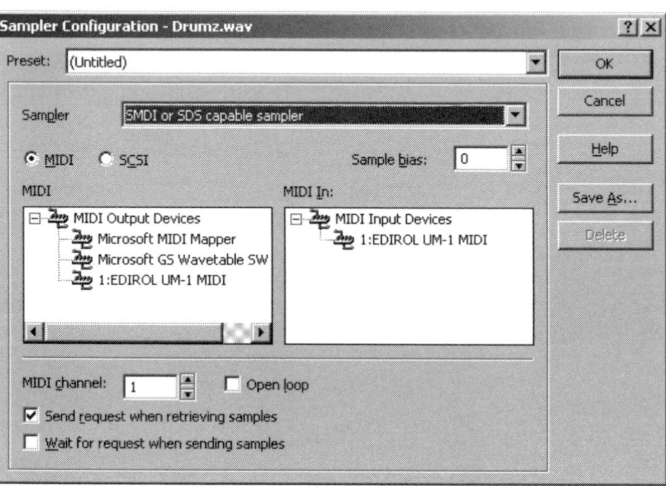

Choose the sampler from the list.

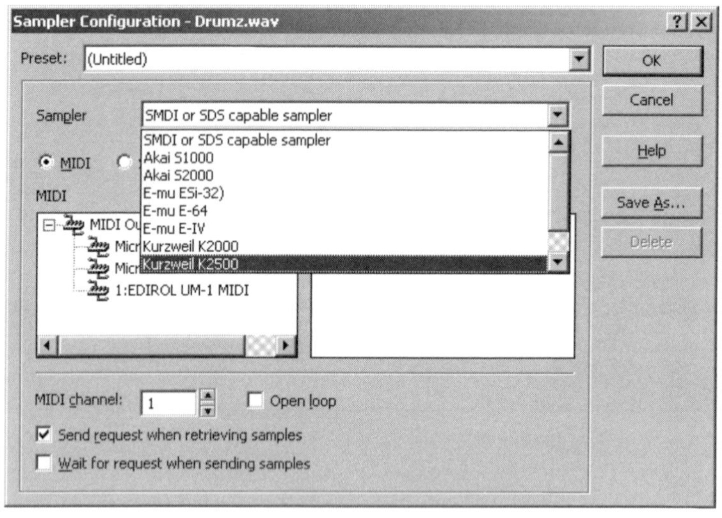

With the sample file loaded up in Sound Forge, make a selection and click Special > Edit Sample or use the shortcut L key.

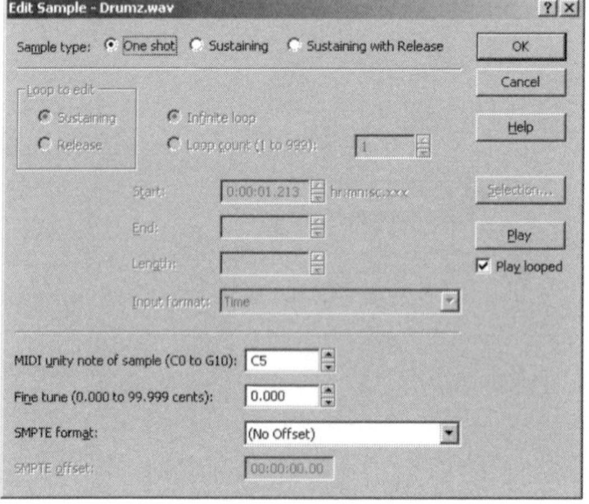

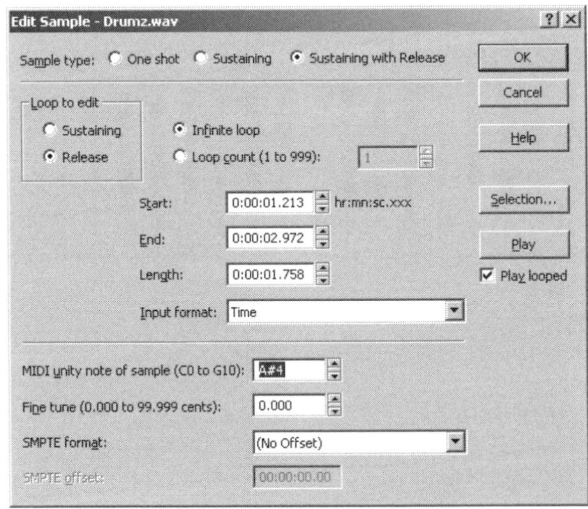

Adjust these settings for the sample including:

- Sample type
- If you select Sustaining or Sustaining with Release there are additional loop tuning tools
- Indicate the MIDI note for the sample and fine tune it, too

Switch to Tools > Sampler to send the sample to the hardware sampler.

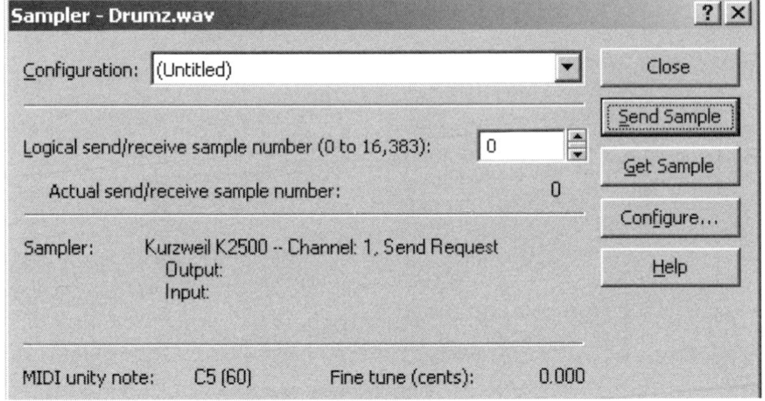

You can use Sound Forge's built-in MIDI keyboard to trigger the sample on the hardware device. Click View > Keyboard. Click the MIDI output button and set the channel accordingly. Play the note to hear the sample.

Other MIDI tools are under the Options menu.

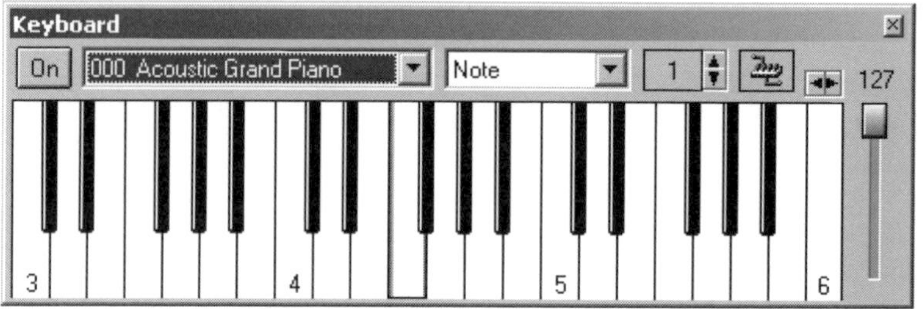

Integration with Vegas

Vegas® is Sony's potent audio multi-track and non-linear video editor application. Although it duplicates some Sound Forge functions, there are many instances where processing a file with Sound Forge makes more sense (e.g. noise reduction). Thankfully, Vegas and Sound Forge get along quite nicely.

In Vegas, click Options > Preferences > Audio Tab and use the Browse button to select Sound Forge as your Preferred audio editor.

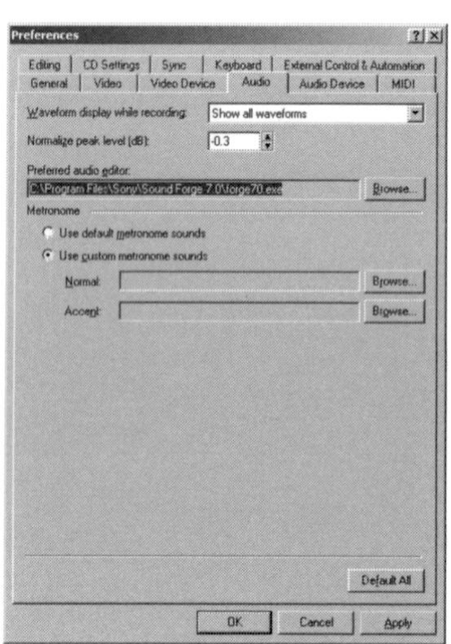

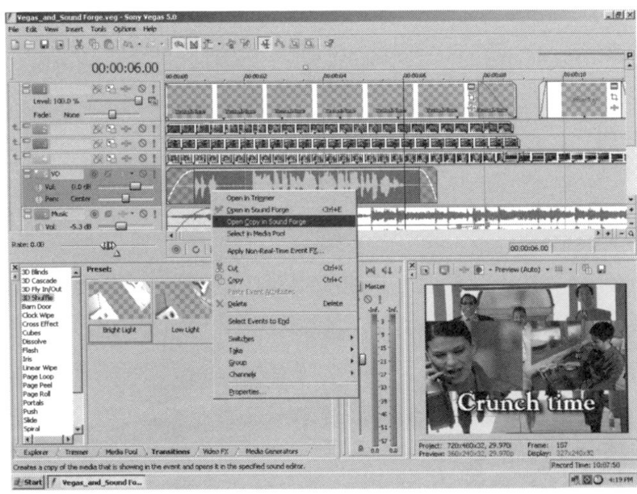

To move a file between Vegas and Sound Forge, have Vegas open, select and right click the audio event, and choose either Open in Sound Forge or Open Copy in Sound Forge.

If you open the file, your processing is destructive. However, if you open a copy of the file, Vegas adds a Take number to the file. Now you can process the copy and keep the original intact.

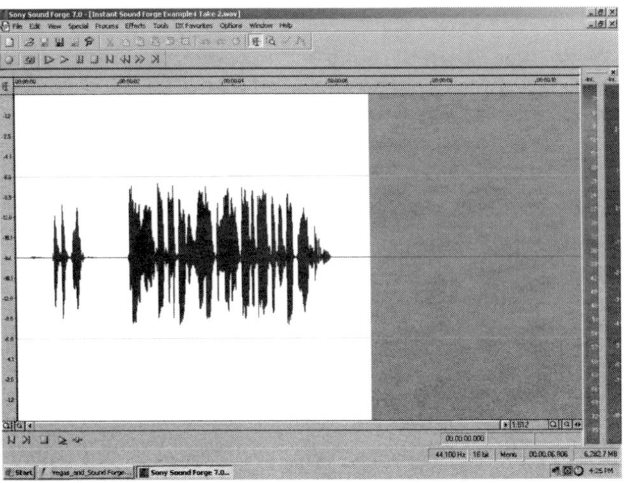

After working on the file and saving it, switch back to Vegas. The new file, with the take extension, will be the active take on the Vegas timeline.

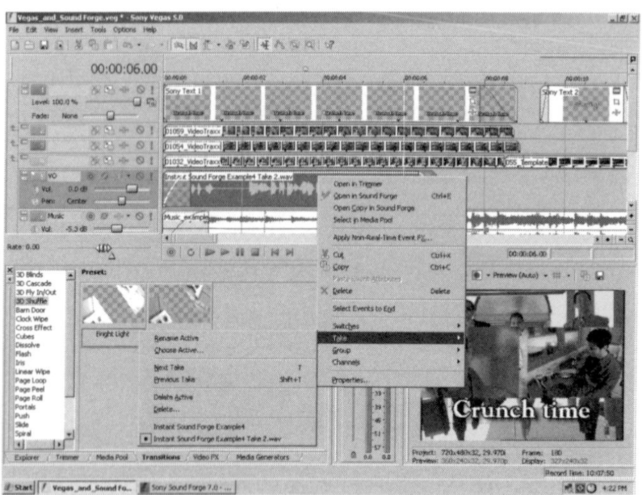

Spectrum Analysis Tools

For critical audio analysis, Sound Forge delivers robust Spectrum Analysis. Use this tool to check the amplitude or level of the frequency content of a file.

Click View > Spectrum Analysis to open the dialog. Play the file to see the result. Alternately, click the Real Time Monitoring option, play the file, and see the result change over time. Note the data window at the bottom and what it tells about the analyzed file.

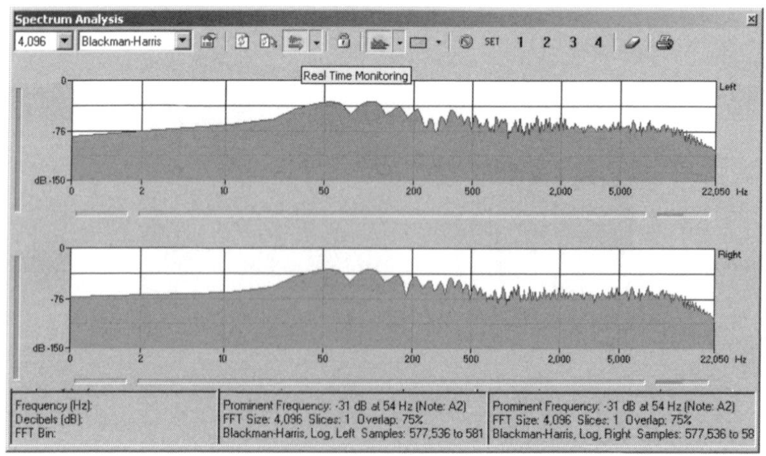

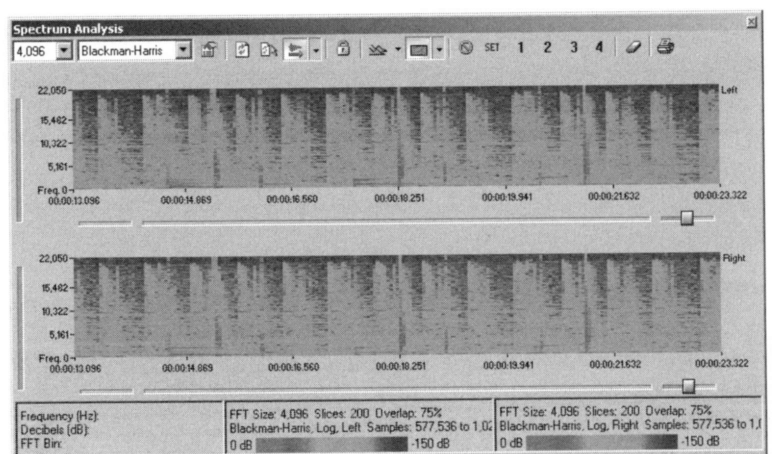

Switch to Sonogram for a different view. The graphs can be printed, too.

Another useful analysis tool is Statistics. With a file open click Tools > Statistics to display critical information about the file. The RMS power is useful for comparing loudness between files.

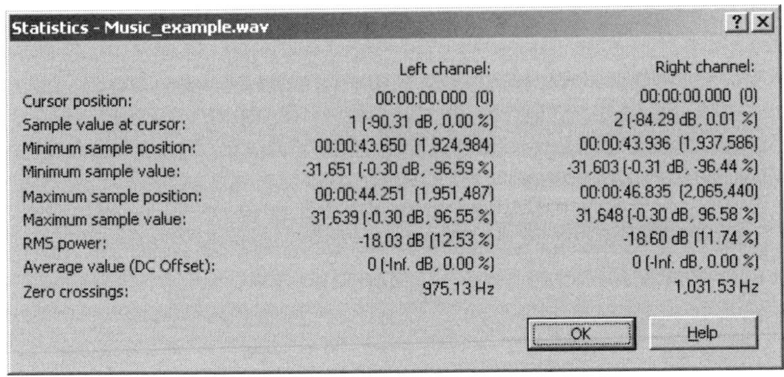

Video Support

Sound Forge can open up video files and their associated audio. While you can't edit the video, you can edit the audio. Be careful not to cut anything or you will lose sync. Instead, use this feature to process and master the audio portion of your video projects.

There are a numerous video save and render options depending on the encoders available on your system. Included are Windows Media and RealMedia. QuickTime is available if you've installed the free tools available from Apple.

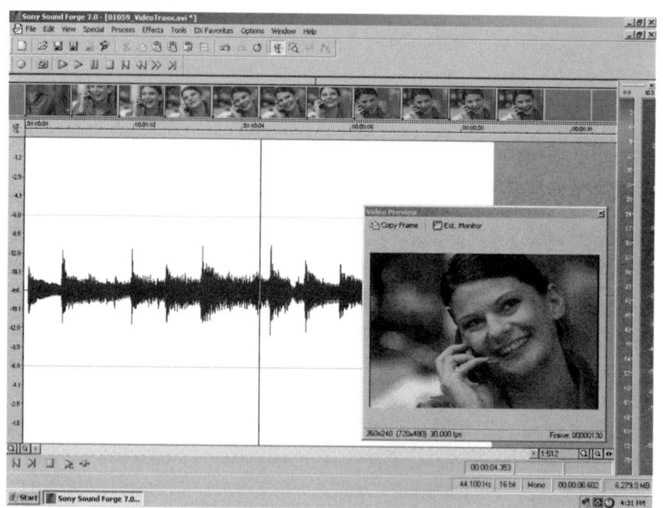

Creating calibration tones and noise

Properly setting up recording gear and monitoring systems requires test tones. Sound Forge can create what you need.

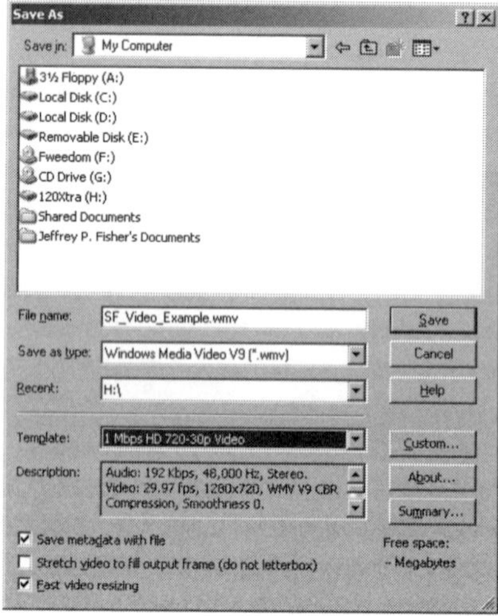

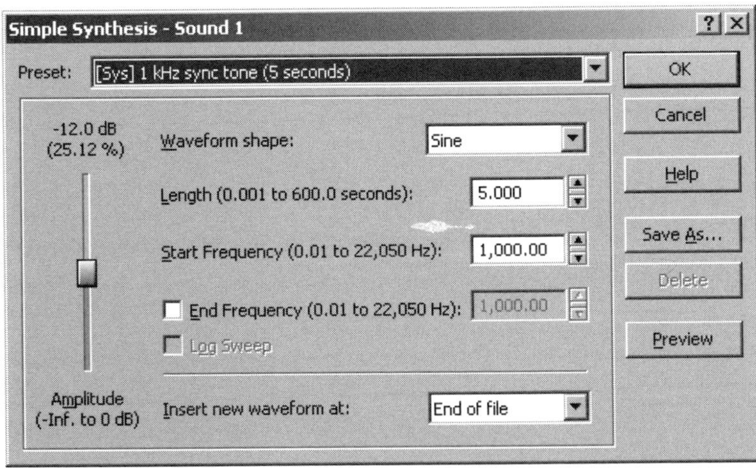

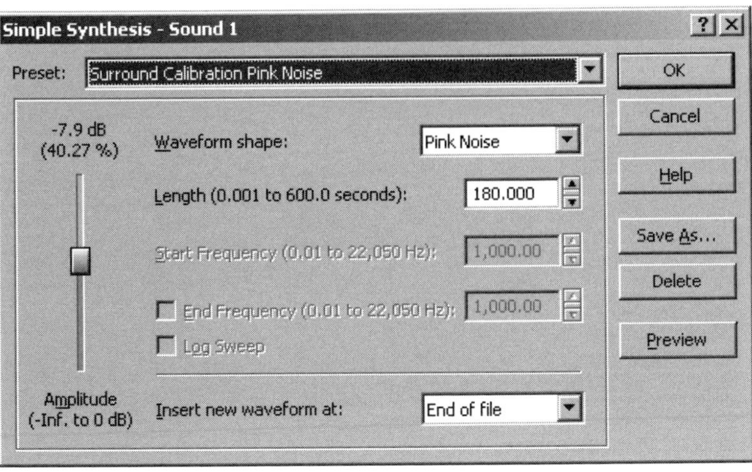

A simple sine wave is useful for setting levels between equipment. With an empty file open (File > New), click Tools > Synthesis > Simple and choose 1kHz sync tone (5 second). Adjust the sliders as required.

For pink noise, useful for calibrating monitors (stereo and surround), create an empty file, click Tools > Synthesis > Simple, and choose Pink Noise as the Waveform shape. Adjust the length to 180 seconds. Adjust the Amplitude to -7.9dB. This creates three minutes of pink noise at -20dB (RMS) for calibrating your monitors, Play this file through each speaker separately and adjust its volume until a sound level meter reads 83dB (C-weighted, slow) at the listening position.

Chapter 11

Conclusion

After finishing this book, I hope you are excited about the possibilities Sound Forge® brings to your audio work. My advice: roll up your sleeves and start working: Record, edit, experiment, encode, and let your ears help you decide what sounds best.

Keep learning, too.

Here are a couple of related resources to further your education:

- Audio Postproduction for Digital Video, by Jay Rose (CMPBooks)
- Musician's Guide to Home Recording, by McIan and Wichman (Simon and Shuster)
- Mastering Audio, by Bob Katz (Focal Press)
- Sound for Film and Television, by Tomlinson Holman (Focal Press)
- Voice-Actors Guide to Home Recording, Fisher and Hogan (Artistpro)
- And the VASST (Video-Audio-Surround-Streaming-Training) home: www.vasst.com

Questions?

If you need additional help with Sound Forge (or general audio issues):

- Drop by the Sound Forge forum on Digital Media Net (www.dmnforums.com).
- Stop by my Web site at www.jeffreypfisher.com
- Or e-mail me at jpf@jeffreypfisher.com

Happy Forge-ing!

Jeffrey P. Fisher

Glossary

Some of these audio terms are relevant to Sony products directly and other terms are related to the audio and video industry in general. Some of the terms are "new" language adapted from the analog world from which many features of Vegas®, ACID®, and Sound Forge® are derived.

2-Pass-An encoding feature, allowing video to be scanned prior to actual encoding. During the first pass, the encoder determines how it will allocate bits during the encoding process. Slower encodes, but generally higher quality in high-motion video. Vegas 5 supports 2-pass encoding.

A/D Converter-Analog to Digital Converter. Many A/D's are also D/A's, which convert Digital back to Analog for monitoring.

AC-3-Dolby's Audio Compression scheme, 3rd generation. Both stereo and 5.1 surround format files may be encoded to AC-3. Encore only supports the encoding of stereo audio, and import of 5.1 AC-3 files.

ACM-Audio Compression Manager, developed by Microsoft as the standard interface for signal processing of audio data in the Windows environment, particularly geared towards the wav file format. Some tools allow custom ACM processes.

ADC-Another name for Analog to Digital Converter

AIFF-Audio Interchange File Format. Can be used for storing audio in high or low resolution formats and sharing them between computer systems.

Aliasing- A form of distortion created when the digital sample rate isn't more than twice the frequencies of the audio being sampled.

The undesired jagged or stair-stepped appearance of unfiltered angled lines in an image, graphic, or text. In video, aliasing also refers to the visual beating effect caused by sampling frequencies of an image being too low to reproduce correctly. Different video aliasing effects include raster scan aliasing (e.g., when sharp horizontal lines cause a flickering effect) and temporal aliasing (e.g., when wheel spokes appear to reverse direction). Contrast with anti-aliasing.

Alpha channel-The fourth channel of a 32-bit RGB image that contains transparency in the image. The other three channels are red, green, and blue.

Amplitude-The height of a waveform measured from the middle, where silence would be indicated. If no waveform is drawn, then the audio section is silent; the measurement from center to the highest point in the graphical drawing is the value of the amplitude. Acoustic amplitude is measured in dB (see decibels) The louder the signal, the higher the amplitude, regardless of the measurement format. (peak, RMS, Instant, etc)

Anchor point-A bitstream location that serves as a random point. An example is a MPEG I-frame.

Anti-aliasing-The manipulation of edges (e.g., those between areas with contrasting colors) in an image, graphic, or text to make the edges appear smoother. Anti-aliased edges appear blurred up close but smooth at average viewing distance. Anti-aliasing is critical when working with high-quality graphics for television display use. Opposite of aliasing.

Artifact-Distortion to a picture or a sound signal. With digital video, artifacts can result from overloading the input device with too much signal, or from excessive or improper compression.

Aspect ratio-Ratio of width to height in dimensions of an image. For example, the frame aspect ratio of NTSC video is 4:3, whereas widescreen frame sizes use the more elongated aspect ratio of 16:9 or 1.85.1

Asset-Any digital file that is part of the library or project is considered an asset.

Audition-Preview audio or video

ATSC-Advanced Television Systems Committee determines voluntary technical standards of acquiring, authoring, distribution and reception of high definition television.

AVI-Abbreviation for Audio-Video Interleaved; the format/scheme created by Microsoft for synchronizing and compressing analog audio and video signals. AVI is also the file format used by Video for Windows.

Attenuate-An analog term, referring to decreasing the audio level. Usually described in Decibels.

Audio File-Audio stored in any digital format is an audio file. Not to be confused with audiophile, an audio affecionado.

B-frame-In inter-frame compression schemes (e.g., MPEG), a highly compressed, bidirectional frame that records the change that occurred between the i-frame before and after it. B frames enable MPEG-compressed video to be played in reverse. Contrast with i frame and p frame.

Balance-The difference in level or apparent loudness between Right and Left in a stereo audio signal. See Panning for additional information.

Balanced Cable-A cable that contains 2 conductors carrying audio, plus a shield for the ground that carries no audio. Professional mic cables are always balanced.

Bandwidth-The range of frequencies in an audio file, EQ, or other signal or device that passes a signal. This term also refers to the datarate of a streaming file.

Bass-Low frequencies in the overall spectrum of sound. Bass is approximated in the 0Hz to 300 Hz region of the frequency spectrum.

Bed-Background music or sound effect laid under a voice over. Typical term in television and radio.

Bitmap-A graphic image comprised of individual pixels, each of which has a value that define its relative brightness and color

Bit-Depth-The number of bits in an audio sample. The greater the number of bits, the greater the resolution of the audio file, and therefore the more accurate the digital file will reproduce the original audio image.

Boost-Raising the volume of an audio signal

Brickwall-When digital audio hits the 0dB threshold, bits are truncated and lost. This is known as 'hitting the brickwall' as there is no recovery from lost bits. Digital form of distortion. See clipping below.

Bright-Descriptive term to describe high frequencies. If a sound is "bright" then it contains a number of high frequencies. If the sound is not bright, it may be considered dull, and contain few high frequencies. Sibilance is typically fairly bright, allowing breath and S's, P's, T's, P's, and other sibilant sounds to be heard.

Bumper-Stock audio identifying the television, radio, or cable station, or perhaps designating a corporate audio ident, such as the famous Intel sound.

Bus-a feature used in hardware mixers and some software mixers to route audio from place to place, such as submixes, effects, or other processes.

Capturing-Refers to capturing source video for use on a computer. If analog, the captured video is converted to digital.

Channel-Each component color that defines a computer graphic image—red, green, and blue—is carried in a separate channel, so each may be adjusted independently. Channels may also be added to a computer graphic file to define masks.

Chapter-A new segment of an existing work, as the work is broken up into subject or scene specific sections. Primarliy used in DV authoring. Chapter points are generated in the Encore Timeline.

Chorus (FX)-A series of short, modulated delays with slight shifts in pitch to create the effect of multiple voices, stemming from one voice. This effect allows a solo instrument to have the sound of an ensemble due to the slight differences in timing and pitch.

Clip-A digitized or captured portion of video.

Clipping-Distortion, given it's name from when audio is 'clipped off' after exceeding maximum levels. Can be caused at input, output or processing stages. In the digital realm, clipping becomes brickwalling. Also: The cropping of peaks (overmodulation) of the white or the black portions of a video signal.

Codec-Contraction of compression/decompression algorithm; used to encode and decode data such as sound and video files. Common codecs include those that convert analog video signals to compressed digital video files (e.g., MPEG), or that convert analog sound signals into digital sound files such as Windows wma file format.

Compilation-term in DVD Architect to define a slideshow or music playlist.

Compress-(dynamic range) To reduce the amount of dynamic range -- difference between the loudest and softest parts -- of an audio signal, making the overall output more consistent. A compressor acts like an automated fader, bringing loud portions of an audio signal to a more quiet point, and raising the level of quiet sections to match louder transient peaks.

Compress-(File size) Resampling, reducing a file size for streaming or sharing over the internet or intranet. Usually a lossy process, causing some loss of audio quality. REAL Media, MPEG, MJPEG, Microsoft wmv/wma are all examples of compressed media. Use Apple's Compressor to compress media.

Copyright-Just as the word implies, the right to copy. Any composition is copyrighted as it's completed. No one has the right to copy the composition, video, or other art forms without the permission of the author of the work.

CTI-Current Time Indicator

Cue-A specific piece of music composed to play at a specific moment in time. The moment the composition is to play is called a Cue Point. A list of Cue Points is called a Cue List, generally determined in the Spotting Session. (see Spotting)
Cue also refers to set up a piece of media (audio or video) to play at a specific trigger, such as a DJ cueing up music or video to play at the press of a button.

Cut-To remove, delete a section from a digital event. Also refers to a composition, typically in album form, with the composition being a 'cut' of an overall album. Also refers to reducing frequencies in an equalizer, as in 'cutting the bass' from a mix meaning to reduce the amount of bass in a mix.

Cutoff Frequency-The frequency that audio is deeply attenuated or reduced. Low-pass and High-pass filters both center around a Cutoff frequency. The higher the cutoff, the less original audio is allowed to be heard.

DAW-Digital Audio Workstation

Decibel (dB) A device of measurement. Describes electrical power referenced to 1 milliwatt so 0dBm is equal to 1 milliwatt, or 1m. dB may refer to dBu, dBv, dBm. To a listener, audio must be 6dB louder to appear to be twice as loud, while electronically, only 3dB of voltage difference are required for the same result. This is why a 200 watt amplifier is not twice as loud as a 100 watt amplifier.

Deinterlace-The process of removing artifacts that result from the nature of two-fields-per-frame (interlaced) video.

Destructive/Non-Destructive-Destructive editing alters the original file, and cannot be recovered. In the DAW and NLE worlds, destructive editing is often used to save disk space. With the cost of hard drives coming down, destructive editing is less prevalent than it was not long ago. Non-destructive editing does not affect the original file regardless of what processes are applied.

Digitize-Converting analog to digital audio or video. The moment analog information is stored on a hard drive by whatever means it arrives there, it becomes digitized.

Distortion-See clipping. The point at which audio no longer maintains it's original integrity, intentionally or not. Audio that exceeds physical or electronic limitations becomes distorted. Also used as an effect, particularly on guitars, violins, and other stringed instruments.

Dolby/Dolby Labs-Founded in 1965, Dolby Laboratories is known for the technologies it has developed for improving audio sound recording and reproduction including their noise reduction systems (e.g., Dolby A, B, and C) and Dolby Digital (AC-3).

Dull-Opposite of Bright. Sound that is dull lacks high frequencies. May be perceived as unexciting.

DV/DV25-Digital Video. The most common form of DV compression. DV25 uses a data rate of 25 megabits per second or 3.6 megabytes per second.

DVD-Digital Versatile Disk, used for storing images, data, audio, and system backups. The standard for MPEG storage and display of moving images.

DVD Start-Sony's nomenclature for the First Play video in a DVD project.

Dynamic Range-The difference between loud and quiet passages in an audio performance. Sometimes referred to in terms of how loud audio is permitted to go without distortion or how quiet audio may go before noise is heard.

Dynamics-Varying levels of amplitude that audio demonstrates throughout the project.

EDL-Edit Decision List

Effects (FX)-Signal processors are referred to as Effects or FX. Reverbs, choruses, delays, phasers, flangers, are all referred to as FX.

End Action-An instruction given to a playlist or video file, indicating what the DVD player should do following the end of a video's play. An end action might instruct the DVD to play the next video on the disc, return to a menu, or simply stop.

Envelope-A graphic display of a volume, pan, or FX control, allowing automated control over the behavior of specific parameters in the mixing of sounds. Also referred to as the acoustical contour of a sound, it's Attack, Decay, Sustain, and Release. (ADSR)

Envelope Point-A handle or node inserted on an envelope in Vegas or Sound Forge, used to control various parameters of volume, pan, and automated FX functions.

Equalizer (EQ) A plugin that allows specific frequencies to be manipulated and controlled. Bass, midrange, treble frequencies are all broken down into specific bands and are controllable via sliders or dials, to cut or boost specific frequencies. This is one of the most important tools found in any DAW or NLE tool, as it allows specific contouring and shaping of audio events to help it fit more easily with other audio events.

Event-Vegas and ACID refer to all media clips on the timeline as events.

Export-Sending media from one application to another, such as exchanging audio from Sound Forge to Vegas or DVD Architect is an export process. See Import.

Fps-Abbreviation for frames per second; the standard for measuring the rate of video playback speed. A rate of 30 fps is considered real-time speed and a rate of 24 fps is considered animation speed. At 12-15 fps, the human eye can detect individual frames causing video to appear jerky.

Fade-A gradual decrease or increase of video or audio. Audio fades from audible to silent, video fades from visible to black. A fade may also be used to transition from one event to another. (crossfade)

Field-One complete vertical scan of a picture that has 262.5 lines. A complete television frame comprises two fields; the lines of field 1 are vertically interlaced with those of field 2 for 525 lines of resolution according to the NTSC standard.

Firewire-An IEEE1394 High bandwidth/high speed interface created by Apple as an industry standard for file I/O, not limited to, but commonly related to video and audio. Also used as a hard drive interface.

Foley-The art of creating ambient sound for film, synchronized with action on the screen. A Foley room used to record audio for film contains various surfaces and equipment to simulate or imitate sounds heard in the field recorded audio for film/video.

Frame-Film moves at 24 frames per second, meaning that 24 individual pictures or 'frames' are required for each second of film/video. An extracted still image or where the playhead parks in Vegas. is referred to as a frame. NTSC video moves at 29.97 frames per second, and PAL video moves at 25.00 frames per second.

Frequency-In audio this refers to how fast a waveform or audio signal repeats itself. Measured in Hertz. Low frequencies are 20Hz to 250Hz, mid-range frequencies are 250Hz to 2000 Hz or 2KHz, and high frequencies are 2KHz to 20KHz.

Gain-The amount that a sound is amplified from its original value; the change in it's its power point. See Amplitude.

GOP-Group of Pictures

Handles-In a captured video file of a specific length, additional time before and after the captured section is captured as well, for editing purposes. The additional media at the beginning and end of the desired media are referred to as "handles."

Hz-Abbreviation for Hertz (cycles per second). Kilo-Hertz is abbreviated KHz, and Megahertz is abbreviated with MHz.

I/O-Abbreviation for In/Out. Relating to Vegas or Sound Forge, generally referring to hardware used to get audio in or out of a computer. See AD Converter.

I-frame-In inter-frame compression schemes (e.g., MPEG), the key frame or reference video frame that acts as a point of comparison to p- and b-frames, and is not rebuilt from another frame. Opposite B frame and P frame.

Import-To open a file in an application that originated in another application. Vegas can import .wav, .aiff, .wma, .wmv, jpg, .png, .mov, m2v, and many other file formats.

Inter-frame compression-A compression algorithm, such as MPEG that reduces the amount of video information by storing only the differences between a frame and those before it.

intra-frame compression-Compression that reduces

the amount of video information in each frame on a frame-by-frame basis. Compare to Inter-frame compression.

KHz-KiloHertz, (1000Hz) abbreviated KHz.

Latency-The processing time between audio's origin or trigger point, and when the signal is actually heard. Latency above 10 milliseconds (ms) is unacceptable in a recording situation, as there is no way to properly match already recorded audio with incoming new audio being recorded, resulting in out-of-time files.

Layback-importing, matching, and dubbing a finished score or soundtrack back to the video master. Exporting audio from ACID and importing to Vegas for final rendering for instance, can be considered a layback.

Layover-Recording audio from an analog source to a multitrack, DAW, or audio portion of an NLE.

Layout-The manner in which a workspace or surface is defined and viewed. Vegas permits single or split-window layouts.

Letterbox-The aspect ratio of motion pictures is wider than those of standard televisions. To preserve the original aspect ratio of a motion picture, a motion picture includes black bars at the top and bottom of the screen when played on television.

Link-the connection between a button or text object in DVD Architect, to a video, still, or audio asset.

Loop-A segment or slice of audio that repeats without any indication of the end of the segment adjoining the beginning of the segment. Looped audio sequences are wonderful for seamless menu looping in DVD Architect and Vegas.

M&E-Industry term for Music and Effects.

Master-The finished product after a final mix has ben created and the final mix components have been finalized with all EQ, compression, and volume settings. The final product on hard disk, tapes, or authored DVD is referred to as "The Master."

Media-Another term for a file, related to audio, video, graphic, etc. in the digital environment.

Mic-Abbreviation for Microphone

Midrange-Audio found in the frequency bandwidths of 250Hz to 2000Hz (2KHz)

Moire-Visual distortion caused by the interference of similar frequencies, or the waving effect produced by the convergence of lines. See Aliasing.

Monitor-Any device that allows audio or video to be seen or heard. Audio monitors are in the form of speakers or headphones. Video monitors are in the form of a television, CRT, or LCD.

Mono-A single channel of audio information as opposed to stereo audio containing 2 channels.

MP3-MPEG Audio Layer 3 compression format. Used to compress files for delivery over the internet or for playback on portable hardware devices to save space and bandwidth.

MPEG-Abbreviation for Motion Picture Experts Group, a group that defined a standard for compression of video or audio media.

MPEG-2-MPEG-2 is an extension of the MPEG-1 compression standard designed to meet the requirements of television broadcast studios. MPEG-2 is the broadcast quality video found on DVDs and requires a hardware decoder (e.g. a DVD-ROM player) for playback.

Multimedia-Media/files that contain audio, video, graphics, midi, animation, or text in any combination. Broadly used term to describe nearly any form of media.

Music Compilation-A series of audio assets that behave like a playlist in DVD Architect.

Mute-A software or hardware switch that prevents audio from being heard on a channel or channels; a specific process in Sound Forge. ACID/Vegas have a mute switch/button on every channel.

Near Field Monitors-Small reference monitors/speakers within close proximity of the engineer/editor. Used in small rooms or for monitoring at low volume levels in larger rooms. Generally less fatiguing to the ear.

NLE-Non-Linear Editor

Normalize-A digital process for increasing the level of an entire audio file file's to a preset level without clipping.

NTSC-National Television Standards Committee. (Sometimes humorously referred to as Never The Same Color)

One shot-An audio file that does not contain looping information, but is intended to play once, not necessarily in time.

Output-Getting audio out of the computer to an analog speaker, digital output via SPDIF, AES/EBU, or other file format external to the computer.

p frame-In interframe compression schemes such as MPEG, the predictive video frame that exhibits the change that occurred compared to the I-frame before it. See I-frame and B-frame.

Pad-Attenuation of the original audio level. See Attenuation.

PAL-Phase Alternation Line. Most all countries use PAL outside of the US and Japan. (Sometimes jokingly referred to as Picture At Last)

Pan-Abbreviation for Panorama, or moving audio across the audio spectrum left to right, front to back, or combination of both. Each channel in Vegas contains a pan control that may be automated.

Peak-Audio level's maximum point in a file.

Pillarbox-The opposite of letterboxing, where black masks are inserted vertically on the sides of an image.

Playback-Listening/monitoring the recording after it's been laid to hard drive or tape. Reviewing the audio file as it's being composed. Also referred to as "Previewing." Which makes no sense, because you are not viewing the video or audio prior to any edit, you are listening or watching video post-edit, making the term 'preview' inaccurate.

Playhead-Where the cursor lies within the DAW or NLE application as relevant to a timeline. Cursor and playhead are generally interchangeable. In Vegas Sound Forge, the playhead is indicated by the vertical line moving across the screen.

PlayList-A set of instructions that tell a linked video how to behave, which audio it should use, when it should play, and what follows after it's playback.

Plug in-DAW or NLE term referring to audio or video processors that may be used to supplement the application's audio or video editing tools.

Preset-Predetermined parameters of a plugin, template, or other predetermined setting for an application.

Preview-Viewing or listening to media from an application. In Vegas, preview is defined by watching video associated with a project and listening to audio loops/compositions assigned to the video, or listening to playback of a musical composition with or without video. See Playback.

Project-A collection of audio files, video files to be assembled for a final product.

Project Overview-DVD Architect 2's window that allows full-time viewing of all assets and actions in a project.

RAM-Abbreviation for Random Access Memory

Region-A predetermined space/time on the Timeline in any DAW or NLE application, controlling playback area/time. A segment of audio or video that may be separately managed for editing.

Render-To blend all multimedia files together in one master file format. Akin to baking a cake from all it's individual ingredients.

RGB-Abbreviation for Red, Green, Blue

Roll Off-The point at which frequencies are filtered out. A low frequency roll-off will rapidly diminish frequencies beginning at the specified point. See Attenuation.

Rumble-Low frequencies too low to actually be clearly heard but taking up audio information space. Footsteps, vibrations, motors all create rumble. Many mixing/recording consoles incorporate rumble filters, set to approximately 60-75Hz, rolling low frequencies off at that point to clean up audio. See Roll off.

Safe title area-The area that comprises the 80 percent of the TV screen measured from the center of the screen outward in all directions. The safe title area is the area within which title credits—no matter how poorly adjusted a monitor or receiver may be—are legible. Vegas displays safe title areas.

Sample Rate-The interval and resolution at which audio is 'photographed' or measured. Audio CD's are sampled at a rate of 44.1K and 16 bits. Sound Forge Vegas is capable of much higher resolutions and sample rates.

Session-A space of time dedicated to recording audio. Each time a new recorded file is created, it may be referred to as a session. Digidesign's ProTools uses this term for their basic document of assembled elements.

SFX-Abbreviation for Sound Effects.

Sibilance-The 'hissing' sounds of the human voice, most noticed in S's, P's, T's, etc. High frequencies, sometimes challenging to control. Use a DeEsser plugin or an EQ to control this phenomenon.

SMPTE-Society of Motion Picture and Television Engineers. Also used as a timecode reference.

Solo-A button or switch that allows a single channel to be monitored. Mutes all other audio during playback when engaged. Vegas offers a solo button on all tracks.

Source Audio-Audio from the original program media. In a video file, this is on-location sound, or audio related to the original source and is often replaced or enhanced.

Spot-Announcement for broadcast, eg; a commercial. Also nick-name of Douglas Spotted Eagle

Spotting-Identifying and documenting cues for music, effects, sound design, or other audio information should occur. See Cue.

Stereo-Two channel audio, consisting of similar or dissimilar audio spread across the left/right spectrum. Two separate mono channels separated to one left and one right, would not be considered stereo, but rather dual mono. Stereo mixes in Vegas consist of placing elements on the multitrack timeline in representations of their occurrence across the left/right spectrum, and then mixed to a two channel/stereo mix reflecting the positioning of audio elements.

Streamer-Slug or graphic overlay on video playback, marking exact points that a cue is to take place. Functions as a visual hit point or Cue. See Cue.

Subwoofer-Speaker enclosure optimized to reproduce sounds from 20Hz to 125Hz.

S-video-Short for Super-video, a technology used for transmitting video signals over a cable by dividing the video information into separated signals: one for luma and one for chroma. (S-Video is synonymous with Y/C video). S-video is a consumer form of component video used primarily with Hi8 and S-VHS equipment.

Sweet Spot-The 'prime' listening area between 2 speakers in a stereo environment or a 5.1 listening environment. This is the point that all audio channels are most precise, arriving at the same location at the same time. A relatively small area in most any listening environment.

Sweeten-Polishing or improving an existing recording through adding other parts to the composition or audio elements. Processing of sound is also considered sweetening. Anything done to original audio in order to enhance it's quality.

Sync-Abbreviation for synchronize. A means of ensuring events consistently occur at the same time. Time Code is generally a common source to assure events being in sync.

T/C-Abbreviation for Time Code.

Temporal compression-A compression method that reduces the data contained within a single video frame by identifying similar areas between individual frames and eliminating the redundancy. See also codec.

Timeline-A component of Vegas and other NLEs where graphic and video elements are placed for purposes of inclusion on the DVD. Timelines include audio, video, and other elements.

Track-An individual line containing audio or video loop elements.

Transfer rate-How fast a disk drive or CD drive can transfer information to the CPU. May be a burst rate or sustained rate. High cache levels (8 meg) or larger assist in providing information to the CPU at fast rates, important when building large composites in Vegas, lots of audio tracks in ACID, and deep menu structures in DVD Architect.

Transient-The difference between the lowest point of decay and highest point of attack in an audio file.

Transport-Play, record, stop, rewind, fast forward, record are all functions of the Transport in Sound Forge Vegas. The Transport tools control position of playback and the playhead.

Treble-The high end of the audio frequency spectrum, generally 2KHz and above.

Underscore-background music, not necessarily musically composed, to create an emotional atmosphere or environment. Similar to, and often called a music bed. See Bed.

USB-Abbreviation for Universal Serial Bus.

Video File- With Sound Forge Vegas, this is relevant to Quicktime, .mpg, .wmv, avi, or m2v files; data files that contain video information.

Volume-The indicator for overall level of a loop, track, or master project output level.

Wave (.wav) The Microsoft designator for audio file formats, a common file type. Used by Windows applications as a file format.

Workspace-The primary work surface in Sound Forge. Vegas., main window where most of the work is performed.